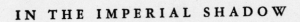

IN THE IMPERIAL SHADOW

IN THE IMPERIAL SHADOW

by

MIRZA MAHMOUD KHAN SAGHAPHI

PAGE TO THE SHAH

GARDEN CITY, NEW YORK

DOUBLEDAY, DORAN & COMPANY, INC.

1928

CONTENTS

PART I

PART II

CONTENTS

PART III

PART I

I

THE BIRTH OF A PERSIAN BOY

IT WAS the 7th of March, the month in which the Queen of Spring is reborn. The peaceful, easy-going Persians were chanting in Arabic the last words of their morning prayer before getting ready to go to their work. The prayer over, each man embraced his wife and children and, standing in the centre of the large court of his house or the smaller one of his hovel, turned his face toward the sky and filled his lungs with a deep draft of the fresh, exhilarating air, laden with the perfume of early violets. The dawn of a new day was enough to make him happy. For the rest, he trusted in the bounty of the Almighty Khoda with the unalterable trust that his faith inspired. The faith of Islam, taught by the Prophet, upon whose soul be the benediction of God!

The first to start his prayer and the last to finish was Mash-hadi Eshagh, a tenant of my father's. In the summer Eshagh made mud bricks with a wooden mould and left them on the ground to dry in the sun. During the fall and winter he was a man of all work. He sold anything for which there was a demand—baked potatoes to pedestrians in the streets or aromatic herbs to the housewives. He worked also during the night, especially in the winter, when the snow was heavy and the air biting. Then he sold tripe. For the past few weeks he had been selling boiled beet-roots in the early morning.

Notwithstanding his meagre revenue he had managed during long years of hard work to turn the courtyard of his

3

little mud-and-straw-covered brick house into a lovely small garden as beautiful as the large gardens and parks of the neighbouring houses. He was a lover of flowers, as most Persians are, and a philosopher and moralist as well. On that particular morning he was looking with interest at the narcissi and hyacinths growing in pots on the window-sills. "Let us see our sabze," he said to himself and walked to his little bedroom window to look with affectionate eyes at slender blades of wheat growing in a large earthen platter. A handful of these grains had been carefully spread two weeks before by the hands of his wife. She had chosen a sunlit spot and anxiously hoped for a full, bushy growth before the 21st of March, the Persian New Year's Day, when the platter was to serve as a decoration for her evening table. "How sweet is the Lord!" murmured Eshagh, who was so occupied with his thoughts that he did not hear his wife calling him to fetch the bowl of boiled beet-roots. He awoke as from a dream when he felt the touch of her hand at his elbow.

A few minutes later, with the bowl on his head, he stepped out into the narrow street running between two high walls. He was a man of forty, tall and vigorous. The bowl of beet-roots made him look taller. He was carrying the largest bowl of a set of three, which comprised all of his culinary equipment. On top of it was a cushion filled with straw, which, although very thick, did not prevent the steam from escaping.

Once in the main street, Eshagh turned towards the Tekkyeh, or Hossein Beyk Square—a central point where four large thoroughfares meet. The streets were still covered with a thin layer of snow which would be gone by the end of the week. When he arrived at the Tekkyeh he walked straight to a majestic old elm tree. Two of the passers-by helped him put down his load. Eshagh thanked them and then uttered a loud good morning to all the shopkeepers and workmen round about. Duly he received an answer in chorus. After this preliminary act of politeness, he uncovered the bowl and let the steam escape. Instantly everybody hurried to his side to be served. He adjusted a small board, which he had carried under his arm, on the bowl. Next, he took out a beet-root and began to peel it with a knife, a delightful procedure to watch. The morning was still young, and in the chilly air the ruby-coloured vegetable seemed deliciously hot. He served every one in his turn and in a solemn and decorous manner. For Eshagh was a gentleman! In Persia any man born of Persian parents and on the soil of Iran, whether in a palace of marble or a hut of mud, is born a gentleman. When some children on their way to school joined the group around Eshagh, he was inspired to sing in his soft and melodious voice the fine quality of his wares. "Come, come, O fathers and uncles of my soul! Come and tell me if any one of you has ever seen a colour so radiant as the lovely hue of these beet-roots. I assure you it will remind you all of the ruby lips of the beloved ones and the wine of Shiraz. Come, come, taste and judge for yourself the delicacy of their flavour. With a little imagination you will be tasting the rosy lips of your beloved."

His singing must have impressed the crowd, for in less than an hour he had sold every beet. He counted his money, all copper coins, and found that he had nearly fifteen shahis. A great deal of money for him! Khoda had been generous. Then, speaking his thoughts aloud, he declared, "To-night there will burn a long and thick candle at the altar of the Haft Dokhteran."

The Haft Dokhteran or shrine of the Seven Daughters, was a beautiful little shrine near the Tekkyeh, where seven Persian sisters of noble birth and saintly reputation were buried more than four hundred years ago. A story in our family relates that before the reign of the Safavi, when one of our ancestors met and fought the Turcomans, his seven daughters seeing that the odds were against their father, begged him to let them fight with him. Upon his refusal the girls changed their clothes, masked their faces and went forth. In the evening when the father returned and saw they were not at home, he went back to the battle field and found their dead bodies. Later the place where they were buried became a shrine which was held in great reverence by the Persian women. When I was a child I was sent every evening with a maid to this shrine to pray, and every Thursday night I was delegated by my family to light seven candles at the altar.

For Eshagh, a beet-root-seller, it was a sacrifice to buy even one candle, especially a long and thick one. It would cost him one fifth of his earnings. But he had made a declaration, which for a Persian, amounts to a vow. The butcher, who had heard his words, touched him on the shoulder. Eshagh turned round and, seeing the butcher, who was a seyyed, or descendant of the Prophet, and therefore a man of some dignity, made a respectful salaam and exclaimed, "O seyyed, it pleases your ancestor that you should always touch my shoulder when my hands are filled with money, earned by honest work."

"O pious and good man," replied the seyyed, "believe me that your exceptional luck this morning is mostly due to the fact that we all expect the happy event of a birth in the house of our beloved and respected arbab."

"God be praised!" cried out Eshagh, "and may you, seyyed, enjoy his care for giving me such joyful news. Come, tell me more about it. I am burning to know the truth."

"Uncle of my soul," replied the seyyed, "do not get excited. I shall tell you as much as I know. Last night in the mosque after prayer was over, the djelowdar bashi"—"chief of the arbab's stable"—"gave out the news to the whole congregation. He promised to tell us just as soon as the pain of our lady, the pure-souled daughter of the Ameri of Firuz-Kuh"— "Turquoise Mount,"—"was over." Then, to impress Eshagh with the truth of his words, the seyyed took him by the shoulder, saying: "Gaze at that beautiful lamb!" He pointed to a white, curly-coated lamb with one end of rope around its neck and the other under a piece of stone in front of his shop. "That finest specimen of all the world's lambs is going to be sacrificed for the safe arrival of the boy."

"Yes, yes," shouted in chorus some of the shopkeepers. "Our seyyed butcher is absolutely right."

The proprietor of the tea-house, who had paid no attention to the conversation between Eshagh and the butcher, now confronted Eshagh with a cup of tea which he used in his hand like a gavel to emphasise his arguments. "Our most respected butcher, besides being an authentic descendant of the Prophet, is a Persian. Therefore he could not tell a lie even if it were necessary to save his life. Our own Persian Prophet Zoroaster told us that 'A lie is the weapon of the coward.' Also His Highness Mohammad, the Arab Prophet, said that whosoever tells a lie goes straight to Hell. And we know for a fact that God never has had the pain of seeing a true Persian in Hell, and, bless our hearts, he never will!" After this the proprietor of the tea-house threw the contents of the cup into the air in confirmation of his reasoning and waited for Eshagh to reply.

Had Eshagh wished, this give and take might have gone on for hours and hours, but he was impatient, and saying, "Please, noble gentlemen, forgive my lack of conversation," he left his bowl where it stood, brushed the seyyed gently aside and ran toward the master's house, shouting as he went, "All the fifteen shahis in my hand shall be spent to-night to buy candles for the altar of the Haft Dokhteran to glorify this joyful event."

At last Eshagh arrived at the Djelow-Khan, a large square

with high walls in front of the mansion belonging to the arbab. The walls were decorated with Sixteenth Century coloured tiles made in Ispahan—tiles mostly yellow and green, with red arabesques interlaced with black lines and curves. In the centre of the front wall the big gate could be seen, bathed in the light of the early sun. Two old men with flowing beards were sitting on raised platforms, one at each side of the entrance. The elder held in his hand a long baton with a gilded top.

Eshagh was a known figure to these venerable men. Therefore after a short greeting and a salaam in Arabic he passed in, made his way to the anderun—the part of the house reserved for the mistress and her entourage—and stopped in front of the heavy curtain. Here he began to expel air from his lungs with as much noise as if he had a coughing fit. Immediately the curtain moved, and the face of a negress appeared. She was the badji, or head of the servants attending her mistress.

"I felt sure it was you," she said to Eshagh in a hushed voice. "You are faithful to this house and have the right of a member of the family. Look!"

Eshagh cautiously pushed aside the curtain and peeped behind it. The courtyard of the anderun was crowded with men and women. The gleam of expectancy shone on their faces. All were whispering. An old woman tiptoed out of the room of Her Grace the Khanom, and made a sign to a group of womenservants. Instantly this group dispersed, and pattered away on muffled feet to carry out her instructions.

"Where is our arbab?" inquired Eshagh.

"Our master is in his room," the badji replied. "He has been in private conference with the most reverend monadj-djem bashi, who since last sunset has been reading the stars and consulting the moon about the fate of the coming little star. There are also the seyyed Andalib and the chief mollah. Moreover, two of the chief mollah's singing boys have been reciting the Koran since last sunset and are nearly at the last chapter." She then made a sign to Eshagh, who bent his head and brought his ear close to her lips. "It is going to be a son," she whispered.

"Oh, glory to the Almighty God!" exclaimed Eshagh. "But tell me how you know the will of Khoda and can you read into destiny? You are not a monadj-djem."

The badji smiled a wise and knowing smile:

"I am Dadeh Zafran Badji, a descendant of the kings of Nubia and Abyssinia," she said. "As a child my eyes have seen the Red Sea and my heart and soul have absorbed the mysteries of the Sahara. I read the stars better than all the astrologers in the world. Listen to me! Last night, when I went to fetch water from the tank, I saw a star fall from the heavens, just above the Khanom's room! I presume that you are old enough to know what that means."

"Aye, aye," answered Eshagh, "do I not—I who am the father of eight! Understand this, my dear and respected lady—"

But the badji, cocking her ears, said, "I hear noises," and without further remark left Eshagh and ran toward the Khanom's room.

At the same instant a young voice rang out, chanting on the roof of the house: "Allaho akbar! Allaho akbar!"— "God is great! God is great!"

Immediately all the doors of the ten or twelve rooms were thrown open and about sixty persons—men, women and children—burst into the court, shouting and kissing one another. They ran toward the Khanom's room, where three strong negro women stretched their arms across the door to prevent anyone from entering.

From the master's room, meanwhile, the famous singer, the seyyed Andalib, nicknamed "Nightingale," ran to a ladder standing against the wall and climbed to the roof of the room of Her Grace the Khanom.

At sight of him the whole crowd became silent and raised their eyes in rapturous expectancy. Soon from the roof of the house rang his voice, clear as a bell, warm as a summer night, soft as the cheek of a child. It was sweet enough to make the angels in heaven and the birds in the air pause in their flight—a marvelous voice believed in Teheran to be the best but one in the whole world.

The Nightingale intoned some exquisite verses of the poet Sadi with such fervour that men and women imagined they were seeing thousands of parys skimming through space, as fairies do, to catch the notes of the song.

Some of the crowd solemnly affirmed that even the new-born child stopped crying and looked as if he were listening! The song told the tale. The whole population of the Hossein Beyk quarter knew that a son had been born unto the family of the most high, most learned, most respected Hadj-Agha, His Excellency Etezad-ol-Atebba, Hadj-Mirza Abdol Baghi, Khan of Saghaphi, son of Hadj Mohammad Esmail Beyk, son of Hadj Agha Baba Beyk, son of Ali-Naghi Beyk, son of Hossein Beyk, son of Mokhtar Ali Beyk, son of Ebrahim Khalil, son of Emir Mohammad Djelal-Od-Din, son of Djelil, son of Khalil, son of Esmail, son of Ebrahim, son of Emir Ahmed Mokhtar Djelal-od-Din, son of Abdol Hamid, son of Abdol Madjid, son of Mokhtar-Ali, son of Mohammad, son of Emir Mohammad-Kemal-od-Din, son of Esmail, son of Assadollah, son of Hossein, son of Ebrahim, son of Hassan, son of Ali, son of Abdollah, son of Emir Assad, son of Emir Rashed, son of Ahmed Mokhtar, the Avenger, Emir of the Faithful, son of Emir Abu-Obeid Saghaphi. Upon his soul be the benediction of God and the Prophet!

My mother was, as I have said, of Ameri blood. From generation to generation it was the custom for the eldest son of my family to choose as his bride a daughter of the Ameri. For a thousand years this great family whom the poet Nezami immortalized in the story of Leila and her lover Madjnoun had been living in the region between Mount Demavend and the Caspian Sea; long before the Tartars invaded Persia, my mother's ancestors occupied a castle-like fortress at Firuz-Kuh, on the top of a rock as sharp and straight as a needle.

Several times on my journies with Nasser-ed-Din Shah, the fourth King of the Kajar dynasty, the great-grandfather of the Ahmed Shah who was recently deposed by the Persian Parliament, I visited Firuz-Kuh. It seemed very strange to me to think that my mother's people lived in that strange castle about which so many uncanny stories swarmed. One of these tells that on stormy nights when lightning flashes, one can see mounted shadows galloping on the edge of the precipice carrying heavy burdens across their saddles. It is believed that the ancient treasure belonging to both the Saghaphi and Ameri families, was buried in that stronghold before the attack of Tchanguis Khan the Mongol. What seems to be a rock is in reality a vast plateau with immense pastures, and the tower itself is only a part of a fortress which, in the old days, could be defended by an army which could live on the pastures for years if necessary. It is said that the treasure hidden was accumulated by one of the Saghaphis who reigned and governed the northern part of the Empire of Persia under the Caliph of Bagdad and his successors. This treasure, so legend says, is destined to be recovered by a male descendant of Saghaphi when the time designated by the hand of Destiny comes, and spent for the good of Persia. Of course I was very much interested in the tales of the phantom cavalry and the treasure and used to sit for hours listening to our peasants, who, twice a year, brought a caravan of provisions to our house in Teheran.

My mother, as a mountaineer and a child of the open air, had a well-poised figure, perfect in its proportions, and was the equal in equestrian skill of any male member of her family or mine. Tall, majestic, with an oval face, she looked like the Madonna Mar-yam, the mother of the little Issa, as Persians say. My father used to call her "The Sun-warmed Marble Lady of the Turquoise Mount," because of her skin, which was unusually white and yet glowing with life. Brown hair and very light brown eyes. Long black lashes, straight eyebrows, also black. A fine and delicate nose, shadowing a small mouth. Beautiful teeth. The only existing likeness of her was a miniature painted on a lacquered pen-box by a master illuminator of manuscripts who was a near relative of hers and a great friend of my father's. In this miniature she had her hair parted in the middle and crowned with a jeweled plume, a buté, as seen in the so-called palm-leaf pattern of Kashmir shawls. Her blouse, with its narrow opening from the neck to the waistline, was of blue silk; her tight-fitting coat, which had long sleeves with turned-up cuffs and fell in wide, rippling folds below the waist, was of purple brocade. A belt of jewels kept the two edges together. That this was my mother's portrait nobody was supposed to know. My father held the pen-box in veneration, and we were not allowed to show it to any one outside the family.

My first memory of my mother goes back to a summer evening just a few minutes after the last note of the music played before sunset had died away. All the Persians were informed by this curious fanfare that the glorious symbol of God, the Sun, had retired for the night and the dark Ahriman was abroad. It is a custom as old as Persia—a part of the religious ceremonies when we were sun-worshippers and believed in the faith of Zoroaster. To me the final note always meant bedtime. I doubt whether any child in any part of the world can figure the supreme pleasure of sleeping on the roof of a house, as we do in Persia in the summertime, with one's mother standing by.

It was a heavenly sensation that night to watch the glittering sky and at the same time to feel my mother's hand touching my face and to hear her melodious voice singing close to my ears the Song of Stars which tells how the stars are loving and beautiful children whom God called back to heaven before they grew into men. They are waiting for their mothers. Every evening they smile and twinkle, inviting their mothers to come and be happy as they are.

At the end of the song I was overcome with a feeling that my swaying hammock was suspended in mid-air. My mother seemed to be an angel, with long wings as white as snow, and eyes like stars. Little by little my own eyes became heavy, my bed swung higher and higher, so near the blue dome that I felt afraid. I called to my mother, and her loving voice answered: "Yes, darling, I am beside you." I tried to open my eyes to make sure, and I had it in my mind to ask her what she was standing on.

But this I did not do. After all, my mother had the right and power to place my bed anywhere she wished to, and could hang it in the sky if she chose. Besides, she might disappear as fairies do, if questioned. So in a last effort to resist the dark Ahriman and the drowsiness that was taking hold of me, I clasped her hand very close in mine and let myself enjoy the swinging of my bed!

The house in which I was born was as old as the Hossein Beyk quarter, one of the oldest districts in Teheran. Early in the Sixteenth Century, when Teheran was still only a tiny village, one of my ancestors decided upon it as a resting-place and army headquarters, and built this house. He had been sent by Shah Ismail Safavi against the Uzbegs— Turkomans who every year at springtime invaded that part of the country, killed the male inhabitants, plundered the villages and carried away the women and children to sell for slaves. This ancestor had the title of beyk, which in his time was borne by only four members of the old nobility. The title gave to the bearer the rank of a reigning prince with privileges equal to those of the Shah himself. Among these privileges was the building of a tekkyeh, a mosque, a cistern, and a caravanserai. Another was the right to carry the family banner in front of his fighting-men and also at the head of the religious processions.

Our house had been so enlarged that it seemed to me, as a child, like a huge maze. Ten or twelve houses were connected by doors, passages or small streets. The idea was to keep members of the same family—even the married children—together under one mighty roof. Each house was provided with one or two underground houses called zir zamin where the whole family lived during the hot weather. They were cool, rather dark, and very mysterious.

At the far end of the garden other buildings were located—the kitchen, storeroom, coal and wood houses, a poultry yard and the private prison, which was more of a joke than a prison, for I could have kicked its door to pieces myself. There was also a place containing many grain cribs always filled with wheat and oats, the principal food for men and horses. There had to be enough stores to enable a community of some hundreds to maintain itself without the necessity of going forth in search of food. This was a matter of prudence for the old families in a country where not only a town but a whole province was subject to periodical famines, invasions, and attacks from nomadic tribes. Thirty years ago the assassination of a Shah, or even his natural death, stirred the populace to revolt and encouraged pretenders to fight for the throne. At such times the big gates of the mansions were closed and the inhabitants, prepared to live on their reserve supply of food, were armed to defend their lives and property.

But the garden, with its fountain, its flower beds, its pomegranates and other trees laden with blossoms or fruit, must not be thought of as given over chiefly to dark storage-caves or buildings stocked with food. I loved to play there among the flowers or in the vineyard, a wonderful spot with old vines transplanted some hundred years ago from Shiraz, the birthplace of the poet Hafiz. My brothers and I used to spend hours jumping from one branch of these vines to another, pretending to be members of a Christian tribe who, we were told, denied the divinity of Issa and were punished by being transformed into monkeys.

When I was a little older, I took part in a play, which we children staged to interpret this story. My little niece played Mar-yam. I, being the smallest, was assigned the part of Issa. It is wonderful to see Persian children in theatricals. Not only do they act well, but each creates his or her own rôle without outside help. They are as a rule very emotional when acting and often shed genuine tears.

Besides my brothers, my cousins and nieces, I had as playmates a negro boy called Mahboub, born on my birthday, another, called Arzagh-Cheshm—Steel-gray Eyes—and a negro girl whose name was Suskeh—Little Black Beetle. These latter were the children of our Abyssinian servants but, being my playmates, were treated as I was treated and lived the same life. Their rank as "Little Master's Companions" gave them a higher standing than that of their parents. They had their meals with us and were waited upon by the servants.

Every morning we attended for one hour a classroom under a Persian woman teacher whose duty it was to make us sit on our bended knees and keep straight. We were too small to be taught anything, but we were given books with pictures and had to make up stories suiting the pictures and tell them well.

The governess told three or four stories every evening, and then it was our turn. Every story-teller commenced with this sentence, "Yeki boud yeki na boud; ghair as Khoda hitchkes na boud," meaning: "One was and one was not; except God there was nobody."

The story was finished with the following verses in Persian:

> We went up; there was buttermilk with water.
> We came down; there was buttermilk with water.
> Our story was not true.

In case a child believed his tale was true, he would finish it by saying:

> We went up; there was buttermilk without water.
> We came down; there was buttermilk without water.
> Our tale was true.

Nearly all of the stories were about a prince and a princess who fell in love with each other, or a prince who loved a pary, or else they were tales of divs, jinnees or Sheytan— Satan himself. They were told with such detail that the governess would gasp with astonishment, and sometimes we would frighten ourselves. In such cases we crowded close to the governess, who would take us in her arms.

II

A VISIT TO MY HOLY UNCLE

EVERY Friday morning I was taken out by my Laleh for a horseback ride. "Laleh" is the title of a gentleman who is attached to a young khan as governor and bodyguard. The physical education, and to some extent the moral education, of the child is entrusted to him. This official is always chosen from amongst the men of the best nomadic tribes of the mountainous provinces. As a rule he is a man of the strictest integrity, and he must be a good fighter. "Mirza Hashem" was the name by which we called my Laleh, but his full name was Hashem Khan Afshar. He was himself head of a band of horsemen and a descendant of Nadir Shah Afshar, who brought back from India to Persia the famous Peacock Throne and the infinitely precious Persian library of Jahangir. I would sit on the saddle in front of Mirza Hashem, clutching the pommel with both hands when trotting, and later I would take the reins myself and guide the horse.

I rode in this way for about six months; then one day for the first time, riding alone, I put the horse to a trot. I was not more than five years old, and Laleh was so pleased that he took me straight to my father and said, "Ghorban," —meaning, "May I be sacrificed,"—"the little master is a full-fledged cavalier and lacks only a horse."

My father looked at me for some minutes as I stood in front of him in the attitude of attendance, arms humbly crossed upon my breast, thus showing all the respect and obedience that I owed to his high person. He finally ad-

17

dressed Laleh, saying, "Yes, yes, we must give him a horse; we must give him a horse."

After repeating the sentence two or three times, he nodded his head to both of us, to indicate that the audience was at an end. Laleh touched me gently and began to retreat backward, like a blue crab, bowing at the same time. I followed his example until we found ourselves outside the door.

Then he put me astride his shoulders and ran to the ande-run where he jumped up and down, showing me to everybody, and shouted: "He must have a horse! Let me into the presence of Her Grace the Khanom."

The sweet voice that I loved called to him, "Mirza Hashem, bring the little master here, quick, quick," and my mother ran out of the room, gathered me into her arms from Laleh's shoulder and kissed my face, murmuring, "Of course my dear little soul shall have his own horse, a most beautiful one, and everybody will see how wonderfully he rides."

"I want many, I want many, four, five, six," I exploded.

"Yes, yes, dear, you will have four, five, six horses, and Mirza Hashem will get his khalat."

The next day my Laleh again put me on his back and took me to all my brothers and sisters-in-law. Each one kissed me and promised to send his best horse to me and a khalat—a gift of a shawl or a robe, made to those who have done great work and deserve distinction—for Mirza Hashem. The third day we went to see every one of my relatives, and they all promised the same thing. We finished the tour by paying a visit to an uncle who was a holy man and a theologian.

He lived in the oldest and remotest quarter of Teheran, called Emamzade Ismail. To get there we had to go through a series of winding streets, sometimes so narrow that two men could not go through abreast. The streets were paved with cobblestones, and a thin stream trickled in a formless and waterworn gutter filled here and there with loose stones and pieces of brick and tile. Sitting on Mirza Hashem's shoulders and clasping his head firmly with my hands, I was jolted as if I had been riding a crazy camel.

At last we arrived at our destination and were received by my aunt, who took my hand and brought me to her husband. He was a learned mollah, or priest, with a large white turban and a long black beard. He was sitting on a sheepskin and looked very solemn and impressive. Laleh had told me beforehand that the knowledge accumulated under his respectable turban was enormous.

With one look at him I understood the truth of what Laleh had told me. He looked so unlike any one I had ever seen before that I could not help feeling embarrassed. His face was kind, but his whole bearing was austere and dignified. My aunt pushed me into his presence, saying, "Sir, it is my little nephew, come to pay his respects to you."

My uncle made no move to arise but drew his hand from under his aba and waited.

"Go, darling, go and kiss the hand of your highly venerable uncle," urged my aunt.

I approached him with a feeling of awe and kissed his hand. He touched my forehead with his lips and said gently, "Be seated, sir!"

I sat down and tried my utmost to remain on my knees and not lose my balance. Somehow I could not do it properly, and I was angry with myself. Happily my uncle moved toward me, and as he did so, his aba slipped from his shoulders and a part of it fell on my knees and covered them. On any other occasion I should have pushed it away, but I was so impressed that I did not think it wise to move my hands, which were clasped and resting on my knees.

Presently he called out, "Mother dear, would it please

you to favour our dear child with some of the gaz sent to us by Zel-es-Soltan, brother of Shah Nasser-ed-Din."

"And yourself, dear sir," answered my aunt, "what does your desire suggest?"

"I shall have a cup of tea in company with our dear guest."

My aunt disappeared, and his holiness took out his rosary, a string of beautiful amber beads, and began counting them while he murmured prayers and repeated in Arabic, "God's benedictions be upon Mohammad and his kin," his eyes half closed and his lips moving almost imperceptibly.

I kept quiet but wished my aunt would make haste and bring the candy. I also thought what a wonderful necklace the rosary would make for my promised horse.

What was very curious to me was the absence of any kind of noise in his house such as I was accustomed to hear in our own home, with its continual running, shuffling, and whisking about of the servants and, above all, their whispering, which sounded like the chirp of birds, yet clear and loud enough for us to hear what they said from one side of the court to the other. It made me very curious. I knew that my aunt had at least ten maidservants, many menservants and also many distant relatives and friends living with her.

Just as I was wondering where my Laleh could be, I heard his holiness say: "I did not forget to ask after the family, but I had to finish some prayers that I started before you arrived. How is the health of the high-ranked sire, Hadj-Agha?"

"By the grace and good wishes of your holiness, he is in perfect health and bounteous condition," I replied.

"And Her Grace the Khanom?"

"Thank God, she is happy and ordered me to submit to your holiness her abiding love and greetings devoid of any calculated design or bias."

He was pleased at the quickness and correctness of my

replies. Arching his eyebrows, he glanced approvingly at me and murmured to himself: "Yes, yes, the sign of our blood and clean lineage, polished as a cut diamond and sharp as a sword. God protect him!"

"May I disturb you, my good sir," said my aunt, coming into the room and taking a large tray from the maid-servant, who turned her head, so as to keep her face covered by her tchador, and disappeared like a spirit, to be followed by another maid, bearing a larger tray with steaming cups of tea.

My aunt sat down and said to me with smiling eyes, "I am sure our dear child is unaccustomed to our lack of ceremony, especially to seeing me perform the servants' duties. His holiness, your venerable and beloved uncle, does not believe in servants, particularly womenservants. He has no taste for anything, be it food served in Heaven to the blessed ones or the food served on earth, that is presented by duty. He only cares for that which is handed to him through love, and——"

"A man receives no better love in this world than that of his wife," my uncle finished.

His wife's cheeks became like roses, and she hid her face behind my shoulder.

My uncle continued, saying: "Remember what our world-famous sages taught us, 'With a good woman a man is borne on angels' wings through this world.'"

"And a bad one?" my aunt asked jestingly.

"A bad woman! There is no such thing," he replied with emphasis.

As if he had forgotten me, he said half apologetically to himself, "Why, we are keeping our child from tasting the gaz."

Somehow, with a piece of candy, I felt more at ease and began to chat in my turn. "Has my high-honoured uncle heard about my riding?" I inquired a little bashfully.

"No; do tell me all about it."

Here my aunt came to my rescue and informed him of what she herself had learned a few minutes before; for my Laleh had been telling it to all the household.

"I am indeed delighted," my uncle declared, "not because our child is riding—riding is in our blood and many of our boys were born on horseback—but because I have been informed of the fact in time to congratulate him."

At this juncture our conversation was interrupted by the most forceful braying of a donkey! Now, a mollah believes that the cries of animals are really songs in praise of the Creator. Hence a silence fell upon us which was not broken until the braying stopped. Then I courageously took up the broken conversation and said that I was going to have a horse, or rather a score of horses, according to the many promises made to me.

My aunt was awaiting some comment from her husband, who, I thought, was still impressed by the donkey's noisy interruption. He noticed her anxiety and nodded as if to say, "Wait a minute." With the rosary in his left hand, he closed his eyes, passed the palm of his right hand thrice over the beads, finally took the string in the middle and, smiling, said: "Aye, my dear mother, it seems to me that the braying of the donkey was not a mere coincidence but the voice of truth! The omen that I took upon the rosary confirms the idea. There is no reason that a creature like me, a total nothingness in the hand of Destiny, less than a dot, humbler than a speck in the vast and infinite arrangement of the creation, should not bend the pride of his ego to that higher and more powerful force that feeds a worm in the heart of a rock and guides a mole to it. Yes, yes, even the cry of an ass can serve one at a given time as an inspiration."

My aunt and I, hushed by this eloquence, tried to look as if we understood. I confess that only the words donkey, ass, worm and mole interested me in the least. All of a sudden His Holiness jumped nimbly to his feet, stretched his powerful body to its full length and said, looking quite boyish, "Heigh, heigh, my child, let us see what you can do." Then he called out in an imperious voice, "Zobeydeh, tell them to bring the donkey here."

Now I understood in what sense the donkey had brayed out the truth. Though I could hardly believe my ears, I joyously took my uncle's hand and tried to make him run. To my immense pleasure he let himself be amused, and together we raced into the court.

The stable was situated at the back of the house, and from there the groom brought in a beautiful, strong, young, white donkey, a high-spirited, fine looking beast, as big as a mule. The maidservants kept themselves behind the curtains in their rooms, and my aunt covered her face a little in the presence of the groom.

My Laleh had been lounging in the room where the servants were having their tea, but now he called to ask if he might be allowed to come out and see the donkey.

My aunt drew the attention of his holiness to Laleh's request.

"Yes, certainly, let him come here; I need him," said my uncle.

Laleh came and stood in attendance.

"What do you think of this donkey?" my uncle inquired.

"Very fine, sir," he answered, with the grimace common with him when he meant what he said.

"Laleh Agha, go and tell them to bring the palan, my own palan," commanded my uncle.

Laleh vanished for a moment and came back with a boy carrying the saddle.

Presently the donkey was ready to be ridden. He looked very proud, as if he knew that he had on his back a most gorgeous saddle with a rug woven by hand especially for him. On his body was a harness covered with silver plates, and around his neck a silver collar and also another one of silk with long fringe at the end. In addition he had two necklaces of blue and red beads, of which I have seen many imitations made into necklaces for women in the West.

"This animal," said my uncle to Laleh, "is a thorougbred of the Kerman strain with an authentic pedigree. It was sent to us by Prince Etezad-es-Sultaneh, and it is worth a pure-bred Arab stallion."

Laleh was already acquainted with these details and more. He confided to me later that this particular donkey was known to all the dealers in Teheran and was worth two bags of gold.

"Now, sir, we shall be pleased if you will try him and see how he receives you," said my uncle.

My heart leaped to my mouth and I ran toward Laleh, who took me up and set me on the saddle, fixing my feet in the stirrups, which had been properly shortened.

The donkey cocked his ears and, when I touched the reins, started a trot called yorgheh, for which animals of his breed were famed throughout the country, a quick step without any jolts and fast as a horse trot. I raced twice around the court. Everybody was filled with enthusiasm, his holiness repeating, "Bah, bah, marhaba, marhaba!"— "Aye, aye, bravo, bravo!" My aunt was devouring me with admiration. The little servant girls with their beautiful eyes were peeping from behind the curtains, and they smiled at me when I passed. My uncle made a motion, and I stopped before him. Both the donkey and I looked to see what he thought of us.

"My boy," he said, "it is a pleasure to see in you the instinct of your forefathers. It is said that no man ever becomes a good horseman without first kissing the ground from the back of a donkey. Having your future at heart,

I advise you to take your share of falls by riding a donkey for the first year of your training."

Everyone seemed to be of the same opinion, and in sign of obedience to his desire I lifted my face to him. He came near and kissed me on the forehead.

"But, Uncle," I cried, "we haven't any donkeys in the stable, and I haven't one myself."

"Are you not sitting on one?" he replied with a twinkle in his eyes.

"Yes, Uncle, but it is not mine."

"Sit fast on it, sir, and ride home on it; the noble donkey, the gift of our faithful friend and Prince, is yours!"

Thus it came about that I was lord and master of a dashing steed in the shape of a donkey, which served me for a whole year, though I had received promises of a score of horses from other members of the family.

"Khoda bozorgast!"—"God is great!" my Laleh said philosophically; "even the great hero of Turan, the famous Afrasiab, rode a donkey before he became known as a rider of wild elephants."

III

MY COUSINS AND I DISTRIBUTE
ALMS TO THE POOR

DINNER in my parents' home was served five hours after sunset, in the apartment where my father rested in the afternoon and read his books. It was a big room with five niches, all, except the one reserved for the money-box, filled with books and a few old china vases. Four Ispahan carpets, two large ones and two runners, covered the floor. There was a long table against the wall in a corner, near one of the doors looking into the court. On this table were heaped some twenty huge bundles. There were pieces of rare old Kashmir shawls, cut into the size of a square tablecloth and containing the everyday wardrobe of my father. All his clothes without exception were made of old shawls, woven either in Kashmir or in Persia, or of rich brocades and fine Persian textiles. The only piece of furniture besides the table was an ancient high chair of ebony with ivory inlay.

At the dinner hour a long tablecloth was spread on the floor in the centre of the room. My mother sat at the head and my father at the foot. There were dishes of stews, bowls of different soups and some twenty or thirty side dishes. The *pièce de résistance* was not roast beef—no Persian in those days would have dreamed of eating beef—but boiled rice. In Persia there is a certain rice called sadry, which is not cultivated elsewhere. For this reason and also because no other cook in the world ever succeeds in boiling rice properly, all the Indian princes and rich people in

26

Turkey and Afghanistan and Syria have Persian cooks and
Persian rice. As for the Persians, they consider the rice
and stews prepared in other countries so much food wasted.
How could it be otherwise? Where, but in Persia, would
a woman work for a whole day to make ready the ingredients needed in the sauce for one stew?

My father and mother expected each member of the
family—brothers and their wives and children, aunts, uncles,
and relatives living with us—to be present at dinner. Altogether there were about thirty persons. They were placed
according to their age, except the youngest, who sat next
to the father—an honour I long enjoyed. As a rule there
were several guests—men with their wives, or bachelors.
Naturally they were near relatives of my parents. I say
naturally because, according to the religious principles of
Islam, male strangers are not admitted to the intimacy of
the anderun. The servants, too, were fed, and, if they had
families living outside, they took home platters for their
wives and children. A score of poor families belonging to
the quarter were also provided with food every night.

It was curious that the meals to be taken away were
served first. This custom, we believed, gave barekat, or
augmentation as a result of charity, to the food that remained. On this subject I have heard a proverb from the
negro woman who was head of the servants attending my
mother. She said, "If you cook enough for ten persons and
first serve two to the poor, you will find the rest sufficient
for twelve."

My governess had another idea about the reward for giving to the poor. She said that when the cook takes the
covers from the bowls of food, the hordes of jinnees that
prowl around in the darkness go to the kitchen and help
themselves. Being invisible, they cannot be dealt with by
human beings. The only protection against them is the
presence of good spirits such as the parys, who are com-

missioned to look after poor men and women in the night and guide them where they will receive food. Accordingly, when a poor person comes to your house for alms, he brings with him an angel, and "Where an angel treads, the devil takes to his heels."

In regard to this as well as most other matters, we children believed what we were told, and seldom contradicted or tried to verify a statement. But it came about that a cousin of mine, several years older than I and very proud of his knowledge, imbued us with the idea of proving the truth of barekat.

One night in the month of Ramazan, when Mohammedans fast except between sunset and sunrise, this cousin, three other boys and I, went into the kitchen, took a bowl of polow (made of rice and chicken), covered it with a basket, and went out of one of the side doors in the garden wall, through a long passage to a small house my father had given to Eshagh, the beet-root seller, and thence to the street. The bowl was set down, and while my cousin kept watch, the three other boys and I went in search of paupers.

The first person we saw was a young man, whose coloured robe, tied with a white scarf, was evidence of his being the son of a merchant and therefore not a pauper. Nevertheless one of the boys called to him, asking, "Are you a poor man?"

The man turned abruptly and looked at him, a frown on his face.

"What of it if I am?" he answered.

Not one of us answered. We felt ashamed. "If he would only go away!" I thought. Seeing that he continued to look inquiringly at us, I ventured to say politely, "You see, sir, we are looking for poor men who would be willing to accept some food from us, and I have no doubt you will excuse our mistake."

Surveying us with more interest, he said with a smile:

"From your manner and words I gather you are well meaning children. In regard to your intentions, you may be assured of my admiration." Then he bowed and walked away.

We were disappointed, and in my annoyance I made a wry face when two big boys and a man approached us. "Best of boys and soul of my soul!" the man called out. "Just the sort of chaps a poor man desires to meet!" Coming closer, he added in a casual and friendly tone while making gestures with his head and hands: "Be sure, boys, that if you have made a vow or wish, you are in the right path. You will never find any of the poor so hungry or meritorious as your humble servant and his praiseworthy friends."

His two praiseworthy friends grinned.

"But are you poor?" inquired one of the boys.

"Do we look like the Shah's sons?" asked the man, bringing his face close to that of my comrade, his head cocked to one side.

"And what about our fine and gorgeous garments?" interrupted one of his companions, throwing the skirt of his torn coat into the air and making a mock salaam with the gesture of a king.

Even if their clothes were poor, their manners were not at all pleasing, but I told them to follow us. When we came up my cousin invited the man and the two big boys to sit. Then he served the rice, imitating the manner of our negro cook, and handed a plate to each. After he had served them, he called us to fetch some more of the hungry, declaring there was enough for ten men.

"Don't trouble yourself, master cook," groaned the man with his mouth full; "remember the Arab proverb, 'If you are bent on being generous, give abundantly.'" He presented his plate three times and his friends did likewise.

"There is still enough food for seven persons," my cousin remarked. "Run, boys, and bring some more."

But, with an uneasy feeling that our long absence would be detected, I remarked that it was time for us to go back home.

"Yes, yes, he is right," the man said. "It is getting late, and everybody, including the poor, will be going home. If you will let me have the rest, I will distribute it."

"How are you going to carry the rice? We have no plate," I replied.

"Very easily; the basket cover will do."

Without a word, my cousin put the basket on the ground, filled it with rice, laid the two remaining chickens on the top and handed it to the man. Then he said to us, "We must hurry."

The man thanked us profusely and declared that the rest of the food would be given to two old women who had many children. He added that if we intended to continue the almsgiving the next evening, he would be glad to see us and bring some very needy persons with him. We told him we were not sure and bade him good night.

We arrived safely, stopped near the kitchen and listened to make certain there was nobody about. Then we put the bowl on its wood-fire bed, covered it with another basket and hurried to our bedroom.

The cocks were beginning to crow. In two hours the servants would be calling us for sahari, the last meal before sunrise. One of the boys suggested that we go back to the kitchen and find out what sort of fairies were going to fill the bowl with rice. But my cousin advised us to keep quiet and feign sleep. He had less faith than the rest of us.

Later we heard whisperings among the servants and then the footsteps of Dadeh, who called for her darlings to get up and make ready for sahari. My cousin was lost in sleep, but the rest of us dressed quickly and went to the dining room where we found my father in an unusually gracious mood. He was very much pleased at our resolution to prove ourselves men by observing the fast of Ramazan, notwithstanding that our age, which was less than eight years, exempted us from the rigidity of going without food for twelve hours.

I thought a great deal about our adventure. When dinner was over and nothing had occurred to give me a clue to whether the bowl had been found empty or filled, I felt that I must ask. There was no one I could address with greater courage than my mother. So, when kissing her good night, I begged her to let me do my Ramazan prayer with her.

"Certainly, darling; I am glad to have you," she replied.

I followed her to the basin and performed the rites of ablution as she did. First the face and mouth were washed; then water was caught in the palm of the right hand and poured on the left arm, and likewise in the palm of the left hand and poured on the right arm. Finally the wet hand was passed over the instep of both feet.

The prayer room reserved for my mother was not so large as ordinary Persian rooms. It contained a very old carved and inlaid chair, with long arms and a tall back, and a single niche holding a half dozen prayer books. In front of the door, which was curtained with a Kashmir shawl, was a small carpet woven in the same design as the shawl. This carpet was covered with a ghadifah, a piece of fine Persian linen of cream colour which had been dipped in the sacred water of the well called Zemzem and spread on the tomb of the bewailed and mourned saints and emams and on the shrine of Hazrate Hossein, most holy of all holy martyrs, by my father, who had made this pilgrimage to Mecca, Medina, Kerbela, Najaf and Meshed. On one side of the ghadifah stood an open, inlaid holder upon which rested a manuscript Koran, an heirloom of rare beauty.

When my mother arrived, I saw that she had changed into garments of fine, white, and almost transparent linen. She looked taller. Her white hands with fine long fingers and her face white as marble—except for her luminous eyes with their long black lashes and her full red lips—were so beautiful that they fascinated me.

She took my chin in her hand and bade me sit on the prayer carpet next to her. Then she opened a brocade handkerchief, which was folded and pinned on the edge of the carpet, and spread it out. In it were a simple rosary of black beads and a little sack of brocade covered with pearls. From this sack she took out two small tablets, which she told me were made of earth taken from the shrine of Hazrate Hossein and inscribed with the name of God and the five sacred names, Mohammad, Ali, Fatima, Hassan and Hossein.

She placed one before me and one before herself. These tablets are an important part of the prayers. When prostrating ourselves on the ground, we place our foreheads upon them. When everything was ready, she began the prayer and I followed her. After the prayer, she put the tablets back in the little sack and folded the handkerchief.

She took the Koran from the holder and touched its cover first with her forehead and then with her lips. Next she presented the sacred book to me and I did the same. After this ceremony she opened it and read this passage in Arabic:

"El djennate tahte eghdamel ommehat"—"Paradise is at the feet of mothers." Although I gave my full attention to the rest of the chapter, this phrase kept repeating itself to me. Finally, when my mother had closed the Koran, I asked, "What about the old Hatieh?" She was a Jewess who used to bring jewelry to my mother and was known as the most honest merchant among her people. "She has a little boy. Is she a mother too?"

"Certainly Hatieh is a mother and is included in the Prophet's words: she too has paradise under her feet."

"Then why did Dadeh tell me not to touch her or go near her or play with her? Because she is a Yahoudi?"

"I think it is because the woman is poorly dressed and her clothes are dusty."

"But you told me that, no matter how poorly men and women are dressed, I must never be afraid to touch them or to be kind to them. Besides, do I not always play with the boys of Mash-hadi Eshagh, who are very dirty and poor?"

My mother looked at me thoughtfully. Then, as if something had come to her mind, she asked me to fetch another holy book from the niche and give it to her. She opened this volume, which she said was the book of Hadiths, or oral teachings of the Prophet, and read to me: "Mohammad taught, nay enforced, as one of the essential teachings of Islam, 'Respect for Women.'" I must know for truth, she herself added, that "Womanhood is divine in any colour, creed or clothes." Then, lowering her voice, she told me that I might even teach this to Dadeh.

I asked if I might go at once and talk to Dadeh.

"No, darling, you are tired out and should go to bed unless there is anything else you wish to ask me."

All at once I thought of what we had done in the early evening. I felt embarrassed, not knowing whether to ask her now or wait till the morrow. "May I ask you something?" I inquired meekly at last.

She nodded.

"Was the small bowl of polow filled or—er—er—"

"Empty!" she replied and smiled as she took my face in both her hands. "The bowl was empty, but twice the quantity of food which you gave to the poor had been added to the contents of the other bowls!"

Then she helped me to my feet and said, "Come along, sweetheart; I shall see you to your room."

IV

LALEH TAKES ME TO SCHOOL

Some time after my seventh birthday, I was informed by Laleh that in a few weeks we should have to think of going to school. By the pronoun "we," he meant me, his little master. "We" is used in Persia instead of "you" in deference or when the subject referred to is considered to be displeasing to a gentleman. I received this news calmly, having no idea of school life. I must even have looked rather pleased; for Laleh smiled and rubbed his hands, saying he would inform the whole household that "I" had decided to attend school.

Of course I liked the thought of having many playmates, all boys, instead of a dozen assorted ones at home, and I was pleased that my preliminary studies were at an end. I could recite poetry from Sadi and Hafiz as if it were my own. I could say my prayers in Arabic without fault. I knew the story of the creation, as taught by the governess. It began on the sixth day of the month of Farvardin. On this day, she told us, Khoda shaped a clay toy that he kept till the sixteenth day of the month of Mehr. Then he blew life into it, and before him stood His Excellency Adam. On this day he also created Havva, or Eve, from one of Adam's left ribs and blew life into all the creatures that live. Also, I was aware that the world was a flat surface made of earth and water and that it rested on the horn of a mighty bull, which, when tired, shifted the world to the other horn. This maneuver happened invariably once a year. I was letter perfect in the story of how Adam ate an apple and after-

34

ward accused Eve of having tempted him, and how Khoda became angry with him, first for having disobeyed, second for pleading so absurd an excuse.

My religious education was now quite equal to that of my governess. I knew that there were seventy-two prophets —the first Adam and the last Hazrate Rassul, or Mohammad. I knew that Moussa, the sage of God, Issa, the spirit of God, and Mohammad, the last messenger of God, were the chosen among the prophets. I knew also that I must never disparage the religious beliefs of others by word or deed and never force them to conversion. When among them or in their temples, I should do as they did. Never should I show by sign or look disbelief or contempt, knowing that Mohammad said, "They have their religion and you have yours."

Laleh and of course my mother and my father, as well as the governess, devoted themselves to my oral education. The rules most stressed by words and pictures were those relating to the immediate needs in life—to ride well, to use arms, to wear only clean clothes and never to·lie. Even the learning of a trade was insisted upon in case I should ever, through some trick of fortune, have to depend on my hands for a livelihood. So I took up woodworking. An old carpenter, who looked very much like a bushman, was especially engaged to teach me. We children were given a large hall to work in, and later this place was made into a real workshop where the man did all the carpentry for our family. He remained with us for years and received a house for himself, his wife, and four children. Another man for more than six months taught me the art of decoration, from the painting of a door to the cutting and making of curtains. I could also mend, sew and cut simple garments. An Armenian tenant of my brother's taught me to make musical instruments such as the tar, setar and seintur. Another Armenian tenant tried to make a cobbler of me, but without success. A third Armenian, who had a liquor shop, wished to show me how to make liquor, but, finding me unresponsive, decided instead to teach me how to cook Armenian food. Both of us later came to the conclusion that it would be simpler to let his mother send some of her cooking to the shop; three or four times a week I had my luncheon with him.

Another Armenian, named Petrus, a very kind and fatherly man with a fine son of my age, had a store where one could buy all sorts of manufactured goods. Though he also wanted me to become interested in his shop, there was nothing to learn, since he did not manufacture any of the goods himself. At last, after much cogitation, he hit upon an idea. Then one day he called me into the shop and showed me a wonderful machine for knitting socks. I had never seen one before and was greatly pleased with it. So, having got my brother's permission, I ordered six of the machines, set up a factory at home and engaged six young men to operate them under the tutelage of the storekeeper's son. The work became a great success and made the old man very happy, since the money I gave him for the machines paid the rent of his shop for many years.

But this was labour at second hand. The chief manual tasks with which I busied myself personally belonged to the care of a horse. To groom it and to make the correct style of knot with its tail were very difficult at first. So was saddling it; for a Persian saddle was an elaborate thing and took a good half hour to make ready.

Even the giving of alms was an art that I, like the one who asks for aid, had to be taught. In this connection I am reminded of an incident having to do with a poor man who once stopped my brother, the Khan Dadash, in the street and asked him for bread.

He stretched out his hand, saying, "O agha of my soul and light of my eyes, turn your eyes to a poor gentleman, give him a piece of bread and know that Khoda will repay you a hundred pieces."

My brother looked displeased. "Are you a fool, you with so tall and sturdy a body, to beg for a piece of bread only? Besides, do I look like a baker that you think I carry bread in my pocket?"

"No, sir, I know you to be the son of the great Hadj-Agha, who never touches a grain of wheat either from the Shah's treasure or from the public store, a generous father and merciful, and—"

"Enough reason that you should ask accordingly," my brother interrupted him.

"Forgive me, sir," the petitioner said apologetically, "my little knowledge of the standard of education built by our poets and thinkers. My insolent and empty stomach has drained my mind for the past six hours, or else I should have remembered the famous percept of Hatem, who said: 'If you have the bad luck to be forced to beg alms from a King on this earth or from God in Heaven, do not beg for anything less than a fortune.' "

My brother then replied with a smile: "Nor do I forget, my good man, the saying of Djelal-od-Din Saghaphi, 'If you give charity, do not heed the man's outward appearance or his immediate need but give according to your own wealth and condition.' "

"Sir, a fine and great man was Djelal-od-Din," the beggar replied.

"You seem to be conversant with our literature and poets," said my brother.

"Has anybody ever know a Persian who was not?" the man inquired.

"Now tell me what I can do for you," urged my brother.

"Very well, sir, give me a roof to shelter my wife and children. Give me clothes to cover my nudity and theirs, and give me also food to eat, so that I shall attain honour in this life, which, by the way, I received without having to ask for it."

My brother roared with laughter and ordered his attendant to look after the man. As a result, he was employed in the dispensary at the garrison of the Cossack regiment, and, after some years, he became a well known and very wealthy doctor.

The principles guiding our relations with other men in later life were also impressed on my mind. Not a day passed that we children did not receive one or two proverbs to memorize. In the evening we discussed them with Laleh and the governess, who would make us understand their practical meaning by anecdotes and illustrations. Laleh and the governess would take turns in interpreting, for example, "Do not wound an enemy or a viper unless it is to kill," or "It is better not to establish friendship with a keeper of elephants unless you have a house with a gate large enough for two elephants to pass through."

On one occasion, when I was being taught how to become a perfect host, I learned a precept said to cover the subject completely: "Never sit a second time at the table of a man who talks about the price of food, or who tells you how to eat, or who sees a hair in the morsel you are bringing to your mouth." Once, and only once, have I been ashamed of myself in this regard. On a Friday I had invited some boys and girls to spend the day. After their departure I gave a report of our doings to my father, and criticised the table manners of some of them. My father looked astonished, put his head down as if in shame and asked, "Did you, sir, invite your friends to partake of food or to learn table manners?"

Another phase of our training in Persia is the instruction we receive at a tender age to prepare us for our future life as husbands and fathers. In truth, I believe that sex consciousness comes very early to a Persian boy. It would not be exaggerating to say that at seven or eight he is as conscious of this aspect of his life as a boy of seventeen or eighteen in the West. Whether our precocity is due to our oral education or to our being compelled to live and behave in childhood as if we were adults, or to climatic conditions, or to all three, I cannot tell. At any rate, rules for behaviour as a husband or a wife were given boys and girls at the age of seven—probably because we were considered to be grown up at the age of nine and a boy, by the law of Islam, could even contract marriage if he so desired.

Among the proverbs taught us, I remember especially, "Never speak about women to men and least of all to women." Another was, "Never flatter a human being unless it happens to be your employer or your wife." There were of course precepts essentially Persian, as: "Love your wife, treat your horse well, take care of your sword, and you may consider yourself a knight. Neglect them and be a knave." One proverb that I always liked immensely as a boy and that is still my favourite with regard to love and marriage, is this: "The shortage of money is said to cause Cupid to fly away; he may just as well fly to Hell!"

My books were chosen for me no less carefully than my first teachers—Laleh and the governess. The volumes I possessed were written by some of our master calligraphers. They were beautifully decorated and had many exquisite miniatures. I was permitted to take them with me anywhere I liked, even to the top of an old apple tree, where I had built a cabin for myself in which to rest in the afternoons and read the famous "Alexander Book," without being disturbed. This volume was an illuminated manuscript, written by my father at the age of eleven and illustrated by the best artists of his time. I was also given beautiful specimens of calligraphy by Mir-Emad and others, to inspect and try to imitate.

So greatly did my father desire to develop in the minds of his children love for art and beauty that, when I asked him to allow me to choose a room for my own study, he said in a courteous voice: "The whole place is yours, sir. A man of your age"—I was seven at the time—"must know his own choice best."

So I called my private council, Mahboub and Arzagh-Cheshm, the two little negro boys, Suskeh, the little negro girl, Dadeh and Laleh and we went through the house to find a room to my liking. Mahboub thought the quietest place would be the room where the walnuts were kept. Suskeh favored a closet in one of the servants' rooms where her mother used to take a nap in the afternoon, and Arzagh voted for the prison-house!

Laleh, who was six feet four inches barefoot, interrupted them all by saying: "I have no desire, sir, but to please you. I must only say that, if the walnut room is selected, I shall have to get a ladder and enter the room through the window. The trap leading to this room is too narrow and low for me to pass through. The closet and the prison are both of no consequence, although I am completely at your command."

All at once I remembered a large room where my doctor brother used to receive visitors. That, I decided, was the place for me. It was a room of rare Persian architecture. Three high, wide, mahogany-framed bay windows of stained glass, cut and painted by hand with a background of royal blue and gold, such as I have seen in some of the cathedrals in the West, opened into an orange grove with tall, graceful trees. The three mahogany doors opening into the biruni, or men's court, in front of the basin and flower beds, were also decorated with stained glass. The ceiling and the walls, with their arched niches holding antique vases of narcissi and blue hyacinths, were ornamented in plaster with floral designs and figures of men. Three antique crystal chandeliers—the central one having seventy branches—hung from the ceiling, and along the walls were smaller chandeliers to match. On every branch sat a blue and silver and gold bird of paradise, and blue and silver were the prevailing tones in the background of the painted cut crystal shades. The floor was covered with fine carpets and rugs. Heavy mokhattehs (huge mattresses a yard and a half long and a yard high, stuffed with cotton and covered with Kashmir shawls and Persian velvet) were placed against the wall and on the floor in a spacious alcove called Shah-Neshin, where the Shah and other distinguished guests would sit when my brother entertained them. The news of my having chosen this beautiful room spread throughout the household. My father seemd pleased with me, and my mother gave her approval. The matter of my study was settled.

On the next day I arose an hour before sunrise, washed, dressed with great care and, prior to eating my simple breakfast of tea and rusks, went for the first time through the regular morning prayer with the full details prescribed for all the Faithful. This is a duty set down by the Shariat for a boy going to school.

Laleh called to escort me. My mother presented me with a manuscript Koran with a beautiful lacquered cover. It was written by the son of Vasal, a master calligrapher, on old paper called termeh. Each page was illuminated, and the spaces between the writing were painted with gold. I took the Koran, which was encased in an envelope made of a shawl and decorated with a band of brocade, respectfully touched the cover with my lips and put the book under my arm. My mother kissed me, wished me great progress in my studies and said, "Remember, darling, what Hazrate Rassul recommended: 'Seek knowledge from the cradle to the bier.' "

Half a dozen womenservants, Dadeh at their head, followed us from the room. Near the curtain they all kissed me lovingly. Dadeh then took her handkerchief out and dried some tears. Finally she blew her nose with great force and made a sign to the others that the scene was finished.

Outside the gates some servants were waiting. One had a fluffy sheepskin on his shoulder. Another held a copper brazier under one arm and a pair of copper tongs in the opposite hand. A third carried a canvas bag filled with charcoal. Laleh took my hand and helped me avoid small patches of snow here and there and ditches filled with water.

When we entered the tekkyeh, all the shopkeepers left their shops and made a circle around us, saying they trusted Khoda that I would pass all other children in knowledge and even surpass my doctor brother, who left his beautiful country with its many world-famed madressehs to study in Faranguestan. "Not that we are resentful—oh, no," they assured me, "but we count on our little master to prove that Iran is a land of culture and that no other boys can be compared with our boys."

Along came the seyyed butcher, with his shaved head and well-trimmed beard. He was a tall, strong man with the chest and arms of a pugilist, a true and real descendant of the Prophet. In one hand he held his scimitar, which looked like a foot-long razor; in the other a rose. He presented me with the rose—it was his custom to decorate the carcasses of sheep with roses—and said: "Here, O son of our master and glory of our tekkyeh, this I give to you before the eyes of all the world"—he drew a circle in the air with his scimitar—"to say that we, the faithful workers under your distinguished family, are ready to uphold you and your family to the last drop of our blood. I, the seyyed butcher of the world and chief of the shopkeepers' organization of this quarter, pledge my head and my scimitar for what I say. Further, to you, O people gathered in this tekkyeh, know that our little master is of age to honour and head our

Dasteh—the Passion Play Procession—for the coming month of Moharram, and that the banner of Tekkyeh Hossein Beyk will be carried to the end of the world, if the whole population of this quarter has to be sacrificed for the cause." He jumped on the platform in the center of the square, tossed up his scimitar, caught it again with a flourish and shouted to everybody, "Now send a salavat to Mohammad!" Some fifty throats burst into a warlike shout: "Allahomma salle ala Mohammad va ale Mohammad!"—"Blessing on him and his faithful descendants and their companions!"

I had known that I was going to have a reception and I was prepared. Laleh without saying a word, took me under the arms and placed me on the same platform. The moment had now arrived for me to proclaim officially to the whole world, as the seyyed butcher had done, that I had entered the sacred circle of manhood.

The seyyed butcher understood. He jumped down and cleared a space before me, and cried out, "Listen, ye people, to what our little master will say."

In the silence that fell, I heard my voice addressing the crowd: "My dear agha and fellow citizens, you and I are all the beloved children of my father, His Honor Hadj-Agha. Although I am not yet as grown up as you are, you may be sure that the honour of this tekkyeh and its banner and the welfare of the people of our quarter will be defended and guarded with a lion's heart and a hero's sword!"

A shout of approval rent the air, and three more salavats were sent to Mohammad. Then Laleh put me on his shoulder, and amid great rejoicing we passed to my schoolroom on the roof of the bazar.

I climbed up the steps, followed by Laleh, and we found ourselves on the flat platform, which commanded a most interesting view. There were as many domes as shops in the bazar, and the outlook suggested a wonderful place for hide-and-seek. But I could not play in public. School, I knew by this time, did not include games: only study, reading, recitation, writing. Wandering, especially, was forbidden; for a pack of wild dogs roamed the roof of the bazar all day long.

These were the night patrols of our district. Every evening four hours after sunset a bugle sounded for the closing of all thoroughfares. Citizens were warned to stay indoors. Then the dogs, savage as wolves, were loosed on the streets. By their howls, they inspired terror in the hearts of thieves and peaceful strangers alike. Even in the daytime they were dangerous. They were fed by the merchants; they knew all the townspeople by sight and smell and were on familiar terms with everyone. But, had Laleh and I trespassed on their holdings, they would have defended their rights with their teeth.

We kept out of their way and presented ourselves before the schoolmaster, Amirza who received us pleasantly and with due respect. Then a servant spread my sheepskin on the floor, and I sat down. The other servant made a charcoal fire in the copper brazier and placed it before me. Laleh whispered for a few minutes in the master's ear, and, after asking permission, bowed and left me. Amirza, who had the title jinnee-catcher—devil-catcher, that is—because he was known to have caught the king of a tribe of jinnees and to be in control of that invisible sovereign and his entire following, was very short, skinny and shriveled, with a long, pointed beard resembling the beard of a goat. His eyes, two black beads of supernormal brilliance, rolled constantly with an alertness that made people uneasy. He looked the wizard to the life. He did not dress in a mollah's costume and turban, as did the other teachers in Persian schools, but affected the aba, a sort of over-all gown, which gave him the appearance of a learned man. On his egg-shaped head he wore a faded imitation lambskin cap. Although comparatively young, he was entirely bald. I had heard that his hair fell out during those meditations in the ruins of Rei, the ancient capital of Persia, which had developed his mysterious powers.

Contrary to what might have been expected, he proved to be an amiable man. My first day at school, he explained, should be spent in conversation with him and in making friends with the other boys. He put aside the Koran and told me stories about the activities of the police dogs, and about Djahannam, or Hell, and its inhabitants. Then he praised my family and told me in a confidential tone that he found my Laleh a man of exceptional intelligence and a well-mannered gentleman, adding: "Yes, sir, a very fine gentleman! And please don't consider yourself bound to me for discretion. You are welcome to repeat my opinion of him to his face!"

I was naturally delighted with my first day at school and eager to give an account of it to my father when I got home. To my surprise when my father learned that no other boy had a copper brazier before him or was fetched for tea, he said, "Very well, sir, you shall see that all the boys are provided with a brazier like yours and are fetched for tea. Equality breeds democracy, and a school is a good place in which to begin." I talked the matter over with my mother and Laleh. My mother agreed that we might give braziers to the boys and provide tea and sugar for them. But she said that their mothers were really too busy to make tea. I took the hint, since I had already got from my father's words my first notion of democracy. "Khanom djounam"—lady of my soul—I said, "I desire to have a sun-baked brazier and will do without tea in the afternoon like all the other boys."

The next morning Laleh and I emerged into the public place without attendants behind us. He carried a clay brazier under one arm and a sack of charcoal. I carried the Koran.

When we reached the centre of the tekkyeh, Eshagh emerged from behind the big tree and greeted me with his usual salaam. He looked rather astonished at sight of the clay brazier. So Laleh whispered an explanation that seemed both to please and satisfy him; he heaved a sigh and commented: "The righteous mind of the father is already moulding that of the son." Then he stooped before me, making himself as small as possible, and said: "Sir, I have sold all my beets and therefore am unable to present you with one. Accept my words instead. With your heart you will win the public's heart. You have won mine. May God protect you."

But the incident had its sequel. On the following day I found a dish of boiled beets with my breakfast. Eshagh had left them for me before going to his work.

I was already aware of the fact that our schoolmaster used his power as jinnee-catcher for the good of the community. He was famed for finding lost articles, children and thieves. Detectives were wont to consult him, and even the judges asked his help in cases where they failed to discover wrongdoers.

"Is it possible," I asked him one day when I knew him better, "for any other man to become a jinnee-catcher like your honourable self?"

"Yes, my son," he replied gently, "it is quite possible. Every man is capable of subduing one or more jinnee. First he must have courage and audacity. Then he must go forth and wander through the subterranean passages in the ruins of Rei, during the nights of the 27th, 28th and 29th of the devil's months—October, November and December—when the jinnees roam in that place. If he will do so, he may be sure of catching one of them."

Although he possessed this extraordinary power, Amirza remained a simple schoolmaster till his last day. He lived on the monthly subscriptions received from the boys, one kran or ten cents, from the sons of working men, two krans from those of merchants and rich shopkeepers, and five krans from the sons of the nobility. His charge for the invocation of the jinnee was left to the generosity of those who solicited his help. His motto was, "Help mortals whenever help is solicited, be they Faranguis [Europeans], Gabres [Zoroastrians], Jews, or Turks, though a single hair of a true believer is worth the whole lot of them!"

One day it chanced that early in the afternoon, just as we had begun to read the Koran, the curtain was pushed aside and a feminine voice called. Amirza signed to one of the boys to answer. A whispered conversation ensued and was repeated to Amirza in whispers.

He nodded, opened the little window overlooking the tekkyeh and shouted to the old cobbler whose shop was directly under the schoolroom, "Dear old uncle, can you tell me what time it is?"

The cobbler jumped from his seat, walked to the centre of the tekkyeh and gazed up at the sky, at the same time stroking the point of his beard. "Most respected teacher," said he, "I should venture my humble conjecture that it is two hours after noon, yet being faithfully cognizant that God alone is all-knowing!"

Amirza closed the window and cried to the woman, who was patiently waiting without, to come in. She made no move to enter. Again, in a softer and lower tone, Amirza said: "My dear lady, I beg of you to enter without hesitation; there are no strangers present. Please consider me to be your old father and the boys your own sons."

This time the curtain was thrust aside and a gorgeously dressed woman came into view, holding her heavy veil over her face with a firm hand.

"Please come and sit near me," Amirza said.

I rose immediately, and the Khanom, with a graceful movement known as "the peacock's-parade step," glided to my place and sat down. Amirza turned his ear to her and put one of his palms behind it in order to catch her words.

She pushed her veil out of the way a tiny bit and spoke in
so low a tone that it was impossible to overhear.

The boy next to me drew my attention to the large gold
plate set with diamonds and emeralds that served as a clasp
to fasten the two ends of the veil behind her head. I nodded
to him in understanding. These clasps, besides being ornaments and the means of keeping the veil in place, were signs
by which the rank of the wearer could be guessed. The
wives of working men and the middle-class generally wore
clasps made of two gold coins with the effigy of the Shah.
As for the Khanom, I knew that her colors of white and
green were those of my own family.

Now the schoolmaster, when the lady had ceased to speak
and had drawn her veil securely over her face once more,
shoved back his hat and placed a forefinger to his forehead.
He was thinking very hard. We all kept rigidly still. A
low panting was heard from the Khanom, who evidently
found it difficult to breathe under the heavy veil. The
silence lasted for about ten minutes and made me uncom-
fortable. Moreover, I had to fight back a cough that was
tickling my throat.

Relief came when Amirza raised his head, looked at us
in a pensive manner and motioned to a negro boy called
Ghahveh to approach. He was a black little fellow with a
flat nose and a very large mouth and an amusing way of
rolling his eyes. He seated himself in front of Amirza and
gazed intently at the veiled face of the lady. Amirza took
from a drawer in the small table before him an inkwell and
a small bottle filled with some kind of oil. Next he cleaned
the nail of Ghahveh's thumb with a handkerchief and, using
his finger with a brush, painted the nail with black ink and
varnished it with the oil.

I heard him say, in a solemn voice, after another consul-
tation with the lady: "They know what is expected of them,
and, I assure you, they have never failed to satisfy me! It

is their sacred duty to me, their master." Thereupon he made a sign to us to keep quiet, and he himself placed his hands on his knees, closed his eyes and remained silent as the dead.

Ghahveh, who had had previous experience, sat up straight, very dignified and grave. He was looking at his thumb with eyes half shut, an inscrutable expression on his face. Great interest, mingled with anxiety and awe was rising in my heart. The silence lasted a long time, but finally, when I thought the schoolmaster must have fallen asleep, a low, deep voice issued from him. It sounded as if it came from the bottom of a well. He was reciting some cabalistic words and verses from the Koran to invoke the presence of a jinnee. The boy's eyes were focused on his varnished thumbnail in an unflinching stare. His breath came hard, and his body was bent as if he carried a heavy load on his shoulders. Suddenly, in a voice louder and more authoritative, Amirza exclaimed: "I, the school teacher of an ancient quarter of an ancient city, the capital of an ancient country; I, the rightful son of an ancient race, lord and master of all the spirits on the earth, jinnee-catcher of the ruins of Rei, in the name of all that is powerful and mysterious, by the spell of my talismanic invocation and because of my unchallenged might and occult knowledge—I command the presence of a jinnee!"

All these words came in one rush and with such hammering emphasis that they took my breath away! A feeling of alarm crept over me; a cold thrill raced down my spine. It was the first time I had ever heard any one invoke the jinnee.

The silence became more oppressive. I thought no jinnee was going to answer the call, especially in a place where so many copies of the Holy Book were in evidence. Amirza repeated his command. This time harshly. The boy opened his eyes wide. Perspiration ran down his face. He looked terrified. It was some time before he spoke: "O master, the jinnee is here! He is staring at me."

The woman gave a jump! I made ready to smash my clay brazier on the head of the first jinnee that would dare to get at her or rather, to be frank, at me. I felt more at ease when I understood, by the subsequent command of Amirza, that the jinnee was not really going to present himself in flesh and blood but would remain on Ghahveh's thumb. I am afraid that in my excitement I jolted the fair lady at my side; for she turned and looked at me through the tiny holes of her veil, which reminded me of the tiled grilles of the windows in our summer house.

Twice again the master recited the invocation, each time demanding the presence of another jinnee. Ghahveh informed him of their appearance and was ordered to instruct them to sweep and sprinkle water on the ground and bring a chair for their king.

Then Amirza groaned a rhythmical string of words, difficult to understand, and commanded the king of the jinnee to come immediately from his nether kingdom. The king evidently obeyed, and Ghahveh seemed more cheerful.

"Tell the officers to bring the long gold trumpets, the sornas and the drums of kingly size to rejoice the hearts of mortal and immortal souls," commanded Amirza.

Although we did not hear a sound, we were sure that Ghahveh was listening to mysterious music. He was actually keeping time with his shoulders as I had seen the negroes do when dancing on Fridays near the great cemetery of Teheran in the "House of the Negroes." Both Amirza and Ghahveh appeared to awake as if from heavy slumber.

Amirza, whose colour had returned, spoke once more in a natural voice: "Give greeting to the king and ask him if he is ready to answer my questions."

Ghahveh delivered this message, appeared to be listening

and then declared that the king said he was at the master's service.

Then Amirza asked: "What has become of the pearl bracelet, composed of sixty-seven pearls, matched and chained together with a gold clasp set with a single emerald? It is an heirloom of the Khanom who is present. She missed it from the safe where she keeps her jewels. She thinks it has been stolen."

Ghahveh repeated the message word for word and waited for an answer. "Master," he said at length, "the king declares that the bracelet has not been stolen."

On hearing this the Khanom, became very much excited and tried to say something, but Amirza would tolerate no interruption. He pointed a finger at her veiled face as if to say, "Keep quiet!"

Thereafter he continued with the séance, inquiring, "What, then, if not stolen?"

"Lost," came the answer.

"Where?" asked the master.

"In the basin in the anderun," was the answer.

"Who lost the bracelet?"

"The Khanom herself!"

The Khanom again made as if to speak but was imperiously commanded to keep silence.

"Convey my regrets to the king for the trouble I have given him, and my gratitude for this information. Tell him he is free to go."

After a few seconds Ghahveh said, "The king thanks you for your generosity in giving him his freedom for to-day, he is leaving."

Then Amirza, having thanked the jinnees for their prompt answer to his call, cleaned Ghahveh's thumb with oil and told him to return to his seat.

Turning to the Khanom, he said: "In the name of the All-knowing and by the powers of the sacred knowledge, we have told you where your bracelet is to be found. Go drain the basin and get your property. Go, and free those whom in your ignorance you accused of being thieves."

The Khanom arose quickly and left the school without speaking.

In the evening, when I related these events to my mother, she said, to my astonishment, that the lady was no other than my own sister-in-law Guelin Khanom and that the bracelet was indeed found in the basin.

I was ashamed at my failure to recognize her, but my mother told me it was quite natural. "We women," said she, "are imprisoned in our tchadors and our veils. I have often passed my daughters-in-law and cousins without guessing who they were."

The finale in the little drama of the jinnee and the bracelet came the next Saturday morning, while I was reading the Koran before the teacher. A servant was ushered into the schoolroom, bearing on his head a large wooden platter covered with a Kashmir shawl. A second servant, having helped take down the platter, handed Amirza a letter. He took it, read it carefully and put it on his desk. Then he ordered one of the boys to receive the gifts. Besides a roll of aghari, an aba from Ispahan, a roll of flowered silk sufficient for a dress for Amirza's wife, there were three conic pieces of sugar, two feet high, ten packages of candles, five flasks of rose water, three boxes of candy from Ispahan and a heavy box of caramel from Kum. In the middle of the platter was a silver bowl, in which there were hundreds of shining silver coins, two krans, piled up like rice. This was handed to Amirza by one of the servants. He took it calmly, poured its contents into a handkerchief and handed the bowl back to the servant, but the man refused to take it, saying his order was to present everything. Amirza just as calmly took the bowl and placed it on his desk. When the platter was empty, the servant folded the shawl and pre-

sented it to Amirza. He looked askance and said to the
man, smiling, "You do not mean to say that you have been
instructed to leave the shawl as well?"

"Certainly, my good master, the Khanom has sent this
wonderful shawl, a gift from the Shah, as a souvenir. We
have to take back only the wooden platter."

Amirza took the shawl and thanked the servants for
their trouble.

Both men fell on their knees and kissed his hands, saying,
"O master of all masters, we are your debtors. All the servants in our house have been under the shadow of suspicion.
We could not swallow our food under its stress; neither
could we look our master in the eyes. You have saved us!"

Then they salaamed to Amirza, bowed to me and left the
room.

V

MAKING READY FOR THE NEW YEAR

THE PERSIAN New Year, which falls on the 21st of March, is a great day. Joyfulness and happiness flutter in the air and the rapture of the occasion is shared by men, animals and plants alike.

The day was instituted as a national holiday by Djemshid the Great, who drank the first toast in wine (till then known as royal medicine), which he quaffed from his famous golden bowl, in which he was reputed to read the future. The day has nothing to do with religion, especially with the religion of Islam. It is a heritage from the ancient life of Iran, the birth land of the Aryans.

A month beforehand every household begins to clean from cellar to garret. I awoke one morning in February to find a dozen menservants taking all the carpets from the house and loading them on mules and donkeys. They were about to hold a rug washing in the stream near the ancient wall of the city, and I begged to be taken along. My famous donkey was saddled and with my Laleh on horseback we started in a long procession through the city. Each mule was burdened twice its size with heavy carpets and the donkeys were so completely hidden under other loads of lighter rugs that only their ears and legs could be seen.

Besides, each mule was further loaded with a man sitting on the top of the carpets and each donkey with a woman. House boys on foot urged the animals forward shouting:

54

"Forward, forward dear souls!" or yelled at the passers-by: "Khabar dar! Khabar dar!"—"Beware, beware!"

After an hour of pushing through the crowded streets and bazaars our caravan halted near the bank of a large stream running between two lines of poplars, where the carpets could be taken to the water without difficulty. Our servants called to a crowd of women who were busy doing their laundry to get their dirty linen out of the way, but they were not to be frightened so easily. Being women, they knew no man would dare to insult or touch them, and so they simply looked at our men with the utmost contempt. Some of the oldest even made faces at them. The head washer was about to start an argument when Laleh intervened.

"My dear old soul and respected creature!" he said to a woman who seemed to be the oldest, "Will you let us help you remove your clothes to a place a little further away? I am afraid these men, clumsy in the art of washing coarse carpets, may hinder you in your admirable labours."

"This is the way one should address a woman," she replied smiling. "Certainly. We shall be glad to make place for you." So saying she arose and called to the others to follow her example.

Meanwhile our animals were unloaded and the carpets spread in the middle of the stream and brushed with long brooms, after which the women trampled them with their feet. I had a great desire to get in the water too, but a look from Laleh made me understand the unseemliness of such an act.

After a while the carpets were taken from the water and spread on gravel beds to dry. Cleansed of dust, they displayed their natural color with more brilliancy than ever. Laleh said that this process of washing the carpets in running water tightened the warp and made them last for centuries.

He was very proud of our beautiful Persian rugs and laughed at the idea of other people trying to copy them.

"Beyond the border of our Empire," said he, "other people, not knowing the secret of vegetable dyes, paint their carpets with chemical dyes." This in his opinion killed the quality of the wool, and if washed with water, as we did ours, the chemical dyes would fade or run into one another.

While this was going on the house itself was receiving repairs where it had suffered from the winter. Mash-hade-Eshagh, the carpenter, and a number of other people under a master mason were working from morning till late in the afternoon. My father used to have a chair placed where he could listen to the master mason, who sang a never ending chantey. Even his orders to his employes were intoned. Thus he called to Eshagh to hand him a brick:

"Oh, my dear old soul and my dear uncle,
Hand me quickly one of the clay bundles,
    You are indeed my help!
Oh, my dear old soul and my dear father,
Throw the lump of mud a little further,
    You are indeed my help!"

I used to amuse my father by playing bricklayer. With bare feet and trousers rolled up to my knees I would paddle in the cool mud and hand Eshagh clay bricks. I was very serious and so was he. Now and then I tried to sing like the master mason, and Eshagh assured me that I was far better than he, but father and the workmen laughed.

Now, too, the gardens were plowed and trees replanted, new shrubbery and bulbs were set out, and basins and pools were drained and cleaned. In addition to this renovation, everyone had to get an entirely new wardrobe, for no one would think of wearing old raiment during the festivities, at least during the thirteen days of the official celebration.

The bazaars and the shops were open from early morning till sunset for bargain hunters of all classes.

The Khanoms alone did not frequent them, but received merchants of all sorts in their own homes. These privileged merchants were very old and respectable men, otherwise they would have been turned away. Many merchants, in order to get the help of their sons in fetching and carrying, urged them to grow beards for the New Year so as to imitate the appearance of old men. Few succeeded. But whether they passed unsuspected or not, none of them could see any other faces in the anderun than those of coloured womenservants too old to wear a veil!

My mother used to receive the merchants in the court-yard of the ladies' house. Besides those invited to bring goods, others came of their own accord and besieged the house. On these occasions my mother was surrounded by the entire household both coloured and white—maids, governesses, wet nurses—some with babies in their arms—lady companions, poor relations living with her, and a dozen or so of her personal friends especially invited to assist at the bargaining. Laleh was also allowed to come in and look after the men in case they got thirsty or craved a water pipe. The vendors opened their bundles and displayed the contents on the ground—textiles, silks, taffetas, flowery or otherwise, brocades, shawls, chintzes of all colours and designs, tissues of Persian make and also of foreign importation were everywhere. Every member of the household from the scullery maid to the Khanom herself had the right to pick and choose.

The choosing of colour was most difficult, for none of the maids would ever select red, knowing that none of the ladies would ever wear it. Even the servants working in the kitchens and pantries scorned it. Exceptions were made in favour of pieces of rare old Persian brocades of great value and exceptional design. Such pieces were often selected for a tunic for the Khanom or a robe with long sleeves for a gentleman.

When these merchants had departed, the Khanom received the tailors, jewelers, embroidery artisans, goldsmiths, vendors of perfumes and ornaments and, finally, the fashion experts.

Moreover, the calendar had to be consulted to see which day was the luckiest to cut the goods, and when that day arrived the whole house was turned into an atelier. In every room one found women cutting, sewing, gossiping, smoking water pipes, and drinking tea. There was no place left for the men of the family! We were compelled to go to our own quarters, the biruni, for our meals and rest. The menservants together with their wives were also taken in and measured for their clothes, the latter whether they were in our service or not.

When all the attendants were taken care of the Khanom was free to think of her own adornment and to receive the Jewesses who brought precious stones and valuable ornaments. It was supposed that they were the only people who had the best.

A temporary workshop was set up at the far end of the garden, in the remotest part possible, where workers were set to clean utensils, and to whiten the inside of the copper bowls and large cauldrons so heavy that a mule could not carry one of them for a hundred yards.

The noise these people made, all day long with their hammering was terrible. All the cats in our house took to the streets or went into other houses and did not come back until after the workmen had left.

Meanwhile a group of women and men were busy making delicacies in the house or going to the sweetmeat bazaar for confections. They bought gaz, a sort of hard nougat, which only a Persian set of teeth can break without damage. They also bought a spun candy looking rather like a white beard, and lawz, a soft mealy sweet, made of sugar, pistachio, and hashed almond, flavoured with perfume of rose or hel (cardamom). There were a number of candies imported from India and Arabia, but the most popular of all delicacies was adjil. This was a collection of nuts, water melon and pumkin seeds, tiny peas of a special kind and pits of quinces all roasted and flavoured with salt or the juice of small limes from Shiraz. Long delicate green Persian raisins were also mixed with it. The eating of adjil was more prevalent than any other habit, even the smoking of cigarettes or chewing of gum among the old women and the coloured servants. It was said that one of the causes of the Persian defeat at the hands of the Arabs under Shah Sultan Hossein Safavi was that they could not refrain from eating adjil even on the battle-field!

The candy shopkeepers in Teheran had to make enough money in this month of festivities to last them for the rest of the year, as the Persians, contrary to what is thought in the West, are not at all fond of sweets. The only other occasion for eating them is during a marriage celebration. This lack of desire for sugar differentiates the Persians from the rest of the Asiatic peoples and is, perhaps, the secret of their strong, white teeth and slender bodies.

On the 14th of March, the "essential arrangements" for the reception of the Queen of Spring began. Among these was the growing of wheat, oat, and other seeds in platters, and bulbs of narcissus and blue hyacinths in special glasses made to order by a man near our tekkyeh, very thin with a round and bulgy bottom and a wide open mouth to accomodate seven bulbs tucked in cotton wool.

But all the preparations in the various households were nothing compared with what Nature herself was doing. Fresh breezes fanned the face of the earth and waked the world of vegetation from its winter slumbers. Trees began to pump sap to all parts of their trunks and tiny buds began to unfold. What struck me most, however, was the fairy sight on the roofs of the houses. They were covered with millions of dots of colour. At first I could not believe they were flowers, as there were no grasses or leaves around them, but Laleh said that when the autumn winds blew, they scattered seeds over the roofs, which are covered with a layer of red clay mixed with straw, and there the seeds slept during the winter under a white blanket of snow. Now with the first breath of spring they were turning the clay roofs into fairyland. Besides the roofs, the mud walls separating one roof from another were alive with flowers.

We children now spent most of our time on the roofs admiring the flowers and, so to speak, taking care of them. None of us ever picked one of them. The God of Zoroaster, the merciful Ahuramazda, had admonished the Persians to protect every living being. To sever a flower from its mother stem was cruel, for the little flowers had their souls, as we had ours. Also we were told not to defile the ground where these beautiful souls were growing. If by accident a child had the misfortune to trample one he felt miserable the rest of the day and was ready to do most anything in the way of atonement. Some burst into tears and prayed to the soul of the flower for forgiveness.

I was told by the famous monadj-djem bashi, chief astrologer, of His Majesty the Shah, whom I met at our house, that on New Year's night the glorious sun passes across the constellation of the Lamb.

For this man I had a great admiration. I wondered if he was a wizard or Magi. I knew that he was no prophet, for Mohammad was the last of the prophets. Explanations from Laleh and my governess were so vague that I asked the astrologer himself how he had learned about the stars. He told me that it was not very difficult. Every man was capable of doing it, only he had to develop his power of thought, which was the key to all mysteries in this world and the one beyond.

"Could I ever develop mine?" I asked.

"Certainly, you or any other man or woman. We are all equally equipped with that gift of God."

When I asked him how I could start he said, "Go on the roof, look at those tiny flowers, think how they come to be there, where they came from, what makes them have different colours and different perfumes. Ask them and they will give you the reason."

The next morning when I set out for the roof to converse with the flowers Dadeh told me I should have to postpone that trip for I must go with my mother to take a grand bath! This was a great event.

We had, of course, our own private bathhouse, which was a large house in itself, with corridors, passages, exterior and interior courts, pools, basins of hot and cold water, large platforms and wide niches, arches and domes and recesses to undress and dress, all decorated with tiled panels. The fuel had to be collected during the summer and stored for the winter. No less than seven men were kept busy for this purpose all year round, not counting two toon-tabs men who kept the furnace going day and night. But the bath of the New Year was different. It must be taken in a public bathhouse. Here a perfect atmosphere of democracy reigned. No one needed an introduction to enter into conversation. A princess rubbed shoulders with the wife of a water carrier and began to gossip with her at once. Here the wife of a great modjtahed—the highest authority in the religion of Islam, sat next to the wife of a lover of wine, drinking more liquor in a week than Omar Khayyam and his followers drank in a month. No woman asked the name or the occupation of her neighbour's husband. It was enough that all belonged to the same sex—daughters of Hazrat Havva, Her Excellency Eve. Seldom did any exterior sign reveal the class or the origin of the bathers. Once in the sanctuary of the interior court, they all were wrapped in the same coloured loin cloth.

It was very early in the morning when Dadeh came to my bedroom and said Her Grace the Khanom, my mother, was ready.

We started off with some twelve other ladies of our household, sisters-in-law, aunts and cousins, with their respective servants. On the street two old men, our gate keepers, walked before us with their heads bent to their chests. I was walking directly behind my mother, who was completely covered by a black silk tchador. The rest of the party came behind us and the tail was brought up by other menservants.

It was so early that the dogs, the official partols of the quarter, barked furiously at us and the sound of the bough, a bugle blown by the master of the public bath to inform people that the bath was ready, filled the air with its shrill and raucous notes. Personally I always hoped to get myself a bough and blow in it on the roof of our own bathhouse. It was such an awful noise!

When we arrived at the bathhouse the first thing that attracted my attention was the picture that is above the door of all Persian bathhouses, representing the famous hero of Persia, Rostam, fighting the white monster of the Mazehderan jungle, which he killed, and whose head he cut off, dried, and put on his helmet as a sign of victory. Rostam was known to the enemies of Persia by this strange headgear. In this picture, although the monster was shown fighting the hero with a great display of violence, Rostam already had the monster's head on his helmet. Later, when I remarked about this to my Dadeh, she said that this white monster was the brother of the first one.

We descended about twenty steps, and stopped before a second door. The menservants remained behind, and we entered a large hall containing a beautiful dome decorated with blue tile, finished with a spacious skylight. In the middle of the hall was a pool with a fountain playfully gushing. All around the hall were niches, affording ample space for thirty persons to sit at once. A thick pole, its ends stuck to the wall, cut the front of each niche where it began to shape itself into an arch. These poles, carved flat on the top, made a resting place for hundreds of glass vases filled with coloured water; red, green, blue, yellow, and mauve.

On the opposite side of the entrance, a wooden throne, decorated with more vases filled with narcissi and hyacinths, was reserved for the bath-mistress, who was at the same time the cashier. She was sitting with crossed legs, her hands resting upon the raised section of the desk, which contained drawers where she kept the money. She arose, bowed before my mother and said a salaam.

We went then to a niche which two of our servants had prepared beforehand. They had brought the usual ghadifah, one for each of us, spread in two lines. These were white cashmere cloths heavily embroidered with coloured and white silk, representing flowers and shrubbery. Dadeh undressed me while the other small boys were attended to by their own Dadehs and my mother and her friends were attended to by their maids. When I was nearly naked Dadeh handed me a cloth of blue and white bath toweling which she helped me to wrap around my body. The ladies wore a similar covering; the attendants wore these too, but Dadeh wore a red towel.

We made our way through a long passage to an immense hall with an arched ceiling and many skylights. This was the hall of baths proper. The floor was very hot and the air was exceedingly dry and hot. In front of us was a colossal cement stairway which led to the hot water pool.

In the hall next to this I could see the cold water pool. Opposite this hall were five steps leading to a compartment in front of a vast swimming pool so deep and wide, and its water so dark, that it was frightening, and I was astonished to see a dozen women jump from a compartment, somersault in the air, and disappear in the deep water. My own Dadeh was among them. I thought she was drowned, but after a while I saw her black face gleaming at the farthest corner, showing her white teeth and making signs to me to look at her. She came back swimming under the water.

When first I entered this hall, the noise of conversation seemed deafening. There were, I believe, some hundred and fifty women, with their long hair streaming on their shoulders and several boys. Private attendants were rushing through the crowd in all directions. I felt giddy.

The noise reverberating against the dome was worse than anything else. In the midst of the confusion I lost sight of my mother and could not find her anywhere. All the women looked alike. The only face I recognized was that of my Dadeh, which was black. After what seemed to me a great while she sent one of the bath attendants to take me in hand. The attendant started the ceremony of washing by rubbing first my back and then my neck with a rough sharp sack of camel's hair which she had slipped over her hand like a glove.

When she had done this she put a small cushion behind my head, and told me to lie down. Then she rubbed every part of my body the same way. I was surprised at the amount of greasy material she got. Next she took a piece of black stone, which looked like a hard sponge, and began to file my feet, taking away a part of epidermis which I always thought was the skin. It tickled so much that I could not help laughing. This caused two other boys of my age, who were with their mothers, to roar with laughter. But here the teaching of my Laleh stood me in good stead, for I immediately got myself under control.

When she did stop, it was only to start another manoeuvre.

She made me sit up again and poured warm water from a pitcher on my head. I was told to stand up. Then a new cloth was spread, and I was allowed to lie down and rest.

My cousin, Touran Khanom, the daughter of my unholy uncle, was sitting near me. She had just finished her rubbing, and was about to have henna put on her head.

I must first explain how henna was applied, because I have never seen it similarly used elsewhere. Henna was the leaf of a plant, and the best grew in Kerman, Ispahan, Shiraz and Kashan. The leaves were dried and ground to powder. A sack containing three pounds of this was the regular portion for each head.

My cousin's attendant poured the contents of the sack into a bowl, and made a thick paste by the addition of water. After the hair had been washed many times with hot water she filled her palm with the paste, applied it to the scalp, taking every strand of hair in turn, saturating it with henna, and laying it on the scalp. My cousin looked like a mollah with a large turban. Her head was then covered with a piece of paper, and she was allowed to lie down on a small straw-filled cushion.

About four hours later I was awakened by Dadeh, who informed me that we were going to have luncheon. Many of the women had left, and only those under the henna treatment remained.

Servants were coming in and out, bearing large platters of delicacies, which they placed before us. It was, of course, a cold luncheon, and the prevailing spirit throughout the meal was that of a group of girls enjoying a party together. My mother asked the other women present to join her in her repast, and, as was the custom, they readily accepted the invitation. Every now and then my mother excused herself for having invited the strangers to such poor fare!

In addition to large bowls of potages made of meat broth

and vegetables, there were cold fish, a sort of omelet known as kou-kou, half a dozen dishes of raw aromatic plants, four different cheeses, dozens of jams and preserves, four different kinds of croquettes with other relishes and pickles. We were served with the recognized dish for luncheon in the bath—the famous ball of hashed meat called koufte tabrizi. This was a formidable looking ball like the turban of a Turkish Mohammedan clergyman. Many pounds of meat, herbs, and spices had been used in its making. It took two persons at least two days to prepare it. About fifty hard-boiled eggs were nesting in its heart, each egg stuffed with a concoction of birds' brains, finely hashed aromatic herbs, and spiced relishes which demanded an admirable chef in the culinary art. This ball was placed in one of the largest Ming China bowls and brought into the bath by the strongest woman attendant. While the guests were eating, servants passed among them carrying decanters of sherbet. After two of the hard boiled eggs I could not eat anything more. My head fell on my mother's lap and I went to sleep.

When I waked the ladies were having the henna washed out of their hair. I observed the washing of my cousin's hair with strictest attention. She sat on a raised platform near the hot pool with her legs dangling. A servant poured hot water on her head in small quantities from a pitcher, while an attendant disentangled her sticky locks. It took both women nearly three-quarters of an hour to get her hair washed. The other ladies going through the same process formed a lovely picture, all sitting on raised platforms with their legs hanging down. Their magnificent tresses, which were now the colour of matured chestnuts, covered their entire bodies, which were glistening and flushed to a lovely hue.

I thought that after this was finished we had only to

undergo the last wash and go home. But alas! we were only in the middle of our ablutionary ceremonies.

The ladies were told to sit in their respective places, and a bowl and a second sack was brought forward, the contents of which were like henna, but of a darker colour, called rang. Henna was never used alone. The red colour that results from it is not appreciated by the Persian women, who consider red a low caste colour. Rang is used to subdue it into that wonderful dark hue which so mystifies the Westerners.

Then we all lay down, and I fell asleep again.

Four hours later I was awakened for the second time by Dadeh who announced that asraneh was ready. This was like the four o'clock tea of the West. I was confronted again with at least thirty plates piled with all sorts of fresh fruits; grapes, apples, pears, peaches and melons. Many of these fruits were of past summers, packed in cotton and kept in air-tight boxes. There were new cucumbers and other fruits grown in hothouses. The bulk of this meal, however, was hearts of lettuce, washed, dried between towels, and heaped on large platters; these were broken with the hand and dipped in different dressings in bowls arranged around the plates. Most of these dressings were made of vinegar and salt and pepper mixed with powdered plants, and others with syrup made of Ispahan quinces, Shiraz lemons and sekandjebin, a beverage made of vinegar and sugar boiled together and flavoured by aromatic herbs. Again sherbets were served, and also tea in glasses, with a few drops of the juice of Shiraz limes in each glass.

After this the ladies' heads were washed again, and they were given an hour's release to do what they liked. Some talked, others went into the swimming pool, and a few started to comb their hair. My cousin and Dadeh took me to the cold water basin, where the water reached only to their waist. I stood between them, with my head barely above the water.

Near the cold water pool, I saw a small door which was closed. Years later I learned that it led to the depilatory room where the attendant prepared a paste with a powder, black in colour, which afterward was applied to the body hair. A minute or two was enough to do its work and then it was washed away with water, and lo! the skin was as clear as a baby's. There was no trace of irritation or roughness on the skin, which now was soft and white. This paste was called Vadjebi.

The legend of the origin of this powder is as follows: When King Solomon fell in love with the Queen of Sheba, he found the poor Queen cursed with an abundance of superfluous hair. None of his viziers, and not even the Royal Physician was able to find a means whereby she could rid herself of this disfigurement. Now King Solomon had under his command a horde of divs, jinnees, devils, and sorcerers, who served him faithfully and carried his throne on their shoulders through space. One of these divs told the King of a mysterious powder used by the feminine monsters of his tribe—whose bodies, as everyone knows, are covered with hair—to cleanse their skins. He was immediately despatched to get some of it and the Queen was delighted with its instantaneous result. This magic powder was what the Persian women and men used as depilatory.

After we had played for some time in the cold water pool, we were called back to the hall.

I sat on the same platform, and was told to shut my eyes. A woman took a large white sack, and put a piece of white, home-made soap and some water into it. She rubbed the sack, and then began to blow with her mouth into it. It swelled, and then she squeezed it above my head, whereupon a great deal of lather oozed out, and I was completely immersed in waves of foam and froth.

Then she rubbed my body all over, as if she were cleaning a glass bowl. I am sure that if it had not been for the soap, she would have taken off my skin. Quantities of hot water were poured on my head, and again, about three or four times more, I was covered with soap and rubbed. I was choking, but I could not protest. When I was completely covered with soap lather, and was closing my eyes for the last time, I lost my loin cloth for some minutes while I was being rubbed; but I found it back in its place when I opened my eyes.

At last I was told to walk into the basin of cool water. Then I was picked up and set on a white cloth. After that professional women masseuses began to rub the ladies, who first sat and then lay, first on one side, then on the other; and finally on their backs. This continued for at least an hour. After a while we dressed and started for home.

I was so tired when we arrived that I refused to go to dinner. I asked Dadeh to help me get to bed.

VI

NEW YEAR'S EVE ARRIVES

THE NEXT day the spring was to be reborn five hours after the setting of the sun, and at its advent a cannon was to be fired to inform the town. Contrary to our usual custom, dinner was served very early, and everyone was sent to rest for a few hours. Meanwhile, Mother and a few servants went about setting the table.

The children were sent to bed, not only to rest but also to give the Queen of Spring an opportunity to present them with beautiful clothes to wear in her honour. This she invariably did when they were fast asleep.

When I was awakened later, I found near my bed a large cashmere shawl made into a bundle. I was not allowed to look inside until after I was washed and rose water had been dashed on my hair and face, but I knew that it contained my New Year's outfit. All my old clothes had disappeared; they had been given to some poor boys of my age and height.

The apex of the luxuries waiting for me was a beautiful coat of deep green brocade, the colour, lustre, and design of which changed with every movement, and a Caucasian leather belt ornamented with silver plates inlaid with gold. Another red covered package contained a new kolah (hat), made of black lambskin, with very fine long curls. In the bundle were also plates of nougats, large and small, round and long, filled with almonds, bits of cocoanuts, pistachios and hel, over which were strewn fresh violets in lavish abundance.

I must say that the newly starched shirt and the brand new squeaking shoes were not quite comfortable, but everything else was wonderful. At that time it was considered very smart to have squeaky shoes; those who could not afford to buy Russian leather shoes used to pay a good price to have a pair of squeakers made.

Dadeh accompanied me to the reception room to meet the Queen of the evening, my mother. The solemnity of the servants and the hushed atmosphere reigning in the house were very impressive. The only light in the house came from the reception room, which had floral decorations in every niche. Rich curtains of brocade were hanging in front of the doors, and the floor was covered with gorgeous carpets.

In the centre of the room was a table with an immaculate white cloth; a decoration of narcissus and hyacinths, with bunches of fresh violets in vases and strewn on the table made it very beautiful. Seven candlesticks in the form of a lozenge were burning on the table. Dishes of sweets and candies were arranged about the flowers, and a long pinched glass bottle of rose water stood at each end of the table. The air was heavily laden with perfume, and from a little silver brazier came the pungent odour of Spand incense. A single high-backed chair of inlay at the head of the table was occupied by my mother, who was covered completely with a white tchador of fine muslin. Only her face could be seen. She seemed transformed into a saint, and I fancied I saw a halo around her head, which was bent over the pages of a Koran, which lay open on the table before her. Her eyes were closed and her hands clasped together. No words can ever describe the beauty of her face. My desire was to run to her and kiss her, but this I dared not lest I should disturb her meditation. I stood near the door, both hands clasped on my breast, and gazed at her with profound love and admiration.

For more than four hours she had been in communion with God, asking His mercy and blessing for her husband and children. For four hours the spirits of all our ancestors had been watching her. She had read more than three chapters of the Koran.

It was the custom in the old Persian families to consider the mother, on the New Year, the head of the family, and a Queen representing Nature, which was second deity after the sun. She was expected to impart her benediction to her husband, children, and kin—a most noble custom which emphasised the rightful position of a woman as mother and wife.

Presently my six brothers joined us and we went inside very quietly.

After a while my mother opened her eyes and smiled at us. We bowed to her and stood silent. Two minutes later the eldest of us spoke:

"May I interrupt you, my own soul? We have only one minute more to wait for the cannon shot, which will announce the New Year."

She made a sign to him that she heard him and closed her eyes again, as we all did, until the cannon boomed. Immediately Mother stood up and in a sweet voice said to us all:

"With Allah's will may this New Year be a happy one for all my children and the children of every mother."

We rushed to her and fell into her outstretched arms, each one trying to embrace her.

Shortly afterward the servants entered to kiss my mother's hands and then mine and my brothers'. Some of the older servants kissed us on the cheek. After this, they took their places around the room. One of them had already lighted the chandeliers.

On the table I could now see that in addition to the sweets, there were seven different kinds of foods whose names started with the letter S to make the haft sin (seven S's). This was necessary for the New Year's table as a talisman against devils and an assurance of the future happiness of the members of the household. The foods were serkah (vinegar), sabzi (green), sumagh (sumach), souhan (a candy), samanou (a sweet), sekandjebin (a syrup), and seer (bulbs of garlic).

No one was allowed to touch anything, until the great Hadj-Agha came, our father, the king of the evening, who had gone to the Shah's palace to be present at his Majesty's reception, and would be back as soon as he had been received by that almighty personage.

Presently a great commotion in the courtyard announced his arrival. He ran to my mother and took her in his arms, kissing her face and her hands; and when he had finished, we came to him in our turn to kiss him and wish him a happy New Year. He was, I thought, a pleasant sight with his high lambskin hat and his long garment of cashmere shawl and sable. The sleeves of the coat, which were two yards long, were pushed back from the wrist, resembling the sleeves of the Western lords in the Middle Ages. Two tassels of fine pearls, fashioned like clusters of grapes, hung from his coat on each side of his chest. He removed his white gloves and took from his large pocket a handful of small red silk sacks of different sizes and presented them to my mother. These sacks, the smaller ones filled with gold and the larger with silver coins, bearing the effigy of the Shah on one side and the date of the New Year on the other, were gifts from the Shah. He handed them to Mother, who presented us each with a sack. From a larger one she distributed both gold and silver to the servants.

A while later we took leave of our parents and gave coins according to their rank and position and to the number of years they had spent in our service to a crowd of servants who were waiting outside for us.

My eldest brother who, like my father, was a doctor, disappeared immediately after we left the room, and twenty minutes later my other brothers and I, together with a crowd of servants, went to his house, which adjourned ours. The same ceremonies were repeated here, with my brother and sister-in-law acting as sovereigns.

The next morning, accompanied by my Laleh, I called on all my near relations, and received coins, and candies, and adjils, and hard-boiled eggs dyed yellow or half red and half yellow, which we preferred to everything else, not because we liked to eat them, but because we could gamble with them later on.

Gambling with eggs was a very ancient game which was supposed to have been invented by children of the street who had no one to look after them.   A child chose an egg, and tested its solidity by hitting the point against his teeth.   If it resounded clearly, it was good to play with; and if it resounded hollowly it showed that the shell was not thick enough to withstand a shock.   The boy then covered the egg with his palm, exposing only its point.   The rival player hit this point with the point of his egg, and the one that broke his opponent's egg was the winner and took the broken egg.   Children sometimes lost as many as fifty eggs at a time.

There were many ways of cheating, but the cheater, when discovered, had to return all his winnings.   He was, moreover, branded as a cheat, and no other boy would play with him.   One method was to leave a fresh egg standing on its head for two or three months in a dry, well-aired corner, during which time the contents became so hard that the head of the egg was insensitive as a stone.   With such an egg, one could crack a hundred ordinary eggs.

The next thirteen days were days of universal merrymaking. All the government offices and schools were closed. In the streets, passers-by stopped to greet one another, whether friends or strangers, in the ancient Persian way, by passing palm against palm. Those who were friends kissed one another on the cheeks, saying, "Lucky be our New Year for you and your family, and all the Persians."

The greatest event came on the thirteenth day, which marked the end of the official merrymaking. This was a national picnic day for all the Persians.

The members of our household arose before sunrise and left the house. Already the streets were crowded with men, women, and children, some on horseback, some on donkeys or mules, and others on foot, all going to different gates of the city. It seemed as if all Teheran was migrating. No one remained in town except the dogs, cats, policemen, and beggars who could not walk.

Outside the gate a mile and a half from the city thousands of people were already assembled: beggars, dervishes, fortune tellers, seers, singers, whistlers, wrestlers, jugglers, acrobats, and boys selling bunches of violets. Hundreds of the crowd consisted of mollahs and seyyeds, some of whom were well known among the clerical body of the city. The day being a great feast day, parents were less strict in enforcing the laws of Islam, which forbid any relations, social or otherwise, between the sexes unless they are members of the same family, and girls and boys were allowed to play together. The girls had thrown aside their veils, but their parents pretended not to notice it.

I was told that many courtships began on this day, and that the marriages resulting were, as a rule, happy ones, because the two young people had looked at each other beforehand, whereas, in the regular marriages arranged by the parents, the man saw his future wife for the first time only after he was safely bound by contract.

As soon as I arrived at the picnic ground Dadeh told me

that I must perform the New Year's ritual. She told me to pick the most beautiful and longest blade of grass I could find. Then she told me to keep it before me, make wishes, and address the following words to it: "O you green, fresh, and beautiful blade of spring grass, you are young and lovely. Please take my bad complexion and any disease in my body for yourself and give me yours instead, which is healthy and filled with youth." When I had repeated the words after her, she bade me tie as many knots as I could in the blade and think hard of my wishes. I was very much amused, and when I had finished the ritual, she took the bit of grass from me, saying: "Look how the green has changed colour and faded. That means that your wishes will be realised."

Presently I joined my brothers, who, with their friends, were playing games. Among these, my favourite was toup arrareh, a very old Persian game, supposed to be the forerunner of baseball. A place was chosen where the grass was soft and thick. Two groups, each under the leadership of a captain, stood at a distance of some hundreds yards apart. A line was drawn in front of each group. The captain of one party, after a private conversation with his men, approached the other captain—the batsman—and threw a ball made of cotton, embroidered with coloured woollen threads. The latter hit it as hard as he could. Immediately the members of his team began to run after it to reach the opposite boundary. If one of the other team caught the ball in the air and hit one of the runners, this lost the game to the batsman's party, and the losers had to bring their opponents back on their shoulders. Children who watched the game were rewarded with a ride on the shoulders of the losers when one of the losers was too weak to carry the winner. I myself got a few long rides on the shoulders of a very stout boy, the captain of one of the teams, who was declared too heavy to carry his own weight. He was one of the best batsmen on the field, but he lost the game and blamed the misfortune on his players. At the end of the game both teams rolled him on the ground for a long distance to punish him for not coaching his players better and then for bringing them on the field and reproaching them. He swore by all the prophets and emams that if he could not find better players by the next year, he would retire from the field and become a merchant of woman's underwear, which calling was considered most degrading for a gentleman.

The women were also having a good time, mostly engaged in making knots in the blades of grass and wishing for things. The servants also partook in the games, with or against their masters, as they chose. On this day everyone was equal, first, because it was a universal holiday, and second, because when people play a game of any sort they are simply players; rank counts for nothing.

At twelve o'clock we were informed that luncheon was served. Then we had to conform to the formalities of home life; that is, the men ate separately on the bank of the stream, and the women inside the luncheon tents. Laleh explained that in view of my rapid progress towards manhood I should take my place with the gentlemen. Only three more springs, and I would be nine springs old and therefore a full-grown man before the eyes of all men and in the interpretation of the Mohammedan laws.

I was seated next to the fat champion of the game, who was devouring plate after plate of rice and stews. He had just asked for a fourth helping when half a dozen white-aproned cooks brought on skewers of lamb which had been roasted over charcoal fires. Completely surfeited myself, I was about to ask Laleh if I could go away when I noticed that an amusing contest had started between the champion and a score of mollahs who were among our guests. These worthy clergymen were renowned for their gluttony; it was jocosely said that when a mollah sits at a table the cats starve.

As the contest waged the belligerents called for more roast. They became so excited and hot that the mollahs took off their turbans and let the abas slip from their shoulders. In a little while they loosened the scarfs around their waists. The stout one kept his hat on, and, since he wore no girdle, merely unbuttoned his long coat. Every few minutes they drank large wooden ladles of sherbet, swallowing it down in one gulp, then more roast and more sherbet, till my brothers, four of them physicians, thought it time to call the match a draw. The contestants were not able to rise. They were helped up and a place was prepared for them to lie down. The champion refused aid, and arose painfully, like a dromedary, remained standing a while, then walked to the nearest tree, leaned against it and called to the mollahs: "I am ready to eat a platter of rice and a whole roasted lamb! Are you?"

There was no response. The mollahs were already snoring.

The guests now went to the other side of the tents to give the servants a chance to sit at table in their turn. By some kind of tacit agreement each servant took possession of his master's place, and, for the moment, assumed his manner and title. It was not unusual to hear the stable boy calling to the equerry of a Khan: "Hey, hey, would Your Highness deign to let free that chicken to glide my way?" Some of the conversation they had heard during our lunch they were now repeating verbatim, imitating the original voices as well as they could. They even had gastronomic champions of their own who impersonated ours and burlesqued the result. A great day was this thirteenth day of the New Year!

VII

TWO EUNUCHS FROM THE SHAH'S
PALACE CALL TO WISH
MY MOTHER A HAPPY
NEW YEAR

IT WAS during the New Year's celebration two years later that I had my first invitation to visit the Shah's palace. It was on a Friday morning, our Mohammedan weekly holiday. My Laleh served me an early breakfast and I dressed in great haste, for I had sent invitations to some of my school friends for luncheon and a ride in the afternoon to call on some of our family who were living outside the city. I dressed myself in my very best and, feeling that I was beginning to know a great deal about life, tilted my new hat of black lambskin at a jaunty angle over my right ear. This was not considered correct by the average conventional Persian family. It was a fashion more or less indulged in by the knights errant, and the more sophisticated young boys with adventurous proclivities. But I felt I had every right to it, because many members of my family had been famous athletes. Two of my cousins were knights champions of our district and their activities had already attracted the attention of well known champions in the city.

When I was fully dressed, I went to my mother.

She was talking to two servants and did not notice my arrival. I was obliged to wait. Although during the day no especial ceremony was observed toward her, we always awaited her permission before sitting in her presence. Finally she saw me, and I was about to speak when a servant, flushed with excitement, hurried in and announced that two eunuchs from the Imperial Harem were on their way to see her ladyship.

It is interesting to note that, although under the laws of Islam, which were strictly observed by the Persians, no man, not even the relations of the wife, except a brother or first cousin, was allowed to frequent the anderun without first being announced, the eunuchs were an exception to the rule. These gentlemen, whether black or white, were entertained in the anderun with little or no ceremony. The ladies received them unveiled.

The curtain was drawn aside, and the two eunuchs, one black and the other white, came into the room and hurried to my mother, who, with the habitual gesture of the Persian ladies, sat up as if she were about to stand, while in actuality no lady ever rises before any male visitors except her parents or relations older than herself. The white eunuch, Hadja Rabi, begged her not to disturb herself, and fell on his knees kissing her hands, wishing her a happy New Year. He was followed by the other eunuch, the black one called Djouhar, who also paid his respects and wished her a most happy New Year, and a hundred more of such years in the future. Mother thanked them gracefully, and then said to me: "Come my soul, make the acquaintance of these two most valued and interesting gentlemen, both of whom are welcome visitors to our humble home."

This phrase was used instead of the word house. No Persian of high birth ever used the word "house" or the pronoun "my." It was considered the height of vulgarity to say "my house" or "my servant"; and worse still to say "my chair," "my cushion," or "my" any article of furni-

ture. The vocabulary of an aristocrat was devoid of the
possessive pronoun in the singular.

Both eunuchs arose, bowed solemnly to me, kissed me
on the cheeks, and wished me a happy New Year. This
done, they sat down again on the floor, and Rabi, looking
in my direction, exclaimed in his voice that was shrill like
a woman's: "It is very strange that our little Khan has
not been presented yet to our dearest Khanom, Her Majesty
the Queen Ghamar-ed-Dowleh"—the Moon of the Empire—
"Why has he not been visiting the imperial harem to make
friends with the ladies and the officials?"

Mother smiled, and said I was yet too young. "My boy
is studying to become a great scholar like his honoured
father," she added.

"But, my dear Khanom," exclaimed the eunuch, "knowledge is hereditary in his family. Both mother and father
are learned, and certainly a son of our high Hadj-Agha, the
greatest scholar in our Empire, is already born a learned man!
I am sure we"—meaning the Shah and his court officials
—"cannot afford to miss the presence of such a fine gentleman in the palace. When our Queen learns of the existence
of the little Khan she certainly will not allow such a jewel
of the first water to waste his time on books and paper!"

Mother smiled again and said: "It is Khoda's pleasure to
decide the future of my boy. He alone does with his creatures as he wills."

Meanwhile two servants, very young and pretty girls,
blushing and trying to hide their faces, notwithstanding the
fact that they were in the presence of eunuchs, brought two
trays holding plates of sweets and adjil, followed by two
others who brought coloured glasses and decanters of sherbets.
Although very shy at first, the girls now, instead of leaving
the room, stood in a line near the door, looking with interest
at the eunuchs.

These girls were distant relations of the family, and though acting as attendants, were ladies themselves and consequently treated as members of the family. The same treatment was tendered the eunuchs, as both were from aristocratic families. The black one was a native Prince of Abyssinia, while Hadja Rabi was the grandson of a Khan and a wealthy landowner in the northern part of the country.

While the eunuchs were busy with the sweets and sherbets, my mother asked them if there was any further reason for their charming visit to her.

"Oh no! oh no!" answered Rabi. "The only object of our visit was to meet your Ladyship and at the same time, if it can be arranged, to pay our respects to the High Master the Hadj-Agha, His Excellency the Etezad-ol-Atebba." This was my father's title, which meant "the arms of all the physicians."

A house boy was despatched to father's head servant to inform my Laleh, who attended also upon my father, that two of his majesty's eunuchs wished to see him. When the messenger returned, saying that the visitors would be welcome, both men arose, kissed my mother's hand, bowed to me, and left the room.

Mother now turned to me: "Darling, you must be tired from having been kept standing all this time."

"It is both a pleasure and an honour for me to be in attendance upon you," I told her. Thereupon she took my hand and bade me sit at her side. Such formality between mother and son may seem very strange to Westerners, but to us it was the most natural thing in the world.

Half an hour later I received my schoolmates in the garden and told them I might be summoned to the harem by the Queen. They all wished they could meet the Shah, before whom, they were told, everyone held his breath. The son of Eshagh, the beet-root seller, who was leaning on the shoulder of another boy who was a cousin of the Shah, heaved a sigh and said: "Be careful, my dear brother, be

careful of the Shah! I have been told that when he is
angry he calls his mir-ghazab and orders wholesale massacre."

"Nonsense," said another boy. "The Shah will not touch
a single hair of the son of Hadj-Agha. Besides, all one has
to do for protection is to invoke the Koran, and say, 'Besmellah Rahman Rahim' "—"in the name of God the Merciful
and the compassionate"—"and blow at him as we do at Sheytan or a wild beast."

"I am not so sure," replied the first boy. "As a fellow
guest, I agree with what you say; but, as a well-wishing
brother to our host, I feel it my duty to warn him to keep
away as much as he can from the Shah."

"And as near as possible to the ladies of the imperial
harem," added my cousin, who was the oldest among us,
and nicknamed "wicked cousin."

VIII

A VISIT TO THE HAREM

At the prospect of visiting the Shah's harem I found myself embarked upon a sea of fantastic dreams. My Dadeh, who had been there many times with my mother, told me that it was an earthly paradise filled with women noted for their beauty and charm, who spent their days parading in rich gowns and splendid jewels, or playing with precious stones as the children of the poor play with pebbles. But this aspect of the harem held no enticement for me. I had seen jewels; they meant little to me. As for brocades and rich garments, our own were as beautiful as any I could imagine, and, as for the lovely women, I knew that none of them could surpass my beloved mother.

What attracted me was the prospect of adventure! How many opportunities might I not have to travel with his court to the far ends of the country, or to hunt wild beasts in the mysterious jungles on the border of the Caspian Sea! These dreams were filling my childish head when one morning I was summoned by my father, who told me I was to accompany him to the palace the following Friday to be presented to the Queen Ghamar-ed-Dowleh who had expressed a desire to see me. The great day arrived and with it a command from Father to be ready at four o'clock in the afternoon. Laleh and I were ready when my father came from his room. He looked truly imposing! He wore a white linen shirt which opened at one side, fastened with a single button on the right shoulder. Over this was an arkhalogh of old Ispahan ghalamkar padded with a thin layer

of cotton wool and quilted with silk thread, another coat
called gheba, of a light blue silk textile named aghari, tight
at the waist and fastened with a button made of knotted
silk thread; a shawl of kerman, long enough to be wound
around his waist three times was wrapped over this garment,
the sleeves of which had pointed cuffs lined with Cashmere
shawl and a narrow border of rare brocade. A long orange-
coloured djobbeh which touched the ground was thrown
over his shoulders. This was the Shah's gift on last New
Year's feast. It was lined with the finest sable, with hundreds of small fluffy tails hanging in fringe-fashion. The
sleeves, which reached the ground, were very wide at
the shoulders and gradually tapered to a narrow opening
through which the hands could with difficulty be squeezed.
As a rule, father used the djobbeh as a cape for ceremonial
visits, and only passed his hands through the sleeves in the
presence of the Shah. He wore a pair of black trousers,
black shoes, and woollen socks of beautiful colours woven
into geometrical designs.

He carried a long walking stick of a rare wood called
arjan which is a light brown and needs no varnishing. The
wood is so flexible that it can be bent double without breaking, yet it is extremely heavy. Father had a great collection
of these sticks which had been accumulating for centuries.
Each had belonged to one of his forefathers and each had
its story. The one which he now carried had saved his life
during his pilgrimage to Mecca when a man attacked him
with a short sword.

Outside the gate our horses were waiting. Father's was
a beautiful white Arab stallion, the gift of Prince Nayeb-es-
Sultaneh, the Shah's third son, then Governor of Teheran.
For more than a year and a half now I had been the proud
possessor of a horse, and my beloved donkey was used by
my little brother. As we approached, an old servant called
the "guardian of the bridles" lifted from the saddle of

father's horse a covering embroidered in purple and black, folded it lengthwise, threw it on his shoulder and walked alongside my father's horse. The carrying of this covering before a mounted gentleman was one of the privileges granted the members of the reigning dynasty and the old nobility. Two servants rode in front at a distance of some hundred yards. Laleh rode behind us.

I was very proud and happy. It was the first time I had ever ridden with my father in formal procession. We crossed the tekkyeh, where all the shop-keepers and pedestrians stood and sent a loud salaam to father who replied to each separately saying: "Salamon-Aleikom"—"greeting unto you." When Amirza the school teacher and jinnee-catcher caught sight of us he opened the window of the schoolroom and pushed his head out waiting for us to pass. When we were near him, he exclaimed: "O high Hadj-Agha, greetings unto you!" Father answered, and I nodded three times. The school children were looking over his shoulder and pleasantly grinning at me.

We pressed our horses forward at greater speed, the two men riding in front clearing the way for us. This was not easy as we were obliged to dodge wide mud-filled ditches and avoid gaps from the underground streams where the horses might easily slip. Riding through Teheran was very thrilling in those days. Here and there I saw women crouching at the edge of the water gaps doing their laundry in the water that was used for drinking purposes. When they saw father some of them ran into the nearest street and waited till we had disappeared, not because they apprehended any reproaches for polluting the water, but simply because they were afraid of the horses. Washing clothes in drinking water was a common practice of theirs, and nothing could make them understand its disastrous consequences to the public health. The public cistern of our tekkyeh and our own private water reservoirs were filled during the night when no one could go in the street. Many other precautions were taken in our household, such as keeping hundreds of goldfish in the cistern, to exterminate germs.

We presently reached the first bazaar, where we were confronted with another difficulty. The shopkeepers, in order to protect themselves against dust, had watered the ground, which had become muddy and slippery. We had to be very careful.

We passed the quarter called Sar-Tcheshmeh and arrived on the great avenue known as Gas Lamp Avenue, a wide thoroughfare filthy beyond description, down the centre of which ran the tracks of a horse car. Lining the street on both sides were shops of all descriptions. Merchants who could not afford to rent a shop displayed their wares along walls or in the middle of the street. Among these latter the roasters of lamb had made a charcoal fire on the ground, and were busy cooking. Heavy clouds of smoke filled the place, and the odour of the burnt meat was strong. Camels and mules were making their way to the gates of the city, and now and then a herd of unbridled donkeys would force their way off in the opposite direction from the one in which they were intended to go.

There was nobody to control the traffic as in the days of ancient Persian kings, when horsemen patrolled the streets in the daytime and forced the riders to go on one side of the street and pedestrians on the other. Now we were governed by the laws of Islam, whose founder, Mohammad, had preached democracy and freedom for all creatures alike. Donkeys were Allah's creatures as well as we.

In half an hour we reached Cannon Square. Here I stopped to admire a building which was called sonorously the Imperial Bank of Persia. The bank had nothing to do with the Persian Government, but was established by the people of Engelestan (Great Britain) for the charitable purpose of teaching the Persians to save their money to buy from the merchants who imported goods from Engelestan. Laleh said that there must be millions of sacks filled with gold in that building, and he wondered how in the name of Sheytan the keeping of gold in safes of the faranguis (foreigners) could possibly help the Persian people.

Cannon Square was as dirty and dusty as the rest of the roads. The ground was broken and bleached white by the sun. In the centre, surrounded by a broken fence that had been constructed by an alignment of some thousand old-fashioned rifles and flintlocks, was a huge basin filled with garbage. At each corner an old cannon with wheels toppling over to one side, stood on a platform. A pile of broken tiles and other debris which had accumulated underneath them was all that kept them from collapsing to the ground. The cannons, it was said, had been taken in war from the Portugese. A piece of shapeless chain attached to one of the broken wheels declared them captured, and warned the stranger that he was in the presence of inanimate prisoners of war,—this to inspire him with admiration for the mighty army of the Shah. Some specimens of this army were to be seen in a dilapidated compound in a corner near the bank. There, under the shadow of a flagpole, upon which no one had ever seen a flag, lay three miserable looking creatures, half naked and ill-fed. They had been smoking opium, and were now sleeping on the ground on their stomachs.

We entered another avenue and finally arrived at the arched entrance to the space before the gate of the imperial harem. Half a dozen untidy men who were lounging in a corner jumped to attention when they sighted us. While I was wondering if they were the guardians of the imperial harem or only beggars, a group of officials appeared in the hall behind the gate of the palace. Their elaborate dress and their crisp and haughty manners made me think better of the Shah's establishment.

Our horsemen jumped nimbly to the ground and stood aside, while the bearer of the purple embroidery held the stirrup as father dismounted. The embroidery was immediately spread over the horse and the saddle. Laleh helped me dismount and we fell behind father, who was now walking very slowly toward the palace.

A commotion was taking place inside the hall as attendants ran to and fro motioning in indication that someone was about to arrive from the palace. This proved to be the supreme head of all the eunuchs, who came in presently out of breath. This was the first glimpse I had of him. He was very stout, very important, very fussy, and in a state of continual agitation and haste, making no progress in any direction. He shouted at everyone, and spun about like a top. At last he seemed to have made up his mind, for he jumped out of the gate and charged at my father with both hands outstretched, and in such a state of devotional enthusiasm that I was afraid he would hurt somebody.

Before he had finished his welcome there was more commotion, more fuss and more noise and Djouhar, the black eunuch, arrived like a whirlwind from the interior of the palace and said that the Khanom was waiting for us.

We passed the waiting gentlemen, who, of course knew my father and were curious to see me. Each bowed to me, and I nodded in return. With Djouhar at my side, the head of the eunuchs at father's, and with a crowd behind us, we crossed the first court, a simple but beautiful place with high walls panelled with blue and yellow tiles, shadowed by old platanes and beauteous cypresses. There was a marble pool with hundreds of goldfish storming toward the fountain in the centre. Hundreds of geraniums in full bloom encircled the pool. About ten or twelve bushes of the wonderful Persian flower yas, with delicate branches laden with tiny blossoms, drooped toward the ground with grace and abandon. The air was heavily-laden with the scent of flowers.

Before us a large staircase led to a balcony in front of a single room with stained glass windows wide open, showing the interior of the room, which was of the ancient type of architecture; that is, the lower part of the walls were covered with blocks of white marble on which floral decorations were painted, while the upper part and the ceiling were lacquered and painted like Persian miniatures. Wide niches cut in the walls were decorated with tiny mirrors which glittered like precious stones. These mirrors formed frames holding paintings by different masters representing hunting scenes, riding scenes, musical parties, or wine drinkings. A single frameless picture on a canvas in the middle of the room was a portrait of the Lord and Master of the Harem, His Majesty Nasser-ed-Din Shah, when he was nineteen years old.

This room, I found later, was reserved for the head of the eunuchs. Here he played chess or tric-trac with some of the other officials when they were off duty. On rare occasions the Shah would favour them with a short visit. A single long-armed, high-backed chair in a corner awaited him. To the left and right of us were other rooms and ante-chambers of more modest nature, which, I learned, belonged to the master of rifles and other officials.

We entered a wide corridor running under a balcony and emerged into another small court, which was quite bare and unpretentious. There was a heavy curtain in front of us which was drawn away by unseen hands as we approached and there was revealed a court so vast that I could not see the end of it.

This place was paved with bricks and shaded with massive platanes. There were no pools nor shrubbery nor flower-beds. All around it were the wide-opened windows of many apartments, all of which seemed to be inhabited.

A boy came out of one room and stood on a little balcony in front of us, surveying us with his head held high with the tolerant amused air of a grand seigneur. He was fingering a long thin dagger that resembled one I had at home but was not allowed to wear. When he saw me, he ran down the staircase toward us and I found to my surprise and pleasure that it was my school friend, Abol-Fath Khan.

Father recognized him and smiled. He came to my side and took my arm in his and walked with us, relating all his news and asking mine. At the end of the court we were confronted with another curtain guarded by two men.

Abol-Fath pressed my hand and slipped away saying that he would meet me again when we had finished our audience. The two guardians looked furtively at the chief eunuch. The latter cleared his throat, and, with the dramatic air of a mighty monarch addressed the guardians of the sanctuary: "His Eminence and Altesse Hadj Hakim Bashi, Etezad-ol-Atebba has been claimed by Her Highness, our beloved Khanom, Ghamar-ed-Dowleh. Announce us and clear the way!"

One of them immediately drew a curtain aside, and remained standing near it. The other crossed the threshold and stepped inside the earthly Eden about which I had heard so much, looked around carefully, then roared like a lion, "OHOY! Kesi-Nabashad! Hear ye! that there be nobody in sight!"

A scene lovelier than any I had dreamed lay before me— a flowered stage, separated into different sections by intricate designs of flowers like a page of arabesque writing, seeming hardly the handiwork of human beings. Numbers of small and large marble pools and basins were scattered like mirrors, and a thousand fountains were playing in the air against the green trees and shrubbery. Thousands of birds of various colours were skimming through the air from tree to tree, displaying their gorgeous plumage, darting arrow-like against the sky. Countless cypresses stood erect and slim like a row of dusky slaves in the presence of Majesty. The ground about these trees was raised, forming small green hills covered with narcissi and Persian hyacinths, the one with creamy petals, very delicate and tender, encircling a gold cup filled with dew, and the other with a single blossom like a badge of azure. The entire scene represented a huge Ispahan carpet. The pools were the medallions. The large one in the centre did not throw water into the air but dispersed it in waves of molten silver from the mouth of a wide fountain. Thousands of gold and silver fish, some so tiny they could hardly be seen, others as large as trout, were storming toward the centre while half a dozen majestic swans towered their beautiful necks above them.

I was so lost in admiration that I paid very little heed to the commotion that followed the roaring of the eunuch. But at the sound of his voice a multitude of women, seemingly all young, ran from all directions toward the apartments around this immense garden, their colourful and diaphanous raiment in the breeze making them like giant rose petals thrown to the wind, or huge butterflies flying close to the ground. A few shuffled away with covered faces to the nearest balconies and corridors.

Presently we halted before a marble stairway leading to a balcony in front of a sunlit room. From this balcony two tall slender women led us to a stained glass door which opened into a luxuriously furnished room, filled with rich carpets and rugs and old and rare brocaded draperies, mostly of a deep rich red colour. There were big cushions (mokhattehs), of velvets and cashmeres embroidered with pearls, in all parts of the immense salon against the walls. Huge candelabra of coloured crystals hung from the ceiling. A round mosaic table stood in the centre of the room, entirely covered with vases of white narcissi and blue hyacinths. A single mosaic chair was in one corner.

As we entered a group of young girls who were sitting or reclining on the cushions, sprang to their feet, very much surprised. They were dressed in the latest fashion, the most interesting feature of which was their ballet skirts. This fashion had been introduced by the Shah, who had taken a fancy to it on the dancers in the Opera House in Paris. These skirts were shorter than those of the ballet dancers, scarcely covering half their thighs, and as those under the top skirt were starched, the group of skirts stood up round their figures like Japanese parasols, showing off the beauty of their bare limbs, which were most lovely and shapely.

A curtain of blue and gold brocade was drawn aside and we entered an antechamber, where four ladies sat on large cushions, near another door. They arose and came to father with words of welcome. One of them I recognized as a Kajar princess who was a great friend of my mother and the chosen messenger of the Queen to bring greetings and good wishes to mother on official occasions.

She kissed me affectionately, and said to father: "Her Majesty has been expecting you and the little Khan for an hour, and has asked for you more than ten times."

"It is indeed a pleasure to hear that her Majesty has deigned to see my little son. We are at her disposal," replied Father.

The eunuchs stepped back. Father and I with these four ladies, walked toward a third curtain, which was drawn aside by the princess herself. Father entered, and I followed.

So far as I could see, there was no one here. The curtains were drawn except one before a wide-open window looking into the green foliage of a tree covered with early blossoms. Father said: "Salamon Aleikom" toward this open window, and I bowed in the same direction without seeing anyone. The silence was making me impatient, when a delightfully thrilling voice spoke, saying: "Oh, how sweet of you to break the monotony of the hours of a lone and wasted soul. Come, come to me!"

I looked in the direction from which the voice seemed to issue, and, for the first time, I saw that someone was in the room! Father approached and motioned me to follow. The Queen was in a bed before the open window. When we approached she sat up and began to arrange a cushion behind her back. "How delightful to break the fast of my eyes with the actual glow of youth!" she continued. "Indeed, all dreams of my youth have been shattered to pieces by realities which I have to suffer. Even my imagination is growing dull. You did well to bring Youth with you, Sire."

"To hear your majesty jesting with the realities of life one would think she had seen more than merely twenty springs," said my father.

"Twenty springs!" she cried, "Oh, say twenty thousand winters! I feel old, and that is what counts in my life!"

"Your majesty is exaggerating, as is the habit of most of our poets," said Father.

She laughed with such a fresh young voice that I felt sure she had no right to say she was old, although to me twenty springs did seem a terrible age for a girl! She motioned Father to sit near the bed. Then she stretched her hand to me. But I did not move. The court ceremony prescribed for a young Khan was to stand erect before the King and Queen and to ignore any familiarity shown to him by his sovereigns. I had been brought up to pay no attention to informal gestures from high personages. She smiled at me, saying to Father: "His princely manner is well-matched by his wonderful looks!" and then to me she said: "Your Queen commands you to take her hand!"

I took it then without hesitation. She bade me sit down near the cushion and kept my hand in hers.

"Your mother," she continued, "was right to pride herself on your education; but I think she has omitted to tell my little Khan that I, too, am about to become . . . "

She stopped, and father finished her sentence, "a mother, if Khoda has willed it."

She blushed and said to me: "Did you hear what your high father said?"

"Yes, Majesty," I replied.

"Then I wish you would look upon me more as a mother than as a Queen."

"I certainly shall; I love my mother!" I replied enthusiastically.

"Then love me too," she said in a soft low voice, which seemed to me to contain a tinge of pathos.

"I shall love you too, Majesty," I replied with great zeal.

"There, there," she said, "now I am sure we shall be great friends. I must tell your father something that will make him angry with me; but, having you near me as a friend and knight protector, I feel more courageous." Then, turning to father, she said: "The Hakim Bashi of the Ayesha Khanom was here the other day to see me."

Father knit his brows, and said: "Hakim Bashi is a learned man and a good physician, but that will not make me alter my instructions that no physician of the court shall be allowed to pay professional visits to your majesty. The delicate rose to which I have given all my efforts is not to be trusted in every hand. By whose order has he been allowed to come here?"

"Do not blame me, my dear," said the Queen. "Her ladyship, the favourite of the Shah, Ayesha Khanom, has been worrying about my health and probably thought she was paying me a compliment by sending her special physician to me. Besides, the Hakim Bashi has been ordered by the Shah to call upon me."

"That is as it should be," said Father. "But, knowing

that his visit always leaves Her Majesty nervous and agitated I cannot but repeat my instructions."

The Queen seemed to me most beautiful. I should not have thought her older than fifteen had I not heard father say she was twenty. She had no wimple on her head. She threw the end of her tchador-nemaz on her head, which only half covered it. Her lovely little face, untouched by rouge or powder, was uncovered. Her eyes were of a dark brown hue which brought to my mind ancient black velvet. Her eyelashes were long and curly, her delicate nose small and straight. The mouth was perfection. I had heard that eyes could speak with the mute language called expression, but her mouth was as eloquent as any eyes I have ever seen. She wore the usual blouse of soft champagne-coloured silk made with long sleeves opening lengthwise. A single ring, a large square emerald mounted on a thin rim of white metal, was her only jewelry.

When her conversation with Father was at an end she turned to me, saying: "You must excuse us for not presenting you any refreshment. Our father"—(meaning my father)—"is so afraid that I may wish to partake of it that I do not dare ask for anything; but wait until . . ." she smiled and gave me a tiny wink as if to say: "wait till we are alone."

Father said, "Does your majesty allow us to take leave of her?"

"Unwillingly and with great reluctance, my dear," she replied, and then to me "I give back your hand; but you are coming again very soon to see how I feel, and afterward, on your return home, you can give an account of my health to the high and great Hadj-Agha!"

"I do not think his presence will be of any great benefit to your majesty if it will keep you from sleep and rest," said father. "Oh, please," she pleaded, "I have slept so much that I stay awake nights. Besides, the company of the little

Khan will brighten the monotony of my life and change my thoughts as well, two purposes which, I am sorry to say, no medicine has ever succeeded in doing."

Father smiled and said: "He shall come as your majesty wishes."

She clapped her hands, and immediately the four ladies in waiting came into the room. We arose, bowed to her, and went out of the room followed by the ladies.

In the second room we found the group of girls who had been so frightened at our entrance, standing in the corner, now considerably more at ease. In the balcony we were given into the charge of the two tall ladies, and in the garden Djouhar Khan and other eunuchs were waiting for us.

When we reached the first court the chief eunuch, Motamed-Harem, asked father to grant him the pleasure of going to his room for rest and refreshment, which invitation father, to my great satisfaction, accepted.

We sat in a circle. Servants brought tea and a water pipe for the eunuch. My father did not smoke. Motamed-Harem said he was delighted to hear that I was going to be a regular visitor to the harem and hoped to have me, whenever he was free, to play a game of chess with him.

What seemed most wonderful to me was the fact that everyone already knew that the Queen had asked my father to allow me to come again, and yet, when she had asked this there was no one else in the room to hear it. Had the ladies-in-waiting been listening at the door? This reminded me that my Laleh had told me repeatedly that in Persia all the doors had ears.

I was deep in thought when my friend Abol-Fath Khan appeared on the balcony and asked the chief eunuch if he might join his little brother without being an intruder.

When the eunuch had given permission and Abol-Fath had

seated himself beside me I asked if he could tell me how everybody knew everything that was said or done.

"Oh," he replied. "Wait till you become acquainted with the harem, and it will no longer seem a mystery. News travels in the air in palaces."

"How wonderful," I marvelled.

"Wonderful indeed," said my companion. "I am sorry that I shall have to give up the life sooner than I thought."

"Are you going away?"

"No, but I shall not be allowed to go inside the harem." That ungraceful creature," he said waving his hand toward the chief eunuch, "thinks I am growing too rapidly. He has decided that in seven months from now I shall become a man. Therefore, not being a boy any longer, I shall not be allowed to wander freely in the harem. Of course I shall be a chamberlain, but my talking with the ladies will be done behind curtains."

"But are you really to be a man in seven months from now?"

"Who can tell?" he answered. "I am not a horse or a eunuch to have my birthday recorded. My age is what the chief eunuch pleases to give me."

"I wonder if he knows his own age?"

"Surely. Dealers in slaves and eunuchs, like horse dealers, always know the ages of their stock; otherwise they could not make sales."

"But in Faranguestan they keep track of men and women's births," I said.

"In Faranguestan they must; they are infidels and no better than animals," he replied arrogantly.

I was thinking about all these things when he said: "Do you know I have never set eyes on the beautiful Queen to whom you were presented to-day?"

"No?" I was very much surprised.

"Never!" he answered sadly. "I am attached to Ayesha

Khanom, the second favourite, and she objects to my visiting other queens." Then he put his lips to my ear and said:
"Besides, she and your Queen are great friends! They love
each other so much that if someone brought news of the
death of one, the other would die of joy!"

"Do not be silly!" I remonstrated. "The Queen Ghamar-
ed-Dowleh is too much of a lady to wish the death of even
her greatest enemy. And I do not believe she can have an
enemy; she is too noble of character and good of heart."

"By all the Sheytans!" he whispered, "you will do wonderfully! Why, if you defend your lady like this you will
make all the others crazy about you. In fact, mine is,
already."

"About whom?" I asked.

"You, of course."

"Did you tell her about me?"

"Listen and judge for yourself." He told me that a few
hours ago he had been called by his queen to give her an
account of my father's arrival; why I was brought to the
Queen; if I could speak French; who my Laleh was; was I
a good shot; could I ride a horse well; could I play music;
if so, who was my master; what day was I free from school;
had I travelled far; would I become frightened were I to
come face to face with a tiger; did I believe in jinnee, div,
and pary; did I know anything about the mysterious medicine prepared from pearl dust possessing properties to keep
ladies young; had I ever seen a ghost; could I love anyone
besides my mother; could I separate two fighting dogs.
There were so many "could I's" and would I's" that Abol-
Fath himself stopped out of breath. I was amazed but
after a moment of silence I asked him what he had answered to all these questions.

"Oh, I said of course that you did all these things and
many more."

Shortly after this Father arose and we departed. We were accompanied by the whole group of eunuchs and court officials to the gate, where we said good-byes and mounted our horses for home.

IX

MY SECOND VISIT TO HER MAJESTY, THE QUEEN

The result of my visit to the harem was that from that day on, a certain Sheik Yaghob, one of the religious attendants of my eldest brother, was introduced to me as a second teacher to enable me to become a more suitable companion to the Queen. He came every evening, and started me on a course of literature and poetry. I had to work very hard, but the prospect of becoming a companion to the Queen proved a tempting incentive. One day three months later, Father said he had received a message from Her Majesty and had arranged my second visit to the harem for the next Friday. He said I was to go alone, and that he would join me later in the afternoon.

When Friday arrived I was brought to the gate of the palace by Laleh, who gave me into the charge of Djouhar Khan to conduct me to the Queen. There was practically no heralding my approach to the garden as on my previous visit. I was received, instead, with more familiarity by the head of the eunuchs and more friendly smiles from the officials and court attendants.

To my great amazement all the women of the harem were assembled in the garden. They made no effort to run away but actually came near and stood in a row along the pathways where I was to pass. A few of the old ones covered their faces, which made them look like sacks of cereal in the market place. The younger ones, with their faces completely uncovered, kept insolently but not unkindly staring at me. Now and then one of them gave me a shy smile. Djouhar, who was my only guide and company, sent some of these curious ones away to mind their own affairs, and introduced me to others as a future agha and a grandee among the Shah's private officials.

On a balcony, hidden by jasimines, the beautiful Queen was lying on a rug reading a book. No one was with her. Djouhar coughed two or three times to draw her attention, and I tried to cough too. I believe my effort made the Queen look up, for she laughed in her musical voice and her eyes filled with mirth like a mischievous child's. "Well tried, my little Khan, well tried," she repeated. "Yours are not so terribly solemn as those of Djouhar, are they?"

I could not help smiling at the Queen's remark.

"I beg your majesty," said Djouhar, "to permit the remark that your slave has to cough at least a hundred times in every twenty-four hours!"

"Poor dear Djouhar," sympathised the Queen. "You should let our great Hadj-Agha prescribe a treatment for you!" She motioned me, "Come and sit near me, I want to see your face."

I approached her and bowed. "Sit down and tell me something quite new about yourself. Djouhar will order some tea and melon."

At this remark Djouhar left the room and, with a low bow, I sat opposite her, very solemn and grave. She astonished me by imitating my expression for at least a minute, and then she burst into laughter: "O you silly boy, do not look like that; you will get lines in your face." Her laughter was contagious, and I laughed too. "That's better!" she remarked. "Now tell me, are you studying very hard?"

"Yes, Majesty, from morning till late at night," I answered.

"That is wonderful for a little boy," she said. "Can you pronounce the Arabic words in your Koran correctly?"

"Oh, that is very difficult. Father said it takes a man forty years to study Arabic and pass an examination in Arabic grammar," I replied.

"And of our poets—what do you know about them?"

"I know them all, and I write poetry myself," I replied very proudly.

"Ah, that is very interesting, but not astonishing. You belong to a family of great scholars, writers, and poets. Your brothers Sadrol-Attebba and Moayedol-Hokama are both renowned poets."

"I shall also become a great poet," I answered, and feeling that the time had come to talk of other things more amusing than poets, I was about to begin a dissertation on hunting and riding, when she asked if I knew Hafiz and Sadi, the two great Persian poets. To end this subject once and for all I replied that I knew their poetry nearly by heart. Contrary to my expectations she began a long discussion about them and ordered Djouhar to sit down and listen. He took off his shoes and sat near the door.

I was overwhelmed at the ease with which she flew from one subject to another, and I wondered if all Persian women were gifted with the same erudition and wit. I was thoroughly fascinated by her charm and the sound of her voice as she quoted:

"When fervid youth mates with Experience, Life's chariot speeds into the Infinite to the goal of Success."

"What poet, by the way, created this magnificent truth?" she asked me with the same pleasing voice.

This was quite out of proportion to the knowledge I had acquired under my schoolmaster and the Sheik Yaghob. The name of this particular poet was unknown to me, but the advice of my Laleh, who told me never to keep a king or a queen waiting for an answer came to my mind.

I replied: "My memory fails to furnish the name of the worthy poet, a fact which surprises me to some extent, unless I shall presume that your majesty's poetical disposition is the source from which she has gathered the quotation!"

She blushed, and replied: "I see that you have inherited your father's worst quality; to flatter my poor and ignorant mind to such an extent that you will make me believe myself in possession of the poetical gift which has been the heritage of all the Persians, and I shall make myself ridiculous."

She was about to continue when the curtain was drawn aside and the princess in waiting announced my father. Djouhar jumped to his feet, and so did I.

"The great Ferdawcy in flesh and blood!" cried the Queen. Ferdawcy was the great epic poet of Persia, author of the Book of the Kings, a tall impressive man whom my father was said to resemble.

"Coming to one of the greatest queens of his time," Father replied. Djouhar, after bowing with solemn austerity, ran to him, took his walking stick and placed it against the wall.

"I was just telling your son how you spoiled me with compliments, which is a very bad example for him. He has been telling me that I was a poetess; and you are calling me one of the greatest queens. Between your highness and your son I shall sooner or later finish by believing myself to be both."

"My son is right," said father. "Your majesty is endowed with the poetic imagination which is the creator of poetry."

"The poetry which awakens the soul," she said mournfully, "flows from those hearts which have known joy, happiness, affection, and love. But my heart has known none of these blessings and perhaps never will."

Her eyes became wet and her lips began to quiver, but after a quick glance at me she threw the fine muslin head-dress which covered her face partly aside, dabbed her eyes with a tiny lace handkerchief and tried to look happy.

Meanwhile two young girls came in with plates holding large slices of Ispahan melon.

"It is not necessary to bring the Samovar here," said the Queen to the girls. "You may pour the tea outside."

Except Djouhar, each of us received a plate with two slices. The melon was separated from the skin upon which it rested and was moreover cut into pieces with a knife as one would cut a loaf of bread, because of our habit of eating with our fingers.

"In the books of our poets we learn that the first lesson of life is love and we search the guiding light. But lo! it takes a long life to realise this! And, even then in some cases, like my own, when we are ready to touch the rim of the cup of wine with our lips the cup is dashed away from us and the light extinguished!"

Soon the girls came back with cups of tea, which we drank, with one or two drops of lime juice from Shiraz. When we finished the melon the girls brought a silver ewer and bowl in which we washed our fingers. All this time Djouhar was silently looking on with his large kind eyes, now at the Queen, then at my father, and then at me.

By this time the Queen was gay again and I was very much pleased when she said to me: "Would you care to hear a story about a little girl named Leila who became a Queen?"

"Oh, I should love to," I replied.

It was a long and mournful tale of how the father of the little girl, a wealthy landowner and khan, had tried in vain to save her from being sacrificed in marriage. The worldly honours offered in return for her by the Shah's uncle, the old Prince-Governor of Shiraz, could not move him, nor the delights of paradise, promised by the Chief Mollah. But against a third suitor, Nasser-ed-Din Shah himself, who had sent as his emissary an agha eunuch, he was helpless: to refuse was rebellion. "Our part of the country is a free land, inhabited by a free race," he said to the child. "The Kajar Shah and his army of mercenaries have to pass over many mountains and many bodies of brave men to reach you. Our horses are swift, our swords sharp, our retainers faithful, and your father willingly places his life at your service. A misfortune has befallen our family, and it must be faced. Take yourself into your own room, light of my eyes; think over our situation and give me your answer."

"The rest of the story," finished the Queen, "is known to everybody. The young daughter of a mountaineer became a Queen of Persia! But what is not known to any one but your father and Djouhar Khan—the Shah's emissary —is that I am that girl, Leila! The Queen! But among how many queens! All these palaces and gardens, all this magnificence of our royal life, cannot satisfy a girl whose ambition was to be loved by the husband of her own choice!"

I felt such sorrow that my eyes must have betrayed my feelings; for she drew me toward her, took my chin in her hand, kissed me and said: "You have a brave little heart. I am sure you are thinking how to help me."

"Your majesty's heart is the bravest of all!" commented my father, who had been listening without saying a word.

"And I," said the eunuch, "I have no heart! I have lost it to your majesty long ago. I have only a black skeleton of a man which I shall willingly burn at your feet, if need be."

"Will that help me?" asked the Queen, addressing herself to me, smiling bravely to hide her emotion.

"Djouhar Khan is a most faithful man," said my father without looking at the Queen. "The summer season is nearing, and a change of air in the country will do her majesty good."

"Oh yes, any change will be welcome," she said to my

father, glad to change the conversation. "By the way, may I take your son with me?"

"He is yours, Majesty, if only he can follow his studies at the same time."

"That is indeed his duty. I shall be only a recreation," replied the Queen.

Thereupon father asked if we were allowed to leave her presence. Interpreting the Queen's silence as a confirmation, he made a sign to me, and we arose.

"Remember," said the Queen to my father, "the summer season is nearing and I need a change."

"I shall remember, Majesty," my father replied. We bowed to her and departed.

The Queen's story was known only to a few of her intimate friends. Nobody outside knew much about any of the women in Nasser-ed-Din Shah's harem; inside very few of them knew anything about one another. Sometimes a queen living in the Sun Palace next to the Palace of Marble, a distance of some five hundred feet did not even know who her rival was. Few of the queens ever bothered with the others. Many were forgotten, and lived obscure lives away from the rest. Only the gifted ones were known more or less universally.

Such was the Queen Ghamar-ed-Dowleh. Her education had been of the best, and her literary and poetic talents were well known.

I could hardly follow her at times when she was talking with my father. It was by the sense of admiration emanating from his person that I knew the Queen must have pleased him with her remarks. Through my father's attitude toward her I came to understand why all the other queens were said to be deadly jealous of her. My Laleh—who had a relation in the harem as one of the Shah's thousand or so concubines—used to tell me the way the four thousand women lived inside the palaces, which formed the sanctuary called by the Arabic name of harem. The fight between these women for supremacy was so great that even the despotic Nasser-ed-Din Shah, upon whose pleasure depended the lives of twelve million people, had to resort to various remedies to defend his peace of mind. The women used every possible weapon. Some tried to win by the sheer force of their corporal beauty. Others tried to outdo their rivals by the subtle art of coquetry. A few had an easy victory because of ancestry more distinguished than the Shah's, which was of low origin and alien in the country.

The public as a whole believed that this earthly paradise was ruled by the inflexible will of Nasser-ed-Din Shah, the most tyrannical of oriental monarchs. But the fact was, so my Laleh told me, His Majesty, the Shadow of Allah, when at the end of his imperial wits would turn to my father to reëstablish peace inside his overpopulated harem. Laleh said also that the Shah, while a very courageous man was thoroughly a coward where women were concerned. This was mainly due to the prediction of a Jewess called Sarah, who had told him that the greatest man in Persia was destined to be assassinated by the hand of a woman! The Shah naturally thought he was the greatest man in Persia, and therefore developed a dread of women which lasted all his life. Besides, some years earlier, he had been attacked on his return from the country, by a group of women, and one of them had fired a pistol at him.

This terror of his was the reason for an elaborate spying supervision which he had established in the palace, especially in the harem. As a result there was a feeling of being spied upon by all who frequented the harem, and an atmosphere of mystery prevailed in that city within a city, with its thousands and thousands of eunuchs, chamberlains, pages, courtiers, officials, guardians, watchmen, spies, door-listeners, detectives, professional confessors, religious men, confidence men and women, seers, star-readers, amateur sorcerers, mascots, interpreters of dreams, lucky and unlucky persons, boys with lucky faces (such as the Queen pretended was the case with my own) which were able to thwart the effect of a bad eye or black eye; and a considerable number of other professionals such as seyyed and mollahs who by prayers and reading of the Koran were there to protect the august person of the Shah and his followers.

The policy of closed doors was severely observed. Even the entry of the nearest relations of the inhabitants of the harem was absolutely forbidden. The merest child among the Shah's children was never allowed to intrude upon the privacy of his mother or enter the dread sanctuary without going through a procession of precautions taken by the head of the eunuchs and other officials. I have seen young princes, sons or grandsons of the Shah, turned away with no excuse or apology. It was a long time before I understood the reason for all these apparently cruel and drastic measures.

Besides, after all, who were these princes who grew like mushrooms in the nursery of the harem? They were the offspring of the Shah's cohabitation with hundreds of women, collected mostly among the provincial gentry and peasants whose parents were delighted to become related to the Shah by marriage and thus escape the tyranny of the men the Shah sent as governors to rule over them. None of the prominent families of Teheran, and very seldom the Persian nobility, would consent to give a daughter in marriage to the Shah. They knew better. So did the Shah, who understood his situation, and therefore obtained the raw material for his daily portion of Oriental felicity among the less prejudiced families. That was a phrase coined by my Laleh, "the raw material!"

Each queen, favourite, or concubine had her own retinue of servants and eunuchs. Each had her own service of spying on the others, and a regiment of men and women to intrigue against her rivals. If a woman was unsuccessful in getting rid of her rival physically, she made efforts to bring her into the Shah's disfavour in some other way. For instance, she would resort to sorcerers, fortune tellers, witches, or dealers in black magic and cabalistic silence. These disreputable persons were smuggled into the harem in spite of the merciless vigilance of the eunuchs, and large sums of money were spent by these silly women to engage their help. Sometimes three or four messengers were sent to get the ingredients which the sorcerers had prescribed for the making up of the magic medicine which would, for example, cause a terrible damage to the complexion of a rival or give her shaky legs or make her fat and unshapely. Sometimes the medicine was to make the Shah enamoured of the lady who had engaged the sorcerer. I believe the effort of these love seekers was one of the reasons why he took such great precautions against poison. Fifty officials were on duty to taste every particle of food destined for the imperial stomach.

One of these medicines, I heard, was a concoction made of the most ridiculous and gruesome substances. For example, a few hairs from the upper lip of a live young leopard, with certain other attributes specified as to the colour of its skin or such and such a spot on its tail or in the centre of its forehead, the navel of a young gazelle cut immediately after it had been attacked by a lion and torn to pieces, the heart of a certain bird which lived only in India, a certain spice not unlike a grain of pepper, from Ceylon, the pulverized teeth of a certain kind of snake, caught alive and killed in such and such a manner that was almost impossible to bring about. These and a score of other uncanny ingredients had to be collected and the mixture exposed to fresh air for so many evenings in the moonlight, while the sorcerer read talismanic words and blew upon it. Afterward it was made into small pills. Whoever took one of these pills was supposed to become wild with love for the lady for whom they were made.

Naturally, it was impossible for the woman to obtain the ingredients herself, and so she would commission a sorcerer, generally an old Jewess, to get them for her at a fabulous price. After many months the sorcerer would present the pills, with a long statement giving details of the expenses for each item, such as sending a man to India for the leopard's hair. Such bills easily ran into hundreds of tomans.

Other expenses had then to be incurred, such as bribing someone to throw one of the pills into his majesty's soup. This emissary, if caught, had to pay the penalty of death, and a wholesale change would ensue in the harem. The lady who had caused the trouble would be thrown into the oblivion of the Shah's disgrace or sent to her parents in exile. Punishment would pursue her family and a dozen other women who were supposed to be accomplices would be divorced in an hour.

In spite of this I am sure the Shah had swallowed many such pills, and I wonder if the periodical stomach pains he used to suffer were not due to them. Father used to think it was due to his passion for eating raw cucumbers in and out of season!

Other ladies less daring and more religious would appeal to the donkeys, the mollahs, (Laleh's word, as he considered all mollahs asses walking on two legs) and also to the seyyeds, who were supposed to be the direct descendants of Mohammad. These worthy representatives of Islam would willingly undertake pilgrimages to the sacred shrines of Ghom and other holy places to induce the spirits of the martyrs to act in the favor of such and such queens before the mighty Shah. Many of these priests, beside being provided with money, were given a horse or a mule to ride to the sacred shrines, and some never came back. My Laleh said they were thieves but the other mollahs and seyyeds soliciting alms from the harem would assure their majesties with solemn oaths that their poor colleagues had sacrificed their holy lives on behalf of the solicitants.

Such practices, as a rule pertained to the ladies of the less refined class, the provincials who were considered nobody by the prominent people in the cities, who were in their turns regarded as nobody by the members of old aristocratic families in Teheran. Outside the harem the Persian women were not, as a rule, such fools as to believe in the seyyeds and mollahs. My own Dadeh used to laugh at the credulity of the Shah's wives.

But this group of clergy not only succeeded in extorting money from the provincial queens and those newly arrived in the harem, but were also ready to collect women discarded from the harem, whom they pestered till they consented to marriage. This was due to the fact that any other man, even the beggar in the street, would not give his hand, much less his name, to a woman discarded from the imperial harem! One of the well known seyyeds living near our quarter granted a divorce to half a dozen of the Shah's wives, who had begun to get fat and ugly, and married the whole lot of them himself for the sake of dowry which the Shah had to give them with the divorce. The Persian laws demand that a man give a dowry to his wife. This is usually a sum of money stipulated in the contract, which the husband has also to give her if he demands a divorce. If the woman demands the divorce, the man is free to give or refuse the dowry. The Shah, always paid it, but the women of lesser importance got very little. Even a mollah would refuse to marry one of them. But he would cheat her in other ways, such as recommending her to a man who did not suspect her origin and thus get a commission from both of them.

All the decent men detested the Shah's polygamy and the Mohammedan clergy's lust for money. Among those who despised him most intensely was my Laleh. He once said to me: "Master of my own heart, try to find out in which part of the infernal harem that unhappy female relation of mine is vegetating. I should love to see her face to face and to send her to the felicity of the great silence with the point of this little dagger, to save her and the dignity of my people!" Laleh, as I have said before was a nobleman from Afshar family and a descendant of Nadir Shah, the conqueror of India, the ravisher of the Peacock throne and the famous diamond "Daryayeh-nour." Besides, he was high-spirited and very quick with his sword. Even if I had the misfortune of finding his relation I should not have had the courage to tell him her whereabouts. I knew perfectly well what he meant to do to her, by the fact that the killing of a daughter, or a sister, or a wife who had the misfortune of dishonouring the name of her family in any way, was considered legitimate and rightful.

Further, the killing of anybody twenty-five years ago was of no importance, least of all to the murderer! A person could kill any one he disliked, especially if he was attached to one of the dignitaries of the Shah's court or was himself powerful and wealthy. There was no such thing as justice. The right of killing was invested in those whom the Shah appointed governors or officers of the Empire; the Moslem clergy had also the right to inflict capital punishment, and it was as easy for the Persian husband to kill his wife for adultery as it was to kill a fly. The clergy would support him. The best of the mollahs could be bought over by putting a small sum of money in the hollow of their holy hands! Another easy way, to avoid punishment was to run to a sacred shrine for refuge. Here protection could be had, even against the Shah.

Aside from these features of life in the harem, I believe the women had very little of which to complain. Materially they had everything they could wish for. Their life was luxurious, such as few women could enjoy unless very rich. They were given jewelry and gorgeous clothes. They had carriages and horses of their own, and they were able to provide their parents and relations with money, positions, and honours which they could not have got in any other way.

I never could understand what pleasure the Shah could have with all these women. As a good Mohammedan, he was, or pretended to be, impartial towards all his wives. The four queens came first in his affection, but there were a thousand others among whom he had to divide equally what was left. There was never anything private about his love-making. No sooner did he set out to lighten the solitude of one of his favourites with his august presence, than the whole harem stirred to frantic agitation. Rival women invoked the holy spirits for something to happen to prevent his majesty from visiting the one he intended to see. The best preventive was to pray that on his way to the apartment of the bride of the evening, somebody would sneeze. In that case his majesty would directly halt the procession and go back to his own apartment.

In Persia a sneeze would halt a declaration of war! A sneeze is a divine warning to abandon one's intention, whatever its nature. War, marriage, divorce, a voyage, the signing of contracts, taking a bath, cutting one's nails or hair—in short, any action has to be abandoned if somebody sneezes. I remember the Shah often abandoned his travelling projects, just as he was about to mount his horse, because he heard someone sneeze. Woe to anybody who ever gave a false sneeze! His head was chopped off instantly, without mercy.

You would think none of the harem women would indulge in such a dangerous game. And yet the contrary was true. Some of the ladies had special women in their service to perform this risky job. The woman was, as a rule, old and in so delicate a state of health that no one could think

of accusing her of having sneezed purposely. This woman
was despatched to waylay the Shah in the garden and sneeze
loud enough to be heard by his majesty. In the meantime
the one he was about to visit had very likely taken measures
to counteract these plots by her own official sneezer, whose
business was to sneeze a second time. A single sneeze was
the divine warning to stop an action but a second sneeze
immediately after the first, even by a different sneezer,
meant to go on and do what was intended.

Every queen had her own system of spying on every other.
Eunuchs and servants were ordered to watch the official
sneezers and pages were directed to look up young girls of
their own age among the suites of the rival queens and make
themselves agreeable to them so as to find out at what hour
his majesty was to pay visit to their queen. It was a most
lively time.

My friend Abol-Fath, told me that once he caught the
official sneezer of one of the ladies and that she happened,
to his great amazement, to be a very young and lovely girl!
He said he saved the situation himself by sneezing falsely.
This girl was so grateful to Abol-Fath and so pleased with
him—and, indeed, he was a most good looking boy—that
she began to sneeze to prevent her mistress from going out
in the evening. This would leave her free to spend her own
evening with Abol in the shady part of the garden, admiring
the blue sky and the shining moon.

Of course it must be understood that his majesty's visit
was literally a visit. That is to say, it lasted only an hour
or two. Then he went to his own apartment where he slept
alone, guarded by some sixty eunuchs and the head of the
imperial watch, a prominent Khan who slept outside the
bedchamber with a naked sword at his side. Sometimes he
spent the early evening visiting two or three of his wives,
and the rest of the night calling on one of the four queens,
with whom he would converse, read poetry, and talk litera-

ture. On such occasions all the officials and chief eunuchs
of the queen were present and the affair was a joyful one.
Anecdotes and stories were told to make him laugh, and
paper and pencil were brought to him with which to draw
sketches. Nasser-ed-Din Shah was a marvellous artist. Some
of his sketches of the heads of his eunuchs in caricature were
very delightful. He frequently sought the company of the
Queen Ghamar-ed-Dowleh because her entertainment was
purely social and at times included music. Since she herself was the daughter of a well known Khan, and of better
birth than the Shah, she never troubled him by asking favours while other women invariably asked for something,
either for themselves or for their relations.

To me the most interesting thing in the harem was the
diversity of character, language, and education of these
women. Some were of high education. The majority knew
how to play at least one musical instrument, such as the
tar, setar, or seinture. A few had wonderful voices. Dancing was out of the question. For a lady to dance was to
lose her dignity as a lady. This part of the entertainment
was reserved for the hundreds of girls who lived in the
harem as "girls in waiting." It took me some time to see
the difference in the ages of the women. Because of the
use of rouge and dye and facial treatments the grandmother
of a girl of fifteen, could be reasonably taken by a boy
unversed in such practices for her granddaughter who as
yet was not allowed to use any artificial means to make
herself more attractive. Very few of the women were fat.
I believe the Persian diet kept them slender.

They seldom ate sweets or pastry, and butter and choco-
late were never used. I myself did not know what choco-
late was! Unmelted butter, except for a special dish—rice
and kabab—was used only in the dispensary, where the doctors mixed it with other medicines to make a paste. Children as a rule were disgusted with butter, and if they saw

a cook or a butter merchant testing butter by tasting it, the sight made them sick! Sugar was very little used, especially by women. Usually a woman drank tea without it or put a tiny bit in her mouth and sipped the tea through it. Sometimes two cups of tea were drunk and the bit of sugar was still in her mouth.

Most Persian women, and especially those in the harem were greatly concerned with keeping themselves beautiful. This was not so much the result of vanity as of a desire to make the best of what nature had bestowed. This desire was shared by all women, even those of the peasantry and nomadic tribes. In our own country place many girls with beautiful fair hair and a few with red hair were working hard to get enough money to buy henna and rang to tint it a darker hue.

The very first cream ever made to keep the skin soft was invented by Persian women, and so was the veil, which was designed to protect the face from dust and heat. The first powder for the face was made in Persia. It came from the special rice called "sadri," cultivated only in Persia and not equalled in the world. So was Persia the origin of the first rouge, which was made by crushing and drying a small insect named "shan-djarf." All the cosmetics of the Persian toilet were made either of animal or vegetable materials. Chemical materials came later and were inventions of the West.

But the young girls who acted as ladies in waiting, keepers of robes, companions, reciters of poetry, readers of books, or simply as decorations in the gorgeous halls and apartments, needed no artificial aids.

Without exception they had wonderful hair, ranging in colour from black to pure yellow gold. The girls ten or twelve years old wore theirs Madonna-fashion. After that age, and especially when they were married, their hair was cut in a fashion as old as Persia, that is to say, combed down the forehead, and cut horizontally about a quarter of an inch above the eyebrows, with two tiny strands coming down on the temples and finished in a curl on either cheek. The rest of the hair was in thick braids, some of which were allowed to fall from the shoulders to the breast. I thought this arrangement very attractive.

All of the women and girls took an interest in clothes that was almost religious in intensity. Each one was her own designer, each had her own fashion. Tailors were called in to carry out designs, not to create them. Each blouse, each wimple, each skirt had to be cut and shaped to fit the individual figure, complexion, colour of hair, shape of head, construction of limbs, height, width, and above all, the personal taste. Such was the case with the cutting of the hair. No fashion was recognised as standard, and no article of dress had a definite length or width. The dress had to follow the figure of the individual woman.

Nowhere else have I seen more beautiful women. The girls in the harem, with their big eyes, small red mouths, beautiful white teeth, and tiny noses, their bangs of brown or chestnut hair escaping from under their wimples and curling on their flushed rosy cheeks, and their lovely, graceful, bare limbs, in complete harmony with the rest of their exquisite, picturesque, and pretty ensemble, made a picture of loveliness that I never can forget. They remind me always of an armful of wild flowers gathered in the open field where sun and light had been their only gardeners and the sky the glass cover of their earthly bed.

PART II

I

LEARNING ABOUT MY ANCESTORS

BEFORE writing about the famous monarch, Nasser-ed-Din Shah, I must acquaint the reader with my father's position and the relation between his family and the Shah.

My father's family had migrated from the place of its origin, Shiraz, some four centuries earlier. Its members established themselves in different parts of the country between the Caspian Sea and the Elburz Mountains. One of my ancestors, known by the name of Hossein, and possessing the title of Beyk—which in his time was borne by only four members of the old nobility—lived in Kazvin when the dynasty of Safavi Shahs was reigning over the Persian Empire. The title gave to the bearer the rank of a reigning prince with privileges equal to those of the Shah himself. The Turcoman invasion of the northern part of the country having become a periodical calamity, Shah Tahmasp, then ruler, ordered Hossein Beyk to go into the interior provinces and fight the invaders. Thus it happened that Hossein Beyk, with his fighting men, came to a small village called Teheran, located near Rei, where he established his headquarters, built for himself a mansion, a tekkyeh, a public cistern, and a mosque.

In fact from time to time members of my family had been commissioned by the Shahs to fight the different invaders of Persia or to quell rebellions among its own inhabitants. The particular enmity of my family for the Usbegs-Turcoman was well known to the Shahs before the reign of the Kajar Dynasty, to which Nasser-ed-Din Shah

121

belonged, and many of its members had lost their lives on
the battle field because of it.   Such was the case of Mokhtar
Ali Beyk, who had been sent by the Shah Ismâil against the
Turcoman and fell in battle near Rei, and was buried in a
garden in the center of Teheran.   This place was known as
Pesta Beyk's Garden, having been named for another prominent warrior.

When I saw this garden, which, in the old days, had been
the marvel of the little village of Teheran, it had become
nothing but a poor reminder of the original.   The entire
estate had been divided into lots for houses to accommodate
the growing population of Teheran, and only a small space,
enclosed within four walls, was left.   The grave, made of
mud and covered with bricks, was located in the centre of
the court—a single fig tree, very old and stately, standing
sentinel, shadowed it.

I remember the day very well.   I had been brought there,
by my Laleh, to pay homage to a famous fighter for the
cause of his country.   Gravely he left me saying, "My little
master, I leave you alone with your ancestor."   Whereupon,
he walked away, backward, and I was alone.

Late afternoon—not a sound was to be heard, and there
was nothing in view but the mud grave, the fig tree, and
those four walls, built up high to hide the buildings outside.   I walked with my arms crossed on my breast, as though
approaching a monarch, and knelt at the side of the grave,
praying to my dead ancestor to make me like himself and
cause me to serve my country as nobly as he had done.   I
do not know how long I knelt there, before I felt a touch
on my shoulder.   It frightened me, as I had never been
frightened before.   I was about to call my Laleh, when a
voice close behind me said, "Steady, my son!   Steady, my
son!   Have no fear; this hand is made of the same flesh
and blood as your own."

I turned around and saw an old man with a long, white

beard and flowing robes such as are worn by the dervishes. He was tall, broad-shouldered, and deep-chested, like an athlete. His bearing was majestic and his eyes, under the shadow of thick brows, were kind and fatherly; a strange glint in them caused me to feel very insignificant.

"A true and faithful copy of the original!" he muttered to himself. Addressing me, he added, "This is the correct hour to pray at a grave. The sun has set, and the spirits are alive and abroad. Do you not think so, my son?"

I agreed with him, but I could not make out what he was doing there. To my great amazement, as if he had read my thoughts he said, "You think I have no right to be here, do you not?"

"Yes," I answered bravely.

He pondered awhile, then turning his face toward the heavens, murmured, "Thanks to you, O almighty and great Khoda, for comforting an old heart, well-nigh beating its last in this aged breast."

He sighed, touching his heart at the same time, and his chest rose as a tower above my head. "It was a good omen —telling me what you thought. Never, oh never, let fear prevent you from speaking the truth or from hearing it."

"You are very gracious, indeed," I responded politely.

"You will live your life like that man, lying there in the grave, and you will serve your country as he served it. What you have asked to-day, from the dead, will be granted to you. But I warn you to prepare yourself for a world of animosity and jealousy. Do you think you can endure that?"

"I will try."

"Take these words" he continued. "Tell the truth—fight for the truth; such will be your homage to the spirit of our ancestors, such your share of service to our beloved home-land."

"Thank you, sir," I answered earnestly.

Stepping back from me, he said, "You will find your

good Laleh at the entrance, waiting. Tell him for me that 'it is a true and faithful copy of the original.' "

Bowing to him, I walked away. Near the entrance, I turned and in the semi-darkness of late evening saw his silhouette bending over the grave where I had left him.

Rushing to Laleh I asked, "Who is that strange man you allowed to come in here?"

"Oh, I forgot to tell you, sir; he comes here every evening. Were you frightened?" he asked me.

"Frightened! I was shaking all over! I was so sure I was alone that I really believed the voice was coming from the grave. Tell me, Laleh dear; who is he?"

"He is a man of God—a holy man."

"Is he a dervish?"

"Oh, no, sir. Nobody knows exactly when and whence he came to this city. But many do know that he serves as one of the high doorkeepers of the Emam-Zade Zeid, in the shrine here."

"But, how did he know who I am?" I questioned.

"I believe he knows everyone in your family."

"But, how could he know what I prayed for just now?" I persisted.

"My own dear little master, I have just told you that the man is a holy man; there is nothing in this world, or in the world to come, that a holy man does not know," Laleh answered in utmost seriousness.

Although there was nothing for me to do but believe my Laleh, I was far from satisfied with his answers. But I did not question him further; silently, we walked home together. "I must learn more about that strange man," I said to myself, "and about my family. Not about my family as it is to-day, but as it was in the past." I planned to speak further with my Laleh that night.

Also, I decided to visit the Shrine of Emam-Zadeh Zeid on the following Thursday, to see if I could meet the holy man again. It was only a quarter of a mile from the old garden. Often, on Thursday evenings (which, according to the Moslem belief, are holy evenings), I had gone there in the company of one of my aunts and some girl cousins to pray and weep.

The reader may think it strange that I say we went there to weep . . . One must be born a Persian to understand the fascination of weeping. Besides the weekly pilgrimages to shrines and other holy places for weeping, the Persians weep for a whole month each year! It is the month of mourning, when Passion Plays are performed throughout the Country.

But to return to my story: After dinner I broached the subject of my ancestry to Laleh. He was unable to satisfy me, but finally he said, "I will tell you where you can secure answers if you give your promise not to mention that I suggested the idea."

I promised.

"Very well, then. The only man who knows well the history of your family—past and present—is your uncle."

"My holy uncle?"

Laleh smiled.

"No. Rather, your *unholy* uncle."

This uncle, Assadollah Khan, my father's brother, was a most unusual man. He possessed neither the Oriental dignity of my father nor the modern characteristics of my brothers. In fact, so far as I could judge, he had nothing Oriental or Occidental about him! One of our great thinkers said of him, "a character!" His life, his thoughts, his ideals, his ambitions for himself and for his country—all, were entirely different from the rest. He had nothing in common with his contemporaries, none of whom equalled him as a man or as a patriot.

The story of his life is long enough to fill a book. I can only introduce him here as the first man whose voice was raised against the tyranny of the Shah. He was the man who originally undertook to open the eyes of the public to the miserable condition in which they lived. Equipped with a poetical gift, he satirized and ridiculed the Shah and his dissolute court, wreaking havoc among the flatterers of the monarch, and so disturbing the Shah himself that he begged Assadollah Khan to make peace with him.

Since my Laleh had told me I should find him in the evening, I chose a Thursday, knowing that my aunt, with her household, would be visiting one of the shrines, and that my uncle would be alone.

I was greeted by the house-boy, known among us children as "The Yellow Monster from Mazenderan." This boy, only twenty years of age, was already noted for his great strength. Like all of his countrymen who had come to Teheran to work, he had travelled on foot from the northern forest of Mazenderan with a donkey driver, with no other wordly belongings than his axe. His remarkable strength and skillful use of it, while chopping wood for the kitchen, had drawn my uncle's attention, and he took the boy into his personal service.

"You are all alone, Master? All by yourself? Nobody behind you?" he asked, very much surprised.

"Why not? I came through the garden," I said to him, by way of quieting his anxiety.

"That is all right, but a young gentleman should always have a nice little friend by his side." And he touched the little pointed dagger hanging from his own belt.

"I know it, Yellow, but I am not allowed to carry one. Where is the Khan Uncle?"

"In his study, working as usual."

"Lead the way to him," said I, fumbling for my step in the dark.

The floor covering in my uncle's study was made of crushed stems of a certain kind of bamboo used, as a rule, in the mosques.   There was not a single rug nor a piece of carpet nor any furniture, except an antique chair and a little, low table covered with books.   My uncle was seated on the floor in the centre of the room before an Ispahan copper candlestick covered with a bulging glass chimney. He was not dressed formally, but was wearing what we call in Persian, "pir-jama," from which the word "pyjamas" is derived.   His feet were bare, and his head was uncovered. Books and sheets of white paper were scattered all around him.   He was busy writing, using his knee as a table.   I took my place opposite him, sitting with my knees bent under me—the correct attitude of a Persian gentleman in the presence of an elder.

Two minutes later, tea was brought in.   My uncle finished his instantly—I wondered how he could drink it so hot— set his cup aside, and said, "Now, my dear nephew, is it a horse, a donkey, a book, a bird or a poem?"

"None of these things, my own dear and respected uncle. I want you to give me extensive information about our family; especially, about our forefather who is buried in the garden of Pesta Beyk."

"Does not the grave strike you as a poor tribute to a great man?" as asked.

"Yes."

"Well, that is how Persia reveres her great men," he replied.

"But I have seen many beautifully decorated graves in the vicinity of sacred places—such as in the Shrine of Hazrate Abdol Azim.   I have even seen one or two old mollahs, engaged to recite the Koran on the graves, soliciting the benediction of visitors and passers-by."

"Those are, mostly, tombs of men who robbed the country," my uncle said calmly.

"And, because our forefathers did not rob, they have merely been buried under a few feet of earth?"   I asked, somewhat puzzled.

"Our forefathers could never rob their motherland! It was ever their aim to punish those dishonest aliens who defiled the honour and traditions of the country, and sapped the vitality of its people. Besides, it is as well that their graves be simple and unpretentious. A warrior falls at the side of the sword and needs no other tribute."

"Well, I wish they *had* robbed the country! They would have, now, beautiful mausoleums, with hundreds of mollahs reciting the Koran and chanting prayers at their graves." I spoke rather to myself than to my uncle.

My uncle looked at me sharply; I thought he was about to say something disagreeable, but he mastered his first impulse and said, "It would not have pleased our fathers to be accorded decorated mausoleums for their remains—nor would you wish it, if you knew the results of dishonesty. Look around you and see in what state the country finds itself to-day—an ugly ruin, with an ignorant, brutal monarch. Its governing class is made of a patched-up aristocracy and a lot of half-witted statesmen, most of whom know not their fathers, or, born of muleteers and donkey-herders, have passed their infancy in stables and kitchens. Our religion is mocked. Our laws are ridiculed! Look at the clergy!—corrupt, fanatic and disreputable, supported by looters and despoilers. Look at the multitude of court desperados doing violence upon men and women! It is an uncivilised land; its self-appointed leaders are all corrupt, all dishonest, all liars, all defilers of human sentiments and of humanity itself!"

My uncle threw away his pen, and sat up on his knees, looking straight at me:

"There, my boy, you have the real picture of your country and its people—hidden behind the false front of the over-painted, gaudy and unsightly panorama of Oriental life displayed before the eyes of the world and before our new generation of boys and girls!"

Here my uncle stopped and called Yellow to bring more tea.   I was astounded.

"Uncle," I said to him, after some reflection, "do you mean that there are no more great men in Persia?   Did not the men who made Persia great in the old days leave a trace of their blood in the new generations?"

"There are only a few patriots left, my boy, and even these, I fear, will soon be dead—or murdered, one by one."

"Murdered?" I interrupted in surprise.

"Yes," he answered curtly.

"But you, yourself, Uncle—do you mean that you are likely to be murdered?"

"Who knows?   I was once a marked man—that was before you were born—so was my brother—your father— and our grandfather before us."

"For what reason?"

"Listen my boy: The men of our family have always been known, above all things, as fighters.   For more than twenty hundred years the fighting spirit has been one of our family, and a desire to fight for righteousness and justice, one of its ambitions; whether under the title of Prince of the Believers, Emir, Khan, Beyk, or, since they are known to-day by titles which the Kajar Shahs force upon the old nobility, as Sultaneh, Dowleh, or Molk, the members of our family have all kept their hereditary title of Upholder of the Truth.

"In the old days they lived and reigned in the part of the world known by the name of Parthia—an ancient, independent kingdom.   Thousands of years ago, some branches of our family emigrated to the West, and there fought and conquered the Arabic tribes, most hardy and noble adversaries, worth conquering and subduing.   These conquerors formed the family of Saghaphi, which brought into the known world a part of the unknown Arabia.

"When Mohammad, the Prophet, and later, the Arab

Caliphs, began conquering the world, our family turned their attention once more to their old homeland and took part in battles to regain what they had willingly left, centuries before.

"Early in the Seventh Century the great fighter, Emir Abu-Obeid Saghaphi, with his warriors, swarmed against the mercenaries of the King Yazdeguerd, who inherited the great empire composed of the countries of Parthia, Medea, Mesopotamia, Egypt, a part of India and many more lands, but who proved unworthy of his trust and incapable of keeping his heritage together under one banner. The battle fought by Emir Abu-Obeid is known in history as the 'Battle of the Bridge,' and bears testimony to the fighting spirit of the Emir.

"Seeing that the fortune of war was against him, Emir Abu-Obeid ordered his army to retreat over a certain bridge, upon which he stood until the last of his men crossed to safety on the opposite side of the river. Notwithstanding this orderly and highly strategic retreat, which, in its details, proved later to be one of the most skillful movements toward subsequent victory ever recorded in the war between the Caliphs and King Yazdeguerd, the Emir considered the delay of his advance upon the enemy as a blight upon his reputation as a fighter and a prince-commander of his men. Therefore, he drew his sword and, single-handed, attacked the enemy who came riding on elephants.

"With one blow, he cut the trunk of the first elephant, and, with a second, he cut its rider in two. But he was trampled by the rush of hundreds of elephants and fell, sword in hand, on the field of honour.

"This cutting the trunk of the elephant became a symbol for his army, who took it as a heavenly sign that the arrogant nose of the King Yazdeguerd would, itself, in the next attack, be likewise cut in two. This would mean his complete defeat. Their prophecy came true in a subsequent battle.

"From that day, the two branches of the family—the Emir's and the one living in Parthia—came together again. Many of the kinsmen reigned in and governed the reconquered countries, either in their own right or on behalf of later kings and caliphs, who appreciated the ability of these men as leaders for governing with justice—creating and safeguarding a national union between the different races and religions composing the Persian Empire.

"Such was the situation when, at the beginning of the Nineteenth Century, my father and the other members of our family in Teheran were forced to renounce the hereditary spirit of their ancestors and exchange the sword for the pen, dedicating their lives to science and scholastic studies. The change was necessary as a result of the ascendancy of the Kajar Shahs to the old, famed throne of Persia.

"These members of an alien tribe succeeded in usurping the throne, not through personal valour, but purely as a result of the lack of national spirit in our people, who, ever since the end of the Safavi Shahs, had been losing the qualities to which the great Empire owed its grandeur and prestige. This Kajar Dynasty, from the nomadic and savage tribes of Turcoman, whose yearly invasion we formerly repelled from our borders, when once in power, started an underhand and systematic war against the old builders of the Empire. The Kajars desired to eliminate the old families, especially the fighters and patriots, in order to strengthen the basis upon which they, the aliens, meant to reign.

"To secure this end, a series of assassinations was plotted, and the victims were replaced in official positions by men from the lawless tribes of Turcoman or other breeds—the lowest imaginable. The history of Persia during this period is filled with stories of cruelty to its old aristocracy.

"The savage rage of these ignorant aliens not only pointed a murderous dagger at the heart of the old families, but tried to root out the traditions, customs, and even the language of the Persians, and put in its place the crippled, barbarous language of Turkey."

Here I took advantage of my uncle's halt—to order more tea—to express my sympathy and sorrow. He interrupted me, however.

"Not yet; I have not finished. The part of the narrative to which I wish you to give full attention is the following: The culmination of the Kajar plot against Persia and the Persians, and the climax in the history of our own family, was the blow dealt us by the present usurper—the Shah Nasser-ed-Din, called the Shadow of Allah! The blasphemy of it! The Shadow of Allah! A blot! A murderer—that is what he really is!"

I was so horrified I could not resist saying, "Oh, dear uncle, what a terrific word you are uttering!"

"I am glad the word pains you," he said, pointing his forefinger right in my face.

"Yellow! Bastard! Where are you?" he shouted toward the door.

Instantly, Yellow came into the room with more tea. He seemed really yellow—or, shall I say, white—in the face, and much agitated. When he had put the cups of tea before my uncle, the latter turned upon him and said, "Were you listening at the door?"

"Yes, Master, I have my ears and feet ever ready for your voice and command."

"Did you hear what I said about the Shah?"

"Yes, Master, I did," replied the boy, with no hesitation.

Turning from him to me, my uncle said, "There, my boy, you have the type of young blood—ignorant and uncultured, but straight as an arrow and sharp as a sword—truthful, as a Persian should be!" And, to Yellow, he said,

"I am pleased with you.   Go to your place and have your ears and feet ready for my voice and command."

Yellow bowed and went out.   I looked after him with some apprehension.   Although my uncle thought me still a child, I had learned by frequenting the palace and the harem many things that it was necessary to know regarding the Shah. . . .   A word—or, sometimes, only a look, not the right sort—would cause the speaker's lips to be torn asunder or his eyes to be gouged out by the Shah's executioner.

Uncle noticed my glance and interpreted it rightly, for he said to me, "Have no fear; this boy is not from that manufactured and bastard aristocracy of the Shah.   He is a simple and pure Persian.   Would that I had thousands of such around me!

"Where was I?" he said to himself.   Then, remembering, "Yes, I was telling you of the blow which was dealt to us by the assassin; by the assassin, I mean the Shah, and by the blow, I mean the assassination of one of the members of our own family, your own kinsman—by name, Mahmoud Khan the Clan-Tar.   He was, at that time, the head of the family, holding our clanship rightly in his hands; a man of great fame and authority, loved by our people.   He would have saved the country from the bastard had he been allowed to live some years longer.   But the luck of Persia was not to endure; its downfall had been written by the hand of destiny."

He continued his story, telling me of the manner of the assassination of Mahmoud Khan by the Shah's professional murderers, and of the Shah, himself, who shared personally in the committing of the crime.

"When the crime had been committed," said my uncle, "news was brought that all of us were in danger of being murdered.   In twenty-four hours, we sent away our women and children to safety, and we, ourselves, left Teheran to seek refuge in the mountainous regions of Mazenderan. Other members of our family had, for centuries, been established in the Province of Mazenderan, in the region called Nour and Kodjour, where they did not live as the Saghaphi Khans but were known, instead, by the new titles of Sultaneh, Dowleh, and other high-sounding words—the Shah's orders. They had been fearful of using their names and rightful family titles and now became more fearful of the Shah's savage anger, heightened by his crime of murdering their kinsman. So they prepared themselves for war.

"Zolfagar Khan, a man of extraordinary intelligence and character, was the Prince-Lord of the famous warriors of Kurd-o-Turk. Another Khan of our family was the head of a famous regiment, known by the name of Khajevand Warriors. The family of our mother, in Firuz-Kuh, also had fled to the mountains. In short, we were scattered all over the country—except in the vicinity of the capital.

"When, finally, the Shah learned that his crime had been a calamity to himself and the country, he retaliated by killing all those who had been in the plot with him and also all those who had advised him to murder the Clan-Tar, whom they accused of being pretender.

"Then, one by one, our family returned to Teheran; some of them, the Shah tried to appease with royal favours. But some never forgave him; one of these was our father—your grandfather—who, although back in the city, decided to dedicate his eldest sons—your father and myself—to study in the madresseh. These were well-known colleges of the old style devoted to ethical, philosophical, and divine study. Thus, we could become scholars—future authorities in the laws of Shariat, then modjtaheds, archbishops in Islamic law and the Mohammedan religion.

"This line of education," continued my uncle, "was necessary, notwithstanding the change in policy of the Shah toward our family. My father knew how worthless were the promises of this Kajar Shah and therefore, at once, placed your father and me in the madresseh built by Ghanbar Ali Khan, of the Saghaphi family. Within a year I had had enough of it. Your father, however, stayed on for nearly twenty years and was rewarded by becoming the greatest scholar of his time—a man sought by all the intelligent people of the world, and even by the ignorant and boorish Shah himself."

To the rest of my uncle's narrative I listened in silence. When he came to the end, Yellow's head appeared at the door, saying that her ladyship, the Khanom, had returned and, having been told that the little Khan was with his uncle, wished to see him.

My uncle looked at me and said, "If you are not wearied by my gossip, you may venture to hear more from your aunt. What do you say?"

"I am not at all tired," I said. "Besides, I must thank you for the trouble you have taken to enlighten me."

"Come, then, let us go to the Khanom."

He threw his aba over his shoulders and pushed his feet into a pair of slippers. We both arose, and he called out to Yellow to bring a light. The court was dark—not even the pool could be seen; it was one of the last days of the month and there was no moon.

Yellow came with a candelabrum; we crossed the court-yard and, at the far corner, entered a passage lighted by an oil lamp stuck half way into the wall. Its flame was not enough to light more than a few feet each way. Presently we arrived at a door, which my uncle opened, and we stepped into the anderun.

My aunt received us with great ceremony, making many short curtsies; I bowed as often. It took some time for us to do honour to each other, each at the same time urging the other to sit down first. We finally decided to sit down at the same time, I near her, and uncle near a low table covered with books.

More tea was brought in. I had already drunk three cups with my uncle, but I knew I must take the many others that were about to follow.

"Very, very welcome are you, my dear," said my aunt.

"Very, very honoured and pleased am I with my call upon your highness," I replied.

"How fares your noble health?" she enquired nicely.

"By the grace of your very kind attention, my health is in a perfect state."

"It is a long time—nay, ages—since I had the honour of your much appreciated company. Methinks you are too economical in bestowing such favours."

"Oh, Khanom," I remonstrated, "how can you conscientiously pretend such a thing? I think I may consider myself, rightfully, the one who has been deprived (though not by his own fault) of feasting his eyes on your charms. I deplore the time which I have lost away from your presence."

"True," she answered. "True. None of your fault and none of mine. The one to blame is your honoured Uncle Khan—the lord of my eyes and heart—who always is busy, and who makes everybody else busy with his thoughts and works."

"There, there!" interrupted my uncle who, until now, had sat quietly amused. "It is wonderful how women can place every fault on the shoulders of the weaker sex."

"No, my dear sir," replied my aunt, "you men are the stronger of the sexes, created thus by Khoda's grace and will. Far be it from us to deny it. We are very happy with things as they are."

"It seemed to me now, as it has seemed on many occasions before, that it is a pity one of our women is not sitting on the throne of Persia instead of the male member of the Kajar Dynasty," remarked my uncle. He did not need to explain to me, for I knew already that my aunt was a Kajar. But she was an extraordinary exception among the Kajar princesses, who were, as a rule, quite homely. Their complexions were of an Eastern hue, and they were invariably fat. Very seldom have I seen one of them as white as the Persian women of our blood. It is said that some slender women can be found in the nomadic regions of Persia, but if this be true, I must presume that the women of Turcoman origin lost their comeliness when transplanted from their wild living to the luxurious life of the reigning class of Persia.

It was growing late, and I suggested that I be allowed to take my leave.

"Oh no, my dear," said my aunt. "You shall honour us at our humble dinner—a very meagre meal, unworthy of such a guest as yourself. Besides, we dine at the usual democratic time, twelve-thirty—half an hour from now."

My uncle also urged me to remain, saying my cousins were out for the evening and my company would, therefore, be more appreciated. Thereupon, he called out, "Ohoy, Yeki biad!"—"Oh, come, one of you!"

Hassan, a fine old man of some sixty summers, with a long, white beard, entered and bowed to the Khanom. He wore the flowing, colourful robe of a well-trained servant, and a Persian hat of light-brown felt, such as is worn by provincial people and peasants.

"Tell someone to go to the house to say that the little Khan dines with his uncle," said my aunt. (My father's home was known simply as the house.)

The old man disappeared as quickly as he had come.

In Persia, it is a rule that no man has a right to dictate, or to order, a single thing in the sanctuary of an anderun. It was quite right for my uncle to call a servant—but to give him instruction, never! The entire management of the anderun is in the hands of the Khanom and the members of her department. The reverse arrangement governs the household of the husband and the biruni.

The lives of husband and wife are lived apart, so far as daily affairs and work are concerned. He passes his time with his friends or attends to his business, whatever its nature, either at his office or at his house, and she passes her time with her friends in her own surroundings. Her relations with her friends and kin are governed by herself; there is no trespassing over the border by her husband.

The only customary contact between husband and wife is in the evening, if there are no guests; otherwise, they may meet for the night. If the wife has guests of her own, or is entertaining a party, her husband is relegated to his own quarter. The reverse is true when the husband entertains.

To the Persian mind there is nothing so vulgar as the continual contact of husband and wife; the lives of Western husbands and wives, forced by the unreasonable claims of Western civilisation to confine themselves and their children within a few square feet of space, called an apartment, is not only amazing to a Persian, but seems unhealthy and immoral, as well. A civilisation which carries with it so ugly a necessity will never make headway in a country like Persia, I am sure.

The interval before the meal was spent in more talk about the social problems of the Persian women—my aunt leading the conversation. Finally, dinner was announced, and we proceeded to the next room, which served as dining-room in the evenings, and as a recreation room for the ladies in the daytime.

The dishes were arranged, in the usual way, on a long piece of Ispahan ghalamakar, spread on the floor. Although we were only three, the tablecloth, covered with dishes, was large and long enough to accommodate twelve persons. Two maids, who were adding the finishing touches, left the room as we entered. Another maidservant held a bowl and water-ewer for us to wash our hands. I did this, after my host and hostess, and sat between them.

My aunt served me with steamed rice and different stews; to my surprise, I discovered that my uncle did not appear to desire any of these for himself. He sat, looking toward the door, as though waiting for someone to come in. Presently Hassan returned with a platter containing a blue clay bowl and a thick, round loaf of bread, which he placed before my uncle. This, I knew, was the coarse peasant bread of barley, which is used only in country places. Then the man brought a long, clay pot, with two handles, black with soot and no larger than a marmalade jar. Thick clouds of steam rose from it and a delicious aroma of food filled the room. My uncle poured out first a sort of soup or gravy and then, into another bowl, the rest of the contents —two pieces of meat and a handful of Persian peas. Then he picked up the loaf of bread—hard and dry—and crumbled some of it with his fingers, throwing the crumbs, one by one, into the bowl, until half the loaf was gone. He sat waiting a minute or two before taking one of the spoons and beginning to eat.

My uncle smiled at me. "This is my only food," he said. "So is it the only food of your father when he is not obliged to eat at the Shah's table."

This was perfectly true, and now I understood why, whenever the great astrologer, manadj-djem-bashi, came to my father, they dined together—not with the rest of us. It was, as a matter of fact, the food of workmen and very poor people who could not afford rice and stew. It was called (from the name given the earthen-baked pot), disy.

When we finished our meal we washed our hands for the second time and went back to the first room, where tea was immediately served. A water-pipe, for my uncle, was brought to him by a maidservant who had decorated the stem with green leaves and perfumed the water inside the crystal bowl with rosewater.

After more tea and still more conversation, I took my leave, kissing my aunt. My uncle, with his hands on my shoulders, accompanied me to the door. As I said goodnight to him, he placed his lips close to my ear and whispered, "Whenever you need information and enlightenment, come to your uncle. He is always at your disposal."

I thanked him, then remembered something:

"Oh, by the way," I whispered, "I quite forgot to tell you about a strange man I saw at the graveyard the other evening." I told him, in a few words, about the way the man had frightened me, and also about his knowledge of my family and his message to Laleh.

"Oh, yes," said my uncle, "I believe I have seen this man. He is, besides being keeper of a sacred shrine, very learned."

"But what of his saying he is of the same flesh and blood as mine?"

"Oh, that is of no particular interest," said uncle. "He probably only meant that all the Persians are as one family."

"Of course I believe all you tell me, dear uncle, but your explanation is of the same nature as that I received from Laleh. That is to say, it does not satisfy me."

"You are most curious," said my uncle, patting me on the shoulder. Then, as though a desire had taken hold of him not to leave me in an uncertain condition of mind, he said, "Look here, dear boy; you know how people's imaginations run fast in this country—how they make mountains out of molehills. The story goes that, after the assassination of Clan-Tar, all his relatives, like ours, left the city. His youngest brother, then a small boy, was hunting somewhere near the Demavend Mountain at the time, and was warned by messenger of the danger of returning to Teheran. He, therefore, went to Mazenderan. It is said that, later on, the Governor of Mazenderan, a Kajar, to win favour, captured the boy and sent his head to the Shah.   And now," uncle turned around to see that no one was near, and whispered closer in my ear, "now, they pretend that this man whom you met at the grave is that boy."

"If that is true, then he is the Clan-Tar of the family," I whispered back.

"Certainly, he would be the only living member of the Clan-Tar's family, in direct line, but nobody knows the truth and this man has never pretended to any such relationship.   In fact, he never talks of himself to anyone, and no one knows anything definite about him, except that he has been the shrine-keeper for years."

II

I VISIT MY FATHER'S COLLEGE

My visits to my "unholy uncle" became a source of considerable information to me. I was most interested in what he had to say about my father's confinement in a madresseh while still a young boy because of the reign of terror that followed the accession of Nasser-ed-Din Shah.

My grandfather's idea in dedicating his children to study was to save them from the fate that had befallen Mahmoud Khan and to show the Shah that, so far as he and his family were concerned, they meant to keep out of government affairs altogether.

I remember well this religious institution or madresseh (one of the most beautiful buildings in Teheran), for I used often to visit it. It was a mile and a half from my home, and in the month of Ramazan—the month of fasting and prayer —all the students were invited to our home for thirty evenings, to join us in our meals; besides this, the student who then occupied my father's old room was donated a pension by my family. Its entrance, with high arch, its dome of blue and gold tiles of fascinating design, were a splendid example of the famous Persian architecture of the Safavi epoch. Two high minarets, at either side of the dome, stretching their graceful columns of extraordinarily lovely faïences, tore aside the thick foliage of stately tchenars and old elms to reach in the air to a place where the blue sky formed a background for their majestic beauty. Behind the entrance was a spacious court and a square basin with water running continually across its surface. Many mollahs

142

and faithful Moslems perched on its stone border to wash their faces and hands before prayers.

Around it were seventy or more small rooms made of red brick, each destined for one student. Here he lived the life of an interne. These rooms, not more than twelve feet square, were very simple in architecture and bare of decoration. Only a part of the wall, near the ground, was covered with white plaster. Besides a few niches for books and other belongings, each room was provided with a closet, which could be shut with a door and locked. The door was of old wood, decorated and painted. Often, verses of the Koran, or lines of poetry from Hafiz or Sadi, were carved in the wood. The floors were covered with crushed bamboo stems, woven by hand, which provided a very cool matting to sit on in summer. The student brought his own bed and, if he liked, a carpet as well. It was a rule that each student swept his room and kept it clean. In fact, life in a madresseh was exactly the same as in a monastery.

In the evenings, the students conned their lessons under the dim lights of earthen lamps with narrow wicks, filled with crude castor oil.

The lamp used by my father for more than fifteen years was afterwards kept at our house as a memento of his student life. I remember that one evening when I complained that the seventy branches of candelabrum, hanging from the ceiling, together with sconces filled with candles, diffused insufficient light for my study, my father said, "Know, my dear sir, that I have studied for more than twenty years with only one thin wick for light!" Even in our own home he never used any light but a candle in the evenings. He read almost incessantly until his last days, and never knew the need of eye-glasses. This special oil lamp of his which had been altered to hold a candle, was made of a piece of crystal with cut facets like a diamond. It was twelve inches long, bored to fit a chiseled top of copper and encrusted with a gold design: a rare piece of Ispahan work of the twelfth century.

The madresseh, although built and consecrated to charity by one of our family, gave no privileges to my father as a student; he lived and studied with no more favour than anyone else. But at the age of sixteen, his works as a scholar began to attract attention. His regular course of study was completed when he was thirty, but even after he had finished, I am told that he sometimes went back to the madresseh and remained for days, completely lost to the world.

Throughout all these years, the watchful eye of the Shah was steadily focused upon him; all his movements, and those of his brothers and father, were continuously shadowed.

My grandfather took care that while my father was pursuing his studies he should also cultivate the art of the Persian pahlevans, or heroes, who were famous for their physical strength in the days of Persia's splendour. In this way my father became a trained athlete, and retained his figure and good health, throughout his life, in perfect condition.

When he became famous as the greatest physician of his time (besides being a philosopher and scholar), the Shah induced him to attach himself to his court. Father, at first, refused by saying he had no desire to live upon the bounty of the sovereign. On the contrary, he begged to be allowed to go either to Najaf or to Kerbela, both famous schools for higher study, but the Shah said he could not afford to lose his knowledge, and induced, or, rather, forced, him to become attached to his sister, Princess Ezzat-ed-Dowleh, the Queen of Persia's women, the Glory of her Country, as her title had it. To this my father unwillingly conceded, but never accepted any monetary favors from the Shah, and refused all his decorations. The Princess attempted to make him accept a certain amount of money, but knowing it would come from the Shah who robbed his country, he refused at first. However, finally, to please her, he consented that a sum of money, ridiculously small, should be sent to him eveny month in a sack. The sack of money, which a eunuch brought, was received by a servant and, after the eunuch was gone, its contents were divided among the poor whom my father received as patients. They soon learned that the first day of the month was, by far, the best time for them to consult the great hakim!

I must say a few words about the noble Princess Ezzat-ed-Dowleh, whose life had been most unhappy. Her first husband, who married her for love, was one of the outstanding figures in the modern history of Persia; but unfortunately for Persia, a man of his character was not desired by the Shah. He met with the same fate as Mahmoud Khan, the Clan-Tar—he was assassinated by the Shah. I believe he was at the time Governor General of the vast province of Aragh and lived in Kashan, the capital of that province. The reason was that when the Shah learned that his brother-in-law's wonderful administration was becoming known throughout the Empire, he became afraid he might prove a rival, and therefore began plotting against his life. He had to wait for an occasion when his official murderers could attack him when the Princess was not present. This was not easy—the Princess feared for her husband's life, and seldom allowed him to go away from her. But the assassins hid themselves and waited. Finally one day when the great Emir went to the bathhouse, which was at some distance from the palace, some of the attendants who had already been bought over by the Shah's emissaries, sent word that Emir was alone. A masked man came to him in the bath, and handed him a cup of coffee from the Shah. This was poisoned, and both knew it. The Emir understood that he had been betrayed, and that there was no escape. He read a paper which the man handed him in which the Shah decreed his death, and asked permission to write a letter to the Princess, his wife. This was denied. The Emir decided to die like a gentleman. He threw away the cup and ordered his barber to open the main vein of his wrist. This done, he was left to bleed to death. With his blood he scrawled a message on the wall of the bathhouse for his wife. Since he was physically robust and very strong, the loss of the blood did not finish him at once and the messenger grew impatient. He reëntered the bath, took hold of the half-unconscious man, covered his face with one of the cushions used in the bath, and so smothered him.

The Princess was said to have felt agitated at that very moment. She believed she actually heard the voice of her husband calling to her. She cried out to her attendants to find him. When told that he was in the bathhouse, she became more disturbed, and asked for my father, to whom she confided her fear. Father ran out of the palace, mounted a horse and galloped to the bathhouse. It was too late! In the passage leading to the bath a masked man pushed him aside and escaped on horseback with his confederate. The Emir was dead.

The Princess arrived at almost the same time. The message on the wall read: "Away from my beloved wife, I die as a man, but God help Persia!'

When I knew the Princess, she had been married again to a certain Mirza Yahya, chosen by the Shah. To render him worthy of his wife, the Shah had made him a noble, giving him the title of Khan, with the additional title of Moshir-ed-Dowleh. He also made him Minister of Foreign Affairs, and this title, after his death, continued to be used by his successors. A palace and park in Shemran were placed at his disposal, where he conducted his office during the summer.

He was a simple soul; a fine old man, courteous, polite, harmless, inefficient, and useless. I never knew who his father and mother were, or what was his origin. He made no claim to any privileges and the Shah had no occasion to become suspicious of him. He knew so well his humble place that he never showed any tinge of superiority. He even had to bow to his offspring, who was a nephew of the Shah, while he himself was nobody in particular.

I used to enjoy visiting them because of a lovely girl, Tuberose, with whom I used to play, who was one of the attendants of the Princess.

But, to return to my father. His greatest pleasure at all times was reading or writing books. His library was known as the best in the country, because each book had been revised and corrected by him with marginal notes. All his books, some eight thousand volumes, were manuscripts with lacquered covers, containing painted miniatures by masters. Later he added some printed books to his collection.

Whenever there was a book in Persian or in Arabic, printed in India, Egypt or Faranguestan, a copy was sent to him, which after it had been read and corrected by him, was considered the best extant.

Later in life, his desire was to go to Engelestan (as he called Great Britain), to live in the great library of the British Museum in London, which he had never seen, but of which he had heard a great deal. It is said that, when the Shah was growing old, he asked my father to accept a favour—anything he liked, whereupon Father requested the Shah to command the Queen of England to order a room built in the Library of London, and to have this room set aside for his use, that he might spend the rest of his life there. The Shah raised many objections and the clergy, also, pronounced it unwise for a man with such high knowledge to soil his reputation by living in an alien country where people ate pigs. Failing in his own efforts, the Shah appealed to the Princess to dissuade him, and my father found it necessary to forego this cherished desire of his life. It was strange that he liked England best of all the countries in Faranguestan—never having seen any of them; perhaps the great library in the British Museum had something to do with it.

Besides my father's other achievements, he was also a master of calligraphy; his writing of Shekaste style was so perfect that, many years after his death, my brothers searched the town for prescriptions which he had written for his patients; these prescriptions were mostly written on any piece of paper which came to his hand (often on ordinary blue paper used for wrapping sugar cones, not more than two inches in length and one inch in width). It was said of his writing that each word looked as though it had been engraved. His Nastaligh (another style of calligraphy) resembled that of Mir, the famous Persian calligraphist.

A miniature on the last page of the book of Alexander the Great—seven huge volumes, which Father started to copy when thirteen years of age, and which required four years to complete—shows him sitting with his right knee raised to form a writing desk. Under it he has written:

I, the poor, the humble, the despondent Abdol Baghi, son of Hadj Esmail of Teheran—may the blessing of God be upon his soul, and his sins forgiven—have penned these volumes.

He made his pilgrimage to Mecca shortly after his study was finished, and the Shah sent with him two desperadoes, as body-guards, and also, his confidant, Hadja Rabi, the famous eunuch.

Rabi, as before mentioned, was a descendant of a Persian Khan, who had been murdered by the Shah. When a baby, he had been made a eunuch, to cut short the continuation of his family. He was brought to court and dedicated to the harem, that he might be kept under the vigilant imperial eye. The case of Hadja Rabi was not unusual; it was a misfortune which could happen to the children of any

Khan, who had risked the anger of that despot. The history of Nasser-ed-Din Shah and the Kajar Shahs before him is filled with such atrocities.

My father's madresseh, like all the colleges in Persia, had its own mosque, with a wide portal of glazed tile looking toward the east. The interior decorations were very simple, which gave a fitting atmosphere to the House of God, where the brotherhood of students gathered three times a day for prayer and meditation.

But, in the niche-like sanctuary where the head priest, or leader of prayer, officiates in the rituals of Namez, the famous Persian craftsmen had wrought a wonder. The entire structure of the niche, some seven feet wide and more than twenty feet high, was of marble and fine glazed tiles. The design was that of a Sixteenth Century Ispahan carpet; its repeated pattern of palmettoes and rosettes boldly interwoven with a fine border of arabesque inscriptions, all set in gorgeous blue background, made it clear that the mosque belonged to the glorious epoch of the Shahs of the Safavi Dynasty, when Persia was its own master in the art of building.

The college, financially, was very rich; it had ample revenue to maintain more than seventy students. Large properties had been dedicated by the Clan-Tar's families for this purpose. Its standing was extremely high when my father became one of its members, but my Laleh said it had greatly changed since that time: The hope of the Persian philanthropists, who had left their fortunes to the education of their fellow countrymen, was shattered by the ascendancy of the Kajar Shah to the throne. As a result, this madresseh, like all the other religious institutions in Persia, was tumbling. The reign of open corruption and encouraged lawlessness was supreme in all national institutions, whether religious or governmental.

III

THE IMPERIAL PRISON

THE PLIGHT of the madresseh made Laleh indignant, but the place of all others that called forth his anger was the Shah's prison in the Tchar-Sou, where the royal torturers and imperial executioners stayed. Every child in Teheran knew this prison; mothers made a habit of pointing to it as a place of horror, and warning their children of the abominations that befell the unfortunate men confined behind its small black door.

This dark, dingy, gloomy hole, I passed every time I went to the bazaars. It was under a balcony where the Darougheh —head of the guardians of the city—sat during the night and received the thieves and outlaws caught by his emissaries, who were scattered through the town. A court of justice, or judges, to inquire into their crimes did not exist. The Darougheh was the only judge, and his open balcony the only court.

The prison had no opening, even for light and air, except the heavy, wooden door, strapped with iron bars, which closed at sunset and opened again in the late morning, after the bazaars began to be crowded. The place was infested with vermin and rats and a thousand other plagues. The ordinary man had no idea of these conditions, nor could he imagine the physical and mental tortures the poor creatures (mostly innocent) endured during the night, while the rest of the town slept quietly in their beds, trusting in the justice and might of the Shah. These prisoners were rarely taken out of their dungeons; some died miserably, others became mad,

a few tried to commit suicide, and many wished to be beheaded.

The passers-by could see only a man or two, near the
opening, pleading with scourged hands for a few coppers.
The coppers were used, it was said, to gain leniency from
the jailer, although they were given, supposedly, to buy
bread. The filth in which the prisoners were kept made
them unrecognisable. Their heads, with long, dirty hair
sticking to their faces, were horrible.

My imagination was aroused to such a degree that I decided to investigate the prison myself. This I could do
without difficulty, since a far cousin of mine, a descendant
of the Clan-Tar, was at this time the Darougheh of Teheran,
and therefore responsible for the safety of the town during
the night. In the daytime he rested, and at night he went
to the Tchar-Sou to sit upon the balcony.

The Tchar-Sou (Tchar, meaning four, and Sou, an ab-
breviation of Sough, meaning bazaar) was the meeting place
of the four greatest bazaars in Teheran. In ancient times,
the tchar-sous were places where the heroes sat and watched
after their fellow countrymen during the night. The stories
of their achievements and exploits, and of their mighty
battles against the alien or native villains, are recorded in
Persian stories and in the book of the Kings, or "Shah Na-
meh."

The space separated by walls was taken by shops, four
in number. One was a drug shop, famous for a legend about
the renowned hero, Rostam, who, it is said, wandered into
Teheran while on a mission for the King. He had spent
all his money and, during the evening, when near the Tchar-
Sou, he felt his hunger. Approaching the shop of the druggist, he asked if the man would lend him some money, saying he would pay it back in the morning, when the town
and its governor discovered that Rostam, the hero of Persia,

the guardian of the throne and defender of the empire, was in the city.

The druggist, an old man and skeptical, looked at the figure of the hero who towered above him, wearing a venerable long beard parted in the middle, and a helmet studded with precious stones, surmounted by the skull of the famous white monster which he had killed in Mazenderan, his chain of mail, immune to any weapon, and his gorgeous armour, his renowned sword, as long as himself, hanging at his side, a bejewelled dagger in his belt, and, above all, his famous cudgel of tempered steel, with which he had battered the heads of the most haughty monarchs in the world. . . .

The druggist looked at all these things and said, "Well, my dear man, you may be the famous Rostam, for all I know—but, I am the drug store man, for all you know! I am not a king who needs heroes to defend him and his empire: I sell drugs and I have no money to give away."

One can easily imagine the consternation of Rostam, the greatest hero of Persia when he heard these words.

"Then will you lend me a few coppers to buy some food?"

"I am not a money-lender," answered the old man, "but you may borrow money, against some security, if you choose to be a borrower. I will take anything."

The hero, seeing nothing else to do, left his cudgel with the man as security and took the money in exchange. But he never came back for his pledge!

Finally, the druggist gave him up as a bad bargain, and, ever after, the cudgel could be seen above his shop, driven half-way into the wall, to show that the shopkeepers in Teheran observed the principle which says: "Do not lend money, even against security, to the greatest of heroes."

On the night we planned to visit the Tchar-Sou, Laleh, who did not quite approve the expedition, four stable boys armed with swords, and I started out. No one knew our mission. Laleh had asked the password for the night from the opium-smoking policeman; so we went without fear of being stopped by the military guards. The few drunken ruffians we met were disposed of, by either threats or kicks. Not a single light showed in the whole town.

I had secretly decided that if I found the jailer torturing those poor prisoners, I should murder him, myself, with a dagger that I had attached to my belt, hidden under my tunic.

When we arrived at our destination, the place was dark, except for a light in a sentry-room. We talked in loud voices to draw the attention of any heroes who might be in the room. Nobody came out! The door of the prison was closed, and there was no sound. Laleh coughed, very loudly, but with no result. I told one of the stable boys to shout, and he roared like a lion. Not an echo answered. Nobody was on the balcony above. The door of the room was ajar, and, in one corner stood a small lamp, smoking like a chimney; a man lay stretched on the floor, snoring.

"One of the heroes!" said my Laleh, sarcastically.

"Hey, animal! Aren't you going to get up?" one of the stable boys shouted.

No answer came, yet the man's loud snoring told us he was not dead.

"Come! Come! O you ass, get up," said the other stable boy. "Don't you see our Khan before you? Get up!"

Laleh looked at the man, and said, "No use to disturb him; he has been smoking opium."

"Now! Let us break open the door of the prison and set those poor souls inside free," I called out to the boys.

"We are ready to do what you desire," said their spokesman, Yadollah, another strong boy from Mazenderan.

"Sir, we had better go home," remonstrated my Laleh. "You see for yourself: We hear no cries nor lamentations from the prisoners. Besides, breaking the door would be of no help to them; they are chained to their places, and some of them are unable to walk. It would not help the prisoners, and it would place your cousin in a bad position before the governor. Come, sir, you can help these people in quite another way."

"In what way?" I asked him eagerly.

"Trust your Laleh to show you the way; have faith in Khoda who will save the people in his time and hour. Shall we go home?"

The boys were disappointed and showed it by kicking the man!

"You must not do that," Laleh remonstrated. "He is not responsible for the misery of the people."

"But where is Darougheh?" I asked.

"You cannot blame him for not staying the whole night in this dreary place!" said Laleh.

"And where are the heroes of whom I read in books?"

"Between the pages of the books," Laleh answered.

"Or half dead with opium, in the corners of the bazaars," said Yadollah.

I looked at the closed, black door.

"But, it seems to me, Laleh, that the prisoners behind this door must be suffering."

"You may be sure, sir, that many of them die for lack of air—but, be sure, too, that those who die are the lucky ones!" said Yadollah.

Laleh glanced significantly at Yadollah, and urged me again to come away, saying, "Come, my soul, let me take you away. I have promised to show you how to help these poor people—you will trust your Laleh."

Reluctantly I turned away and we started back in the same direction we had come. We had not gone far when in the darkness of the long bazaar I saw a light approaching. Who could it be? Perhaps a thief, a night marauder, or, possibly, a warrior coming to visit the tall Darougheh of the Tchar-Sou. At any rate, it might bring some change in the evening, which had, so far, been disappointing.

After about ten minutes' walk we made out three men coming toward us. The first had a small oilskin lantern in his hand; the second was waving a walking stick in the air, the third man was so small I thought he was a child. At some distance, we halted, and, having no light, we must have looked like shadows.

"Who are you?" called a harsh and growling voice from the man whom I had thought a child.

"And, please, who are you, to ask us who we are?" shouted back Yadollah.

"What!" cried the little man, jumping as though he had been stung, and rushing, like a mad dog, toward us, club in hand.

"Hey! Hey! Quiet! Quiet! Do not make such a fuss and commotion! Bring them here," commanded the man whose face was hidden behind the light.

I recognized the voice and cried, "Why! It is my cousin, Darougheh!"

"Is it you, my soul?" he replied, while the disagreeable little man dropped his club and gaped at us, like an undersized chimpanzee.

I ran to my cousin. "We have been to the Tchar-Sou to see you, but we found no one except a man asleep on the floor."

"It is as well that he sleeps," said my cousin. "But, what was it you wanted to see me for, my soul?"

"Oh, nothing in particular," answered Laleh. "The little Master has been sleepless so we decided to let him see the Tchar-Sou in the night."

"Not a good remedy for sleeplessness, and the Tchar-Sou is not the proper place to pay me a visit," he said, with a little laugh, and then, "Go your way, you boys; I shall be there, after a while."

They left immediately, carrying the lantern with them, and we were again in the gloomy darkness of the bazaar.

Djafar Khan took my hand in his and said, "I shall walk back a short distance with you, before going to the Tchar-Sou."

In his position as a Darougheh, and a Khan, he made it understood to the rest of my companions that they should keep a distance behind us. To my Laleh, he said, "Laleh Agha, you come with us."

When far enough to not be heard by our boys, he said, "Laleh Agha, you should not have brought your master to the Tchar-Sou in the night, and with no light."

I replied for Laleh. "I wanted to go there, to see if it is true that the prisoners were tortured during the night!"

"Did you find that they were?"

"No, but they are alive in a grave behind that closed door," I replied.

"You mean dead," he said calmly.

I was about to say something unpleasant when Laleh interrupted me. "Your Khan cousin did not mean actually dead."

"To God!" cried the Darougheh, "I wish they were!"

"Then are you, also, a cruel man?" I asked, in surprise.

"Ah, my little soul," he answered patiently, "I would that your Laleh should enlighten you so as to spare you missing sleep and wasting your time. Not my time, for I swear I am very glad to see you, to see anyone in a dreary place like this." He emphasised each word with an increasing grip of my hand, nearly crushing my fingers.

"I do my duty, sir, but my little master is growing. He is, indeed, beyond me," said Laleh.

My cousin said, "I will tell you this: People were tortured centuries ago, and are tortured to-day, but for a year, there has been no torturing in the Tchar-Sou prison. No Darougheh has ever been a torturer of his own children.

The people of this metropolis are the rightful children of a Darougheh—even those miserable ones in prisons. Remember, too, that for ages the post of Darougheh has been entrusted to our family; not that we care for any position under the Shah Nasser-ed-Din, but because the call of the unfortunate people of this town is stronger to us than our personal feelings."

"But, was it not in your time that a poor man was tortured nearly to death in prison, and then handed over to the executioner to be beheaded? Only, God was with him and a mashdi, or knight, saved him from the dagger," I said.

"Unfortunately, it was," he confessed.

"Then, what difference did it make to the man that you were Darougheh?"

"A great difference, my own soul," he answered kindly. "If your cousin had not been Darougheh, that man would have been dead, and those helping him would have been in prison in his stead. That man is living to-day, in safety, and those who staged the street fight to save him are free, only because their identities are not known to the governor and his farrashes."

I understood, now, and felt very proud of my cousin.

"I should like you to know," he continued, "that the service that runs under my command is the most powerful in the city. Not one drop of water is drunk without my knowledge; every single mashdi and member of the underworld is known to me; the man who escaped the executioner two years ago—I can put my hands on him at any time I choose."

"And those who saved him?"

"Akbar and his men!" he answered me promptly, and shortly after bade us farewell.

IV

A GLIMPSE OF THE SHAH AND A VISIT TO THE SUMMER PALACE

My summers, from early childhood, were spent in Shemran, a country place some six miles from Teheran, composed of two villages, one, called high Rostam-abad, where the Shah's sister lived, and the second, called Low Rostam-abad, where other members of her suite and one of her sons lived. Shemran was close by another summer resort, called Golohak, the Deauville of Teheran, where the foreign legations had their summer residences. I lived in a charming little house, with a small but beautiful garden, near the palace of the Princess.

Here my father stayed all summer, to be near her and to avoid the noise and bustle of Teheran, in order to read and write in peace. At this time I was the only member of his family privileged to live with him in his summer seclusion. His object was to have me under his exclusive tutorship. It was very pleasant for me; no servants, no outside teachers, no mollahs, none of the score of bashis whose duty it was to further my education. Laleh was with us (the astrologer had taught him how to make the broth Father liked), and I had my donkey. The rest of the family had their own country places in the same vicinity, where they lived and entertained their guests during the summer months. Now and then, one of them would come to visit my father, but none of my brothers was anxious to remain with us more than a day or two, because we were living very simply.

One of the greatest excitements of the village was the

yearly visit of the Shah, which as I grew older, was of little interest to me, since I knew that I should some day meet him personally. But when I was a small boy and saw him for the first time, the pomp and magnificence of his procession filled me with awe. The circumstances follow:

One day in the month of June, news ran through the country that His Imperial Majesty the Shah, was going, according to his usual custom, to pay a visit to his sister, the Princess Ezzat-ed-Dowleh. The inhabitants of the village began their preparations to receive him, and on the day of his arrival the entire population, in great excitement, gathered in the public square before the little mosque. The village belles were in their best raiment; the scene was gay and colourful, and the girls themselves charming. At that time, the peasant women still wore long skirts, reaching to the ground and covered themselves with pieces of printed chintz; they wore no veils.

By four o'clock in the afternoon all the thoroughfares were crowded, the women standing in front with the men behind them. Laleh chose a place near a large tree, opposite the Princess's palace, and set me astride his shoulders. The streets, always dusty, were sprinkled with water for the occasion. Water had also been splashed against the mud walls, to make them look cool and fresh. The butcher had hung up a few joints of mutton, decorated with field flowers, and himself appeared in his Friday best suit—a short, blue tunic, a fresh white shirt, black trousers, sockless feet in a pair of guiveh, with a round, grey felt hat, which covered his bobbed hair and shaved neck.

The tea room proprietor covered the space in front of his shop with rugs, placed vases of flowers near each bench and heralded an invitation to all his fellow villagers to free tea and sherbets, in honour of the Shah, from the minute he set foot in the village until his departure.

In front of the palace stood a regiment of eunuchs (black

and white), equerries, attendants, guardians, house boys, stable chiefs accompanied by their many employees, the chief cook with his bodyguard of scores of scullery boys, and, behind, the nazer, supreme head of the kitchen and taster of all foods. There were a few mollahs, the chanter of Azan, the head gardener and the innumerable rest of the palace retinue.

I looked carefully around, for I knew my father would call upon us to give an account of the ceremony later in the evening. He, during all this time, would be lying upon his wooden platform, called a throne, in his garden, before a cool pool, reading and frightening away swarms of flies with his palm leaf fan.

Presently a horseman, galloping at full speed, dashed in, jumped from his horse, and ran toward the palace, shouting that his imperial majesty's cavalcade was near! A chorus of shrieks from the eunuchs rent the air, and a commotion began. The girls pushed one another excitedly, and I tried to sit higher on Laleh's shoulders.

Ten minutes passed, then a dozen warrior guardians galloped up, dismounted, threw their reins over the saddles, frightened the horses away with their hands, and took their places among the line of courtiers. Behind them came a dozen eunuchs riding Arab chargers with beautifully coloured saddles and gold and silver harness. They, too, dismounted, and their horses were taken away by the Princess's stable boys.

Following the eunuchs came a single horseman, a white eunuch riding a fine, white Arabian horse, which danced in the air and reared; its tail was painted red. This gentle half-man and half-woman was shrieking at the top of his voice:

"Ohoy, Pas-berid, Pas-berid!" "Go away, go away!" to the same imaginary crowd! A loud murmur, such as of mighty waves upon the beach, filled the air.

HIS IMPERIAL MAJESTY!

A pair of white horses, covered with glorious gold embroidery, wearing bejewelled harnesses of massive gold, with high aigrettes of red plumage adorned with precious stones, advanced very slowly; then another pair, and a third. The coachmen were gorgeous in their purple clothes with gold straps all over their shoulders and waists.

In a gold coach, lined with purple velvet, the Shadow of Allah, The Emperor of all the Emperors, reclined on a soft cushion. Four runners, two on each side of the coach, walked on foot—shaters, they were called. They wore purple coats, embroidered with gold, white breeches, and red silk socks and guiveh; the most marvellous article of their attire were the purple crowns on their heads, crowns such as were worn in old times by kings.

A silence fell on the waiting crowd. The imperial coach stopped at the gate—so did the cavalcade of hundreds of men who brought up the rear of the procession. The door of the coach was opened by a court minister, and the Shah was helped by two high officials to alight. His majesty was dressed in a coat of grey and orange brocade; under this was a doublet made of a purple shawl, and a leather belt studded with huge diamonds. His trousers were black and his military boots were brightly varnished. His Persian lamb hat, tilted to one side, was adorned by a single diamond as large as an egg! In his hand he carried a walking stick of rare wood, with a single emerald at the top. He was impressive and majestic: black hair, bobbed; black, straight eyebrows and striking eyes; long nose and a dashing, dagger-like moustache. What interested me most was the farangui collar, attached to his white shirt by a narrow, black tie knotted like an artist's bow. And it was strange, too, that he was wearing, at this summer season, a coat lined with sable! He held his head high, as though the whole world belonged to him. And as a matter of fact, he seriously believed that such was the case, as did most of his subjects. His eyes seemed always sleepy, except when he opened them to look at some one who interested him; then he would stare, with his head cocked appraisingly on one side, like a beast of prey.

The Shah's own summer palace, which I visited shortly after this under very curious circumstances, was a most beautiful place. With high walls and majestic gates of gold and yellow tiles, it looked like one of the ancient palaces of Persia.

The most gorgeous of its buildings was in front of the main entrance. It was built around a court in the centre of which was the famous pool of marble that was the pride of Nasser-ed-Din Shah. It was said that the entire pool was made of a single piece of marble. Although many times I paddled in its water, I cannot verify the truth of this saying. The most splendid detail of the palace itself was its floor, which was made entirely of crystal blocks! Each was the usual size of Persian tile, and four inches thick. In the centre of each a bouquet of flowers was chiseled, no two of the designs alike.

His majesty sometimes would lie in front of the pool, while a hundred beautiful girls of his harem, scantily clad, danced on the second balcony, to give him an illusion of the Prophet's Paradise, with its myriad houris. When one of these houris especially attracted the attention of his majesty, he would make a sign and the beautiful butterfly would throw herself upon a marble chute, gliding down just in front of him—and sometimes on him! This little detail was kept secret. The eyes which beheld this imperial recreation would have been torn out of their sockets by the sharp point of the executioner's dagger.

All this part of the palace was to be seen by the public when the Shah was in town. The section which was never seen by the public was the part reserved for the harem, situated at the back of the first palace. It was completely secluded from intrusion by any man, hidden behind a wall, surrounded by a desert. Beyond the desert were wild hills and beyond them high mountains. This was the one place that I wanted to explore. I had no excuse for going there, but I was always thinking of it. Finally a day came when I was not only allowed to go near it, but actually was begged to go there with my father! The following is the story of the extraordinary circumstances which led to my visit:

Father, as I have said before, was free from the lust and greed which brought so many of his contemporaries to the feet of the Shah. One of his sayings which I have never forgotten was: "Be just and never fear God. Be unjust and fear man." He tried to teach me not to be afraid of anybody, especially the Shah. Although the accepted rule for the behaviour of a gentleman was that of equality with those beneath him, and humility toward the humble and poor, with regard to the Shah and the aristocracy, my father reminded his children now and again of these words: "Do not bend your head before a King, even if he be a just King!" He used to practice what he preached, and he gave me more than once a vivid example of his actions according to this principle.

One afternoon in the country, when he was lying on his wooden throne reading, there arose a great commotion in the passage leading from the street to the house. Laleh came in hurriedly saying that two messengers had arrived on horseback from His Majesty the Shah. At the same moment Hadja Rabi, and a Nubian called Safran Khan, the favourite eunuch of the Shah, were ushered in with a great to-do. Both started talking at the same time, and one of them ran to fetch my father's clothes.

"What is all this bustle?" inquired my father.

"Agha Djounam"—master of our souls—"please get up, quick, quick! His majesty our beloved lord is feeling ill and has ordered us to accompany you to the palace at once. We have nearly killed our horses and ourselves. We have no breath left. Please get up quick, Djounam, quick!"

My father was lying on his side, with his elbow on a cushion, and his book before him.

"Come, come, sirs, do not be so excited," he said, very gently. "Is it again the same illness that his majesty is wont to suffer when he indulges in eating unripe fruits? Or too many raw cucumbers?"

The eyes of the eunuchs bulged. They were doubtful if they had heard aright! Why, the Shadow of God, the Eyes of the Universe, the Lord of the Seas and Continents, was suffering, and Hadj-Agha was calmly lying down, reading a book!

"Djounam, Ghorban, Azizam"—"may we be sacrificed, our soul!" they cried again, "the Shah has commanded your presence!"

"What of it? Do you not see I am reading one of the most cherished books of my life?—the famous *Tchehar Maghaleh*, translated from Arabic to Persian by one of the great Orientalists, Professor Brown of Cambridge, Engelestan, and you came here to disturb me because the Shah of Shahs feels ill in his stomach?"

They both brought their hands to their throats as if they were choking.

"O, God Almighty, what has happened to our dear Hadj-Agha, and, O God, what will happen to us for being late! Oh, Oh, Oh!" Safran Khan ran out of the room crying that he was going to the Princess to see if she could help persuade Hadj-Agha to arise. "I am sure it is the end of the world. Oh, we shall all be murdered, all beheaded. Oh, Oh!"

Hadja Rabi, more calm, was a spiritual brother of my father by a sacred decree from one of the greatest of the seyyed modjtahed (the religious heads of Islam), and a

fellow brother in Hadj. That is to say he had made the
pilgrimage to Mecca in the company of my father. In those
days when two companions were to start on a pilgrimage
they used to bind themselves before a high clergyman as
brothers, one to the other, until death. Besides, he loved
my father and believed in him as his "spiritual guide and
light."

He went to my father and sat next to him, then he took
his hand, and kissed it. Then very gently, as if speaking
to a child, he said: "What is it, Master?"

"Oh, nothing," answered my father. He put the book
aside.

"Come, Djounam, there is no such word as 'Nothing' in
our vocabulary. Say something to your brother."

"I am tired of the Shah and his Shah-Basy"—meaning
a Shah who is a counterfeit. "A man of vulgar nature and
vulgar descent, with none of the morals created by God or
developed by civilisation. I am sick of him!"

"Patience, brother, he is only one of the incidents in
our national life, and oh, such a puny incident, so petty,
so insignificant!"

"And yet it is sucking the sap of our national tree,"
answered my father.

"True, very true," murmured Rabi, and then added with
emphasis, "You are right, brother. Pray to God that the
unseen hand shall redeem the country!"

At this point my Laleh, who was standing all the time
in attendance, coughed and said: "Ghorban, I hear people
arriving."

"Let them come," replied my father. Rabi was looking
at my father's face. He seemed not to have heard the remark of Laleh nor the answer of my father.

In rushed the little Princess, Afsar-es-Sultaneh, the daughter of the Shah's sister. She went directly to Father and
begged him not to slight the command of his majesty.

But nothing would change my father's mind. He refused to move. "I am ill myself, at heart. Go and send another hakim to his majesty. I am not in the mood to attend a patient."

What astonished the little Princess was that the emissary of the Shah, the eunuch Hadja Rabi, who had all to lose if in disgrace, said nothing to induce father to follow him.

"Why do you not say something?" said the little Princess to him.

"My dear soul, I am unable to move a mountain of will, such as God has bestowed on my respected master." He pointed to Father. "I am ready to die, if that be the whim of his majesty, but I will not intrude myself upon Hadj-Agha's thoughts. There is nothing I can do, except take Hakim Hadj Mirza Ali, who is in Saheb-Gharanyeh, to his majesty instead." Thereupon he jumped to his feet and went out of the house, and I heard the galloping of his horse toward the north.

This Hakim, or Doctor Hadj Mirza Ali, was the well known wealthy man who went to the Faranguestan once, to learn the methods of Farangui doctors. He brought back a million francs worth of books and modern articles manufactured in France, to present as gifts to the Shah and his courtiers. He later was poisoned, and died a madman. This was the man whom some of our Persians believed was "le grand Persan" mentioned in a French novel called *Le Fantôme de l'Opera*.

After the departure of Hadja Rabi, the Princess and the eunuch also left. I could see that both were worried.

I was worried too. I told Laleh of my fear. He smiled and shook his head. "The days when the Shah could murder men such as the Clan-Tar are past. He is afraid of his own shadow! He has always to come back to my master!"

Nothing happened, but as days went on I had an idea that Father was still unwilling to obey the orders of the

Shah, and that Hadja Rabi was trying to induce him to go
to the palace to put an end to the disagreeable situation. This
he always succeeded in doing after such incidents, which were
more or less frequent. Indeed, he came back one day with
a message which could not fail to appeal to my father: "My
respected brother and master, I have come to ask you to
go with me to Her Majesty the Queen Ghamar-ed-Dowleh
who I think is expecting . . . . " Here he put his lips to
father's ear and whispered something which I could not hear
or guess.

Father seemed pleased, and smiled to Rabi.

"I knew you would be glad," said the eunuch, "and if
pleasant for you, we may go at once." Then looking at
me, he said: "Oh, I forgot to tell you that our little Khanom
Princess Taj-es-Sultaneh"—his majesty's daughter—"has
asked me many times to bring the little Khan to her. She
wants to show him to her teacher, the Mollah-Bashi."

"I think we may leave the boy out; he will have plenty
of opportunity to see the humdrum of the court," said my
father.

"But believe me, Djounam," said the eunuch, "she will
be disappointed if I do not bring our little friend."

"Very well, he may come, only this must not be repeated
in the future," my father answered.

Half an hour later, father and the eunuch, with Laleh
on horseback and I on my donkey, started on our way to
Sultanat-Abad. It was before noon. The air was fresh and
the ride very pleasant. My donkey kept a good space in
front of the others. It took us three-quarters of an hour
to arrive at our destination. We passed the front gate of
the summer palace and a half a mile away turned around
the wall toward the back of the garden, for the harem.
Half an hour more and we arrived at the back where tents
were pitched one after another, as if a large army were
quartering there. Stable after stable, kitchen tent after

kitchen tent, followed one another as far as I could see. We passed between long lines of tents, and finally came in front of the gate of the harem. The crowd of eunuchs and officials at this place seemed more numerous and formal than in Teheran. Many guardians with their gorgeous purple costumes were on duty, and hundreds of warriors and gholams armed to the teeth were passing and repassing in front of the gate. The chorus of noise, shouts, and cries, made me think of a mosque in the month of Ramazan.

Servants ran to us and I was trusted to the hands of a eunuch to bring me to the tent of the Mollah-Bashi. Father and Rabi disappeared inside the gate. I followed the guide into a maze of alleys and passages among the tents, and finally stopped before a large double tent, with the front part in the shape of doors, now opened wide. We crossed the first tent and entered a second smaller one lined with red cloth. The Mollah-Bashi met me near the entrance. "Salamon Aleikom, Agha"—"Good day, sir"—he said to me. "Welcome, welcome. Come in, please come in. Here is Her Highness the Princess!" I returned his salaam and bowed to a little girl sitting on her knees in the far corner of the tent, covered entirely by a black taffeta tchador. There was not a single part of her to be seen—just like a small black sack. I wondered if she could see me! We approached her with great respect. Mollah-Bashi showed me my place near her and he sat on a sheepskin in his usual place, five feet away.

The Arabic grammar of which I hated the sight was open before her. "Poor little girl," I thought to myself, "she is suffering as I do when in town." I believe my sympathy was appreciated, for presently I heard a soft, sweet voice asking very shyly: "Are you the son of our great Hadj-Agha?"

"Yes, Khanom," I answered, feeling as shy as she and looking sideways to find out if there was anything to be seen of her. But no! the sack was closed. She must be feeling very hot under that black thing, I thought to myself. She had no veil.

"Yes, Khanom," said the Mollah-Bashi. "The little Khan is a very studious gentleman. I am glad he has come to your highness. There is no better company for you."

"Indeed, indeed," said the shy voice of the Princess. "Who's son can be better than the child of our Hadj-Agha? Himself a model for our men, it is just that his children shall be models for other children!"

"By all the jinnees!" I said to myself. "What eloquence!" Although I was told she was eight years of age, nearly a woman!

"I am sure he knows his grammar by heart," said the mollah.

"Oh, dear," I thought to myself, "I hope the silly ass is not going to ask me the conjugation of any verbs. I am ruined if he does." And curse the devil, he did that very thing! I was so embarrassed that I had it in my mind to get up and run away, but happily there came an unexpected event which saved the situation.

"Salamon Aleikom," said a farrash who put his head inside the tent, not daring to show his whole self before the eyes of the Princess. "The presence of your honourship is called by our Khanom."

"My presence?" asked the mollah hastily, "are you sure it is my presence?"

"Yes, your honourship," affirmed the farrash.

"I am at her sacred order," the mollah said, jumping to his feet. Excusing himself to the Princess, he vanished like a jinnee.

When we were left alone I heard a giggle under the black taffeta sack, and presently caught through an aperture a single eye full of mirth, looking at me, but still very shy.

I smiled at the eye, intimating with my face an unspoken phrase to this effect: "Aha, I see you!"

She understood, and let the tchador fall back so that I could see her face.

It took all her courage to open her eyes and look up at me, as she was breaking the whole code of the law of Islam, but we both smiled and little by little began to chat on anything that came to our minds.

"Do you really know all the Arabic verbs?" she asked sorrowfully.

"Not a single one!" I confessed.

Her eyes opened as wide as they could. She looked absolutely astonished, and perfectly lovely.

"How brave you are to tell me the truth! Now I know you are the son of our Hadj-Agha."

I smiled again at her.

"I wish Hadj-Agha would bring you with him whenever he comes," she said.

"I wish so, too, but he seems always so reluctant to come," I replied.

"I do not blame him. Always the same! Monotonous as the cry of a crow and uninteresting as the page of a prayer book. I wish I could run away."

"I shall take you away," I said. "I know all the good places around here. Besides I am not afraid of anybody in the world."

"And if his majesty sends people to take us back, I will not go!" she said petulantly.

"Let me have you next to me, my gun in my hands, and my donkey ready to ride, then I should like to see anyone try to get you back!" I said gravely.

"And what would happen?" she asked.

"None of them would ever live, even to tell the news," I said proudly.

"It is lovely to hear you," she replied frankly, "but I believe the life in the harem has made a coward of me."

She was about to say more when Mollah-Bashi was seen coming into the outer tent. Immediately the black taffeta closed its folds over the lovely little mouth and the velvety eyes bent once more over the Arab grammar.

"Ah!" said the mollah, "her Highness the Khanom wanted to know how you two were getting on and if the little Khan knew all the Arabic verbs."

At the mention of the Arabic verbs goose flesh covered me and I wished Khoda would strike the mollah with lightning.

"He is simply marvellous," said the soft voice of the Princess from under her cover. "With your honour as teacher, and our little Khan as company, I cannot help but go further than anybody in the harem."

"Your highness is very gracious to her humble teacher," said the mollah, "and I have no doubt you will go very far."

"Yes, very far," affirmed the Princess.

Thereupon two eunuchs and another farrash came into the tent. One of the eunuchs said: "Luncheon time, your highness."

The Princess stood up and so did we.

"I hope to meet you again," she said to me.

I bowed without saying anything. We followed her outside the tent. An old man opened a purple parasol and handed it to her. She held it above her head, and then with a graceful step, she walked slowly away, the two eunuchs in front of her, and the farrash behind. Another man cried out: "Ohoy, Pas-berid, kour-beshid!"—"O, get away, become blinds!" I watched her until she disappeared behind the gate.

V

"LOOKING THE TIGER IN THE EYES"

I HAD been in attendance upon the Shah for more than a year and had seen him many times in his official position and also in his private life in the harem before I was presented to him.

Many people who had been for years in the palace had never met the Shah face to face or, as the expression went, "looked the Tiger in the eyes." Moreover, the Shah never knew exactly the number of his retinue, which ran to thousands and thousands, much less their names. It was common practice to present one man to him over and over again, sometimes as often as three or four times during the same week. People often called this forgetfulness a pose of his majesty, but I think it would have been impossible for any man in his position to remember the names, or even the faces, of such a crowd.

The manner of my presentation was such that it was impossible for him to forget me for the rest of his life, which was nearer its end than he then realised.

One Friday afternoon when I was reading to the Queen Ghamar-ed-Dowleh some of the poems of Hafiz, the eunuch Djouhar came in quietly and whispered a message to her. She immediately called for servants and gave many instructions. I decided it would be better for me to take my leave. Besides, Djouhar had with a sign indicated to me that I should go. I bowed to the Queen, asking her permission to take my departure.

"No, no, you must stay; I want to present you." But

she did not say to whom, and etiquette did not allow me to question her.

I noticed that the whole balcony in front of the rooms had become deserted, as if the place had been stricken by a plague. A dead silence prevailed. The Queen walked out on the balcony with Djouhar and me as her escort, and stood motionless at the top of the steps that led down into the garden.

Djouhar looked at me with an expression of doubt and worry. Clearly he was dissatisfied, and I thought it was because he did not think it wise for me to remain. However, I had no alternative, since her majesty had ordered me.

A nervous tremor shook the figure of Djouhar Khan as he strained his neck, behind the Queen toward the thick foliage of the twining branches of the jasmine trees which hid the garden from our view.

I heard footsteps. Presently the sound came nearer and in another moment, mounting the stairs, I saw the same figure which I had beheld, for the first time, three years ago in the country; His Majesty the Shah! I do not know why, but a chill ran along my spine as I watched his approach.

Clad in a short tunic, tightened at the waist by a belt with a ghameh (short sword) hanging from it, a long dark military coat hung over his shoulder, top boots, a riding whip in his hand, he stood in front of us, a superb figure of an Oriental monarch. The skirt of his coat, on the left side, was thrown back, displaying the vivid purple colour of its lining, which made a striking background for the sheath of his sword; a dash of black in a pool of blood.

He looked at us with his abnormally large eyes, glittering and dark; the "imperial stare" was of such magnetic power that it was said that neither man nor beast could stand before it.

An English writer whose name I do not remember, after

visiting the Shah, wrote in his book: "It is true; a man has difficulty to stand the Shah's glare!"

But, being a curious boy, and not well versed in the stories about his glare, I firmly withstood his gaze, knowing that I should be able to talk about it later to my friends. For a full minute he glared and then—if uttering growls like an angry animal can be called speaking—he began to speak:

"Ho ho ho ho ho, hohoho." By which he meant, "How, how, how is it?" He continued, "Halton Tchetore?"—"How are you?"

"By the fortune of your imperial majesty, these humble servitors in attendance at the heavenly gate, are well," replied the Queen.

"Khoub, khoub, khoub"—"Good, good, good" were his Majesty's next growls.

This manner of growling was known as the "imperial way of speaking!" All the Persian Shahs of the Kajar Dynasty before him talked in this way, and so did the Shahs who succeeded him. His entourage only guessed the meaning of these growls, and many were those who paid with their lives for interpreting their meaning wrongly.

"Bidjelo, bidjelo"—"Come near, come near" he growled again.

Her Majesty, the Queen, stepped forward, but Djouhar and I kept our places.

Then he looked at me and said: "Tohambia, Tohambia, Biabiabia"—"Thou also come, come, come, come."

I went a few steps toward him and stood still again.

"Nanana djelo, djelo,"—"No, no, no, near, near!"

I went still nearer, almost in a line with the Queen.

In the same manner he growled out again, meaning this time: "Who is this boy?"

"Ghorban, it is the child of the highly honoured and

faithful man, your imperial majesty's Hakim Bashi," answered the Queen.

"Ho! Ho! Ho!" he cried out. "Our Hakim Bashi! Our Hakim Bashi! Ho, Ho! He looks like his father!"

"Yes, Ghorban, very much like his father," repeated the Queen.

"Thou art a big boy," his majesty said to me, and this time he changed the intonation of the word "thou" to that by which he addressed his intimate entourage.

I bowed again and said nothing. My education, in regard to the court manner (in case I should meet the Shah) had taught me that any word spoken by him was final and should be acknowledged as such by a bow or by suitable words whether his statement be true or false.

"Dost thou learn lessons?" (He meant, was I studying.)

"Yes, Ghorban," I answered this time.

"His knowledge of Persian literature and poetry is most remarkable," said the Queen.

"Yap, Yap, Yap," growled the Shah. "Son of our Hadj-Agha, he will be like him." And then, as he wanted to show special honour to me:

"Thou, thy father, thy family, all have been and still are guardians of our health and well-being."

"Your majesty's words are the truth in all its glory," answered the Queen.

"We are starting for Mazenderan now," said the Shah, changing the subject.

"God be with your majesty," replied the Queen.

"Very soon you will follow the ordou," growled the Shah in such unusually incomprehensible words that I could not, until the Queen repeated it, understand what he meant. The ordou was the imperial caravan that went north for the summer.

"Yes, Ghorban, we all will follow the ordou and the high

perched and divine cavalcading camping," acquiesced the Queen.

My attention must have been attracted to the handsome, short sword at the Shah's belt, and he must have noticed it, for presently he turned to me and said:

"Ho, Ho, Ho, Ho, Yeh, Geh, Geh,"—"Thou shalt have one, thou shalt!" Thereupon, without saying more, he turned around, cocked his head, looked at the courtyard before him, scrutinising all its sides and corners, then descended the stairs and walked away, while the Queen made a curtsy and I bowed. After he had taken his departure I turned to see what Djouhar was doing; I found his body still doubled up in a position as when one prays—I believe he did not even know his master had gone, for he now straightened his body and looked as if he were coming to himself after a long fainting spell.

The Queen addressed him: "When is the ordou moving to the north?"

"In a week or two," he answered. "His majesty will spend a week hunting in Djadjoroud and then will start for the north; the imperial harem will join his majesty near Nour."

"It will be pleasant, to roam once more in the fields of Mazenderan and breathe the cool sweet air on the green hill-sides of Nour and Kodjour!" said the Queen. "It will bring back my girlhood to hear again happy birds on the branches, singing all day, and men reading verses under the shade of weeping willows, the silver tinkle of tiny streams in their ears and the love of Persian maids in their hearts; women playing setars, to accompany the voices of their younger sisters; children playing in the clear waters of little pools." She stopped short and sighed: "Oh, what a difference it would have made to me and to thousands like me, if the whole of Persia were only as I then pictured it in my mind! So we are all going away!"

She touched my cheek with her finger and said: "We are leaving soon for the north."

"Yes, Majesty, I wish I were going too."

"But you are going, my boy," she cried.

I began to stammer, not understanding her quite clearly. "But I am to go with my father to the country place, very soon!"

"No, you are going with us! Did you not hear his majesty say, 'Very soon you *all* follow the ordou?' You were included."

Thus my dream of adventure through the jungle in the wake of the Shah was at last about to be a reality! Riding, hunting, who knows, maybe fighting, all were to be mine, and all in a few days! Yet something had happened. I was now completely indifferent to my dream. Was it a childish whim? Or a reaction? I could not say.

Perhaps there was another reason—one difficult to speak of, even after so many years. My mother, with the perfume of whose name every breath of my life was mingled, had died a little while before; and desolately I knew that, whether I went out from my father's house or came back into it, I must do so forevermore without the blessing of her lips or hands.

Her majesty perceived my dejection and, taking my hand in hers, asked me why I was not happy: "I, myself, am as happy as a boy like you should be, now that I am to travel at the skirts of the high mountains, inhaling the cool air that floats down from those heights where nothing can be seen but the white snow standing out in clear high peaks against the blue sky."

"I doubt if Father will like interrupting my study," I answered.

The Queen saw that this was a subterfuge and said: "Did you not once declare you would do anything for your Queen?"

"Yes, Majesty."

"Very well, then, your Queen desires that you should go with the ordou."

"I shall go," I answered promptly. She seemed really happy, and Djouhar also gave signs of pleasure.

"You may go now to Hadj-Agha and give him this bit of news: Djouhar will go to his house to-morrow, and I shall see him some time next week," the Queen said very kindly.

I bowed to her and was leaving the room when a thought came into my mind. Taking my courage in hand I asked the Queen if I might say something.

"You may," she said.

"I have no ghameh to attach to my belt!"

"Oh, I see!" She laughed. "You are reminding me of his majesty's order to give you a weapon. You shall have it."

VI

PREPARATIONS FOR THE IMPERIAL ORDOU

THAT evening I spent the time between my afternoon prayers and dinner in my study alone. I wanted to think over my journey with the Shah before mentioning it to Father.

I had, of course, heard many stories of the Shah. I knew that some people, my unholy uncle, for instance, considered him really insane. A more impartial judgement was made by my father, who had studied him very closely. He thought the Shah was of a neurasthenic and hysterical disposition, and that in anger he became demented. Otherwise it would be impossible to reconcile the conflicting elements which made up his daily life. He was cruel, savage, barbarous, without morals or principles, ignorant of truthfulness or trustworthiness. He lied alike to his friends and foes, and yet he was a perfect gentleman in his words and manner, when he chose to be. He was a marvellous logician in conversation, a passable poet, an excellent artist at drawing, witty, humorous, courageous, a dashing horseman, a most able shot, and a great hunter. My father believed that, had his youthful days been spent in a better atmosphere, he might have made a very acceptable monarch for the country.

Yet even when a young boy this extraordinary man showed symptoms of becoming a heartless man; at the age of nineteen, when he mounted the throne, he already possessed the despotic eccentricities of his forefathers and the greedy instincts of nomadic, half savage tribes for usurping what belonged to others. As Crown Prince of Persia he had been given the governorship of the important province of Azerbaijan, in the northwest part of the country, when he was only ten years old. Thus from a tender age he had been surrounded by a corrupt group whose hands were red with blood of the poor and unprotected. Scores of old families were ruined under his youthful governorship.

In the beginning of his reign, when half the people in different parts of the country were said to be in rebellion, he was busy, day and night, receiving reports from various governors and officials who, every day, found a plot or two against his life and government. Of course half these plots were the creations of the ministers and officials who reported them in the hope of getting rid of their rivals and advancing their own positions with the new monarch. At this time, hundreds of men were killed in the most dastardly ways: scores of people had their eyes gouged out and others had their hands and legs amputated or their tongues cut out.

The aristocracy was decimated, and educated people found it necessary to hide themselves or to pretend to be crazy or irresponsible. There were many who resorted to this second ruse. I, personally, knew a few of them. A book could be written on these "fools" who were the only sane people in the land of the Lion and the Sun.

One day news was brought to the Shah that a group of young students in the modern college every night held meetings at different places. This was at the time when the Shah, in search of unlicensed pleasure, used to go out at night and force his entrance into the houses of unprotected citizens. First it was decided to send the farrash to deliver these young men into the hands of the executioner. But, being in one of his crazy moods, the Shah decided to do justice in person. He dressed himself as a ruffian and in company with a dozen or more of his dare-devils invaded the house where forty peaceful young men, unarmed and innocent, sat preparing their French lesson for the next day. Many of them fell by the sword of the crazy Shah.

Another quality of Nasser-ed-Din Shah, much talked about among his attendants, was something which made all animals, wild or domestic, tremble at his approach. Stories were told which are so preposterous that I am afraid no one will believe them; I would not have given credit to them myself had I not seen similar instances during the short time I had occasion to watch him.

There was one story which was told me by the Supreme Head of His Majesty's Equerries, a fine old gentleman and pure-blooded Persian of high birth. His reason for trusting me is another subject and a story apart. His official duty was to choose the proper horse for the Shah on all occasions. His other duty was to hold the Shah's stirrup for him to mount! He said that, notwithstanding the Shah's three hundred stallions (all Arabs with the highest authentic pedigrees, and the cream of some four thousand horses belonging to the Shah alone) he always picked out the most quiet and spiritless charger for his majesty because he knew that no high-spirited animal would bear the look in his eye. He swore to me that when he presented the stirrup to his master the poor animal would begin to shudder as if cornered by a tiger. And stranger still, as soon as the Shah was in the saddle, the quiet horse, otherwise as meek as a camel, would instantly behave as if he were being scorched with hot iron.

Did the Shah really possess an uncanny nature? And could this be detected by animals? Did his gaze in reality possess such powerful magnetism that it subdued other human beings and turned them, temporarily, into cowards? Or was all this due to the abnormally large, deep, clear and strangely attractive eyes that he flashed like searchlights, knowing their power, upon all people who came face to face with him? Even the late Queen Victoria was said to have noticed the magnetic power of the Shah's eyes and to have been, at times, disturbed by his uncanny gaze.

Such was the Shah, Nasser-ed-Din, as I pictured him to myself.

After the first few hours of hesitation about going north with his imperial camp, the idea of adventure took possession of me once more and I became engrossed in plans. During the two weeks before the time fixed for the departure, I had many dreams about it, day and night. I had already, in my own mind, made a selection of servants to accompany me on my future trips—the head of my stable, the chief of my kitchen, my secretary, my poet, my story-teller, my joker, and my fool.

It was the correct thing for every gentleman to maintain a fool; to have more than one was considered very smart. The Shah had a score and so had all the great Khans and the old grandees. The demand for fools created a class of people who trained for the profession; in fact, many who had failed to attain high-salaried political posts threw all pretence away and became fools. Some succeeded so well that they deceived not only the Shah but the country as well and grew fat at the expense of the ignorant people.

But my heart was set upon having a genuine fool, like one named Ali who was employed by my eldest brother. This poor man was gifted with a splendid insanity! He was known to all the gentlemen of the Shah's court and lived in perfect freedom with my brother's retinue of servants.

In summer when the Cossack regiment retired to the Kajar palace, outside Teheran, where it camped for the season, Ali, the madman, accompanied my brother. His duty was to amuse him during the evenings. On these occasions he was made to drink champagne in such quantities that my Laleh said it would have made any man crazy. The mad Ali would then jump up and down, completely naked, and dance like a possessed savage, or attack the servants. At this performance the guests would roar with laughter and clap their hands in applause.

I remember one evening when the whole party, feeling very warm and happy with wine, called for Ali. He was brought in by his keepers; one of the officers drew his shush-geh (a Cossack sword) and handed it to Ali. The lunatic took the weapon eagerly, swinging it and testing its weight like a connoisseur. Suddenly he tore himself free and rushed out of the tent. The party laughed and thought no more about him. Ten minutes later a wild scrimmage and a chorus of shouts was heard outside. Ali had attacked the nearest sentinel, had wounded another man, and was now fighting all comers. At this news the officers drank a toast to the lunatic and laughed themselves to tears! No one attempted to stop him; he was official fool to my brother and, there-fore, as free and as important as any of the officials of the army.

Finally, through my Laleh, my brother issued an order for his capture and he was, with great difficulty, brought in, but not before he had wounded a score of Cossacks and a number of servants. It took four men to keep him in hand.

I wished my fool to be like Ali, only a bit less dangerous! I thought of Nazi. Nazi was tall and majestic, with long curly hair falling about his head; he wore a most vener-able beard cut according to the rules laid down for the followers of the Prophet. Nazi! The fool of the district! Yes!

The trimming of his beard was done by the barber of our district as a religious duty. This barber had a zeal for his work, believing that he was doing a service to the community at large. He tried his best to make every one within the scope of his practice, appear, at least, as a decent Moslem, and he saw no reason why the district fool should escape him. On these occasions, if Nazi objected, some other fellow, as good a Moslem as the barber, lent a hand to keep him quiet during the operation. To complete the fool's toilet, the proprietor of the drug store, who also sold perfumes, would fill the hollow of his hand with rose water and use it generously as a lotion for Nazi's beard.

Nazi appeared sane enough except for his dislike for clothing. He wore only a piece of rag wrapped around his loins and would tolerate nothing more. He was allowed to live in a ruin near the tekkyeh where people threw their garbage. His only company was a pack of a dozen or more wild dogs who formed a sort of bodyguard to keep away the children who otherwise might have annoyed him.

During the day Nazi begged his food and every shopkeeper gave generously. He roamed through the streets and bazaars in complete freedom, choosing what food he fancied—an apple, a piece of cheese, a roll, a few nuts, or a coloured egg which he knew, by instinct, was hard boiled and ready to eat. All shopkeepers considered his visits a sign of good luck. For in their opinion a madman was favoured by Allah who, in His graciousness, had spared him the sordid drudgery of life and had deadened his senses so that he was not only immune from craving this world's goods but was also free from care.

"Verily the fools are the happiest of all God's creatures and much wiser than our Shahs," said the shopkeepers.

To Nazi money meant nothing and so he would throw it away. He enjoyed not only the freedom of the city at large but was also kindly treated at many different houses. Our own was one of the places where he found a welcome. He would walk in, unannounced. None of the servants ever tried to keep him back—he was mad and thus half holy in their eyes.

He could do nothing like the other fools in the Shah's court. His only amusing feat (and this he performed only on rare occasions), was a sort of a grotesque dance for the children in which he imitated a camel. But even this he was never asked to give in our house. My mother objected: "Let the poor man alone, do not disturb him in his thoughts."

This was the man I selected in my mind to become my own official fool, and having arranged, in my imagination, all the details of what I chose to term my entourage, I began to consider myself already a member of the Shah's suite, and the best equipped among them all!

But an unexpected difficulty lay ahead.

I did not find it at all easy to obtain my father's consent. He considered my studies my first duty and, besides, he feared that too early acquaintance with court life and with the vagaries of a Kajar monarch might spoil my mind and prevent me from developing into a peaceful citizen and a man of culture.

But, apart from my grief at the death of my mother, which seemed unassuageable within the walls of the house that lacked her presence, there were three reasons for my father's finally changing his mind. The first was the Shah's tyrannic desire to keep boys of the old Persian families as ignorant of European ideas as possible. Various incidents gave irrefutable proof of his attitude. For example, he had emphatically refused my father's request that my next older, or fifth, brother might be allowed to go to Engelestan for study. Even when father sent my brother to the Madresseh Yengueh-Donya—College of the Nether Part of the World, that is, the American College—instead, he was far from pleased. Accordingly, father, fearing further unpleasantness, placed my brother, with me, as a student in the Imperial College of All the Sciences, an institution directed by the Shah's government, where my second and fourth brothers were teaching.

I, being too young yet for the other classes, attended a French class. The professor in charge was a Farangui whose

name, if I remember rightly, was Barnaout. In addition to
his French courses M. Barnaout, a short, stout, kindly old
man with a little grey beard, had a shop where he sold
French books and Dutch tulips. He was particularly kind
to me, first because I made quick progress in learning to
speak his language, and secondly because I was visiting the
Shah's palace and the imperial harem and could therefore
recommend to the ladies his beautiful tulips. When I had
gone through the first French book and could read it pass-
ably, I was given a volume called *Télémaque*. I was so fond
of it that by the end of the season I had memorized half
of it.

At this time, while the question of my following the ordou
was in the air, it was whispered about that his majesty
would pay a visit to the college. Everybody was agitated.
The professors were absorbed in preparing their classes for
the event. The classrooms were swept and spattered with
water daily for a week, in case his majesty should arrive
without warning, and the food served at noon to the students
was becoming nearly eatable.

It was a Thursday when the imperial inspection finally
took place. Our French classroom was the first to be favoured with a call. M. Barnaout, proud of my work and
also of my being already known to his majesty, had chosen
me to perform the leading number. It was understood that
I should read for the Shah from a book handed to me
with the pages opened by chance. We all stood in our places
with the califeh, or head inspector, of our class, at the door,
wearing his long military tunic buttoned up to the chin.
He was very tall, and it was because of his height, together
with his baritone voice, with which he could roar like a
lion, that he qualified for his position.

A bugle sounded outside! The Shah! He was actually
in the sanctuary of the Imperial College of All the Sciences.
Dead silence fell over the class. One heard only the hard

breathing of those students who for the first time were to
see the Shah with their own eyes! This was no jest! The
Shah of Persia! The Shadow of Allah! I have seen the
most courageous people breathe like trapped animals when
standing fifty yards from him. "Khabar dar!" the inspector
roared out, more from fright than in duty, "His Imperial
Majesty, the Shah!"

Before us stood an ominous and arrogant figure. A pair
of large, velvety eyes was focused burningly upon us all!
All the students were shaking, cold sweat on their brows,
and the professor was unconsciously munching the end of
his dusty beard. The figure stepped quickly in and walked
to the middle of the room, uttering the imperial growls!

M. Barnaout approached, almost trembling, and said something polite, but quite unintelligible, in French. Then he
looked in my direction, as if asking for help through the
impending ordeal, and motioned to me to come forward.

The eyes of the other students bulged from their sockets
when they saw me standing before the Shah, actually alive!
The professor walked to a table piled high with books from
his shop, selected one and, passing his palm along its edge,
opened it at random and, in the same nonchalant manner,
pointed to a passage as if by sheer hazard. The book was
my own worn-out copy of *Télémaque!* I had read it through
and through and was especially fond of this page to which
it automatically opened from long usage. My recital of such
a passage, telling, as it did, about the despotic government
of Greece in the days when a certain young man called
Télémachus made a search for his father, would have had
terrible consequences for the innocent professor had he not
been a farangui.

"Burrr, burrr, huhuh, huh, hunfg!" came from his majesty. This meant, "Very good, very good!" Then he asked,
"Where is your father?"

"At home, your majesty, and at your sublime feet," I answered.

I believe everybody, the professor included, was thunderstruck by this time. His majesty actually speaking to one of the boys about his father!

"Bo-m, bo-m, bo-m bur, bur!" finished the Shah. "Go home, go home!"

I bowed to him and retired to my place. The examination was at an end. Thereupon the Shah turned his eyes upon the professor, growled "Very good!" and walked out of the room.

"Bravo! bravo! mon cher élève," said M. Barnaout to me delightedly; "vous avez bien passé!"

But his pleasure in me was short-lived. In a week from that time it was announced, as the opinion of the council of professors of the institution, that the book called *Télémaque* was too difficult a study and would hereafter be set aside—on the index. At the same time, Father suddenly changed his mind and thought, though I was not told why, that I had better study at home and discontinue going to the Imperial College of All the Sciences.

The second reason for Father's altered views was that my third brother also had decided to accompany the Shah. This was a most happy opportunity to travel with the ordou and still be with my brother, who was very fond of me. Moreover, my education would not be neglected. My brother would take charge of my French and other modern studies, and the mollah teacher of the governor's two sons would see to my Arabic and the reading of the Koran.

Since my brother had travelled many times in Mazanderan and knew the country well, all the problems of my equipment were left to him. Unfortunately one of my schemes had to be given up, namely, the taking of a fool. My brother said I would find plenty of fools in the imperial camp and need not take one with me.

Horses now had to be chosen for me—my own beautiful Arab with the long tail dyed red, the royal colour, was deemed unfit for travel in the mountain passes and through the country known for its treacherous swamps. This was the only discordant note in my happiness, for she was a glorious animal, a gift of the Sultan of Turkey to the Shah, who in turn had given her to his sister, the Princess Ezzat-ed-Dowleh, from whom she was passed on to my father, to be later reserved for my sole benefit. I was enormously proud and fond of her and disliked leaving her behind. But for the journey to Mazanderan horses with Turcoman blood were required, because they were the only animals besides the mules which had the necessary endurance for that wild country.

I learned to attend to my own horse, to mend saddles and other equipment and—what later on proved more valuable than anything else—to stand in complete darkness for an hour at a time without moving a muscle. It was said that Persian children were afraid in the dark. Their fear was due to a common superstition that evil spirits and the jinnees fly abroad in the night, ready to strangle wayward little boys and girls. I had to overcome this fear. When, with great difficulty, I had at last succeeded in doing so, I was made to walk in the dark without stopping or hesitating. In consequence, I could make my way through a forest at night without being scratched by the branches of trees; I could do so as easily and as quickly as in the daytime; I could feel a branch fifty inches before my face without seeing it.

The third reason for Father's consent to my going away was the reassuring fact that Akbar, the terrifying swordsman, had agreed to be my guardian during my adventure in the wild forests and high mountains of Mazenderon.

AKBAR, THE KNIGHT ERRANT

EVEN Her Majesty welcomed the news that Akbar was to be my guardian with a smile like the gleam reflected for an instant from a delicately beautiful memory image. I had heard that her father knew Akbar well. Could she possibly have seen him in her happy childhood when she sat in her father's garden, reading the poetry of Hafiz and dreaming of love? In any case, whatever she may have known or thought about this man who already seemed to me like a legendary hero, she gave me pleasure by her obvious approval of him as my new protector.

The fact that Akbar was going with me was the only thing that reconciled Laleh to my departure. Laleh himself was to remain behind.

It would take much space to give all the titles of this extraordinary man, Akbar, the Mysterious Knight, but I must mention a few which were well known to everybody in Teheran: Akbar, the Lootee (Dare-Devil); Akbar, the Mashdi (Knight Errant); Akbar, the Farrash; Akbar, the Noblest and Kindest of Men upon Earth, the Perfect Gentleman, the Fighter, the Just, the Wise, the Faithful, the Fearless, the Indomitable, the Prince Protector of the Poor and Unprotected! Yet with all these titles and his wide reputation, his actual identity was unknown and he, himself, a mystery!

Even his intimate friends knew nothing about his family. Not even its name. It was said that only three men knew who he was: my father, my unholy uncle, and the head of the mehtars (the stable warriors) of the Princess Ezzat-ed-Dowleh. A fourth man, it was said, had ample suspicion about Akbar's identity, but kept the secret to himself. This fourth man was His Imperial Majesty, the Shah.

Attributing this knowledge to the Shah was more or less a guess, owing to Akbar's awe-inspiring reputation of having been bastinadoed many times by Nasser-ed-Din Shah, and each time, while being flogged, of having had the courage to hurl insults at the Shah; these included some very personal affronts to the imperial and august personage and to his family, yet strangely enough, each time Akbar had been released. The fact that the Shah never ordered his executioner to cut off Akbar's head strengthened the suspicion that there was a reason for his leniency.

From early childhood I had noticed Akbar coming to our house and being received cordially by everyone. During the month of Moharram (the month of weeping), he was always a regular visitor, helping with the programs for the Passion Play and with the distribution of food to the poor. On the New Year's Day, he was received by my father with all the respect due a gentleman of high birth and culture. Aside from this, I had heard many tales of him. It was said that he had been a highwayman, robbing many caravans on the lonely deserts in Persia. It was said also that he had been a terror to the Shah's cavalry troop, whose duty it was to guard the empire, but who, in reality, were the worst robbers ever encountered on the highways. Akbar was also accused of rebellion, in some vague part of the country, against the Shah and his officials, all of whom he despised with all his heart. He had been caught when young in one of these so-called rebellions, and brought to Teheran. But his indomitable spirit had not been broken. His life in Teheran had been spent in the underworld. He had even been called, at times, the Madman—and who knows? Perhaps he was one who feigned madness. For a year or two

I had seen much of him, and I remember now that from the day I started to go to the palace his visits, first to the servants or to my Laleh, had become steadily more frequent.

Akbar took charge of me for some little time before our start. One of the first things he did was to start me in a course of sword-fighting. This training in the way mashdis used their swords was entirely different from what I had received from Laleh. A knowledge of a vast number of points about fighting and wrestling had to be acquired by practice—the most important among these being, as Akbar expressed it, the development of my major will, to subdue and control my minor will. There were also exercises for endurance, such as fasting day after day or riding hour after hour without food or water. Being a good Mahommedan, I was already so accustomed to fasting—I never had broken my fast during the month of Ramazan—that this endurance exercise precribed by Akbar was not too difficult, although I was a growing boy.

I could never tell by what means Akbar lived. Laleh said: "Oh! Akbar lives by the point of his sword!" But this meant nothing to me.

Finally he became one of the regular servants of our house without being officially called one. So far as I know, he never received any salary for his services.

On two occasions I saw him fighting: once with the dasteh (procession) of our tekkyeh, when we met another dasteh from the district of Sangue-Ladje and each demanded that the other make way. The parley proving unsuccessful, our men attacked the men of the opposite dasteh and a terrible battle ensued. I, being a boy, and representing father under the fold of our banner, was very much upset. The seyyed butcher, descendant of Mohammad, was behind me, with a deadly scimitar in his hand. It was the same weapon he used for cutting mutton!

I watched eagerly and presently saw that our men were

running back. Immediately the seyyed butcher brandished his scimitar in the air alarmingly and rushed at the party of wild looking men who came on, shouting at the tops of their voices and hurling insults at us, their naked swords high above their heads. Their idea was to capture our banner. This would have been a most terrible insult to the Tekkyeh of Hossein Beyk, to all the inhabitants of our district and, moreover, a fearful blight on the name of my family.

On that particular day I had no time to think about this! I was tired and very hungry. I had been walking, since early morning, from one district to another, from one tekkyeh to another, tramping through muddy and dusty streets, with my shirt purposely rent by Laleh and with bare feet, as a sign of my mourning for the death of Hossein, the great Martyr, who, I was told, had given his life for freedom. I was a true and sincere mourner for Hossein— but when I saw the seyyed and his followers going forth to fight, I forgot my mourning and my hunger entirely! My one thought was for safety. I, into whose custody the banner had been given for safe keeping! I had nothing in my hand except a string of beads for saying my prayers, and a wild-looking creature, shouting like a madman, was rushing toward me, his long sword whipping the air. I looked behind me; only a few followers were left—mostly old men and servants with walking sticks in their hands. I *knew* this was going to be my end! I steadied myself and thought of Hossein, the Martyr! "Ya, Hossein," I murmured aloud, "Here stands one of your mourners and here is the banner which has upheld your name for centuries! Please save us both!" I was sincere in my belief and my prayer. I simply stood in my place waiting for one of two alternatives: either Hossein would save me or the wild man would kill me. I closed my eyes.

Only a second passed before I heard above my very head

the clashing of swords! Then another sound as if a bronze bowl had been smashed against a stone wall followed immediately by an awful cry of agony, then the thud of a heavy mass falling at my feet. I opened my eyes and saw the back of a man standing before me, parrying the points of a dozen swords drawn against him. He was shielding me and the banner with his body and fighting in the way I had read about in the book of Alexander, but which I had never seen before. With his free hand he was pushing me back, inch by inch, until we were close to the opening of a narrow street. Those behind me went first into this narrow passage; after them the carrier of the banner. Soon we all stood in the passage—the fighting man, in front, blocking its entrance.

Having achieved this position for us, he performed, then, a feat which I shall never forget. Crying for a stick, which was immediately handed to him by a man behind me, he jumped from the passage into the open and plunged his sword straight through the man in front of him; a cry; a thud! He leapt back to his place and after a few seconds darted out again and brought a second man to the ground. He used the stick to parry the point of his adversary's sword, at the same time plunging his own into the body of the nearest of his foes. Thus he put out of the fight six of his adversaries.

When our enemies were in full retreat I ran from the passage and saw for the first time the face of the man who had saved my life and those of the twenty unarmed men behind me: It was Akbar!

I was about to say something to him when he turned to me and said: "Hossein, our beloved Martyr, saved you." And without another word he threw his stick on the ground and went away.

The second time I saw Akbar fight was during an altercation in a Jewish quarter between my Laleh and a mollah, the latter raising hell against the Jews because his donkey had slipped into a ditch. At first this was only an insignificant street row, of a sort not uncommon in Teheran; but soon enough it developed into a regular battle. The mollah received help and so did my Laleh! Hundreds of fanatics took the part of the holy man, and other men, mostly our own stable boys, received them with swords and clubs. When we were surrounded, Akbar appeared on the scene, shouting his own name and attributes to foes and friends alike: "Oh, you sons of dogs and burned fathers! Beating the peaceful Jews because you are Moslems! Fighting as well, a son of the father of this holy district, because he protects them! You cads! You low, unbridled cutthroats! All right, you are welcome! But know, I am Akbar! In flesh and blood, before your hungry hordes!"

In a second the place became the scene of a most ridiculous commotion; people rushed, for safety, in all directions. The mollah was hurriedly helped to his donkey, and he scuttled away as if fleeing from hurricane!

For a reason which has nothing to do with my present book, there existed a misunderstanding between my eldest brother and the mollahs. They supported the restrictions imposed upon the Jews, sanctioned in the secret consistory of the ecclesiastical college, while my brother insisted that they be treated as they had been during the Clan-Tarship of Mahmoud Khan, and considered faithful citizens of the country, as was the case of other religious minorities. Be that as it may, this gallant Knight Errant saved me a second time, and my Laleh as well, who probably otherwise, would have been torn into pieces.

To me, Akbar had already taken the form of a legendary hero, such as those about whom I was reading in the Book of the Kings. I believed him capable of defeating an army, single handed! I was sure that with him as my bodyguard, I could do no less than reconquer the whole country from the Shah! Now that he was going to take the place of Laleh I thought I should see more of him. But, to my great surprise, he came less and less to the house, and yet I frequently saw him in places where I least expected to.

For example: One afternoon I went to the palace to talk over my coming trip with some of the officials. I noticed that a man, dressed like a farrash, kept close to the group of officials who were speaking to me, and that now and then he deliberately listened to them. Nobody was paying attention to him.

I watched him for a while—I had never seen him before —and when I left the group to visit Ghahveh-Tchi Bashi, who was mixing sherbets, I saw him again standing in front of the room looking at the sky with his back turned to us. In itself, this was not unusual. I have seen people absorbed in looking at the sky for hours, and when they are asked why, the answer has been invariably the same: "The sky is so beautiful!" But instinct told me this man had come to listen to the conversation between Ghahveh-Tchi and me.

"Who is that man?" I asked my host.

"Oh, he is one of the Shah's mule-drivers."

"I have never seen him before."

"No," he answered, "mule-drivers have no right to come into the palace. But as the ordou is to start for the north and the head master of the royal camp is here, he receives his men in his office, which is just opposite mine. From now until the day we start, you will see hundreds of these mule-drivers; in fact, the whole palace looks like a stable!"

After thanking him profusely for the drink, I proceeded to the harem; the man was still looking at the sky!

In the evening when I came out of the palace to join my Laleh, who was waiting outside the gate, I saw the sky-gazer engaged in conversation with Akbar! I wanted to draw Laleh's attention to Akbar, but he was riding too far in front of me. Since I had begun inhaling the imperial atmosphere of the Shah's harem, Laleh, to advertise this fact to the passer-by, stretched the conventional distance between master and servant by riding some hundred yards in advance of me.

Later I told him I had seen Akbar near the palace and asked if he was busy with some job there. "Not that I know of, sir, but Akbar is a jinnee; he is everywhere at the same time."

This answer was sufficient for me. I assumed that the mule-driver was some friend of Akbar and thought no more about it. But day after day, I saw Akbar in different places where I happened to go; if he was not there himself, one of his friends was sure to be near. A most interesting thing about Akbar was his reputation for being a great friend of the beggars of Teheran. "Akbar is their favourite," Laleh said, "and I believe that if he ever found himself very poor any beggar would be delighted to help him. He has saved more than fifty persons from the city prison and more than ten from the sword of the executioner.

"Some time ago," he continued, "a man was ordered by the Governor of Teheran to be beheaded to inspire the on-lookers with awe and respect for the Governor and his officials. Two farrashs took him by the arms and were dragging him toward the ghapogh, while the executioner walked in front. It was planned to stick his head on the end of a long pole in the middle of the ghapogh and keep it there for two weeks, so all the inhabitants of the city would understand how justice was done in the Shah's empire. It happened that Akbar knew this man to be a simple farmer outside a town next to where the Governor's Farrash Bashi owned a small land holding. The Farrash Bashi offered to buy the land for a tenth of its value. The farmer refused to sell and became involved in difficulties with the Farrash Bashi which lasted for years, with the result that the poor man was accused of robbery, rebellion and, worst of all, a refusal to pay his taxes. Finally a murder was accredited to him and he was confined for six months in the prison in the Tchar-Sou. There he was tortured systematically by the jailer, and offered money by the Farrash Bashi if he would confess the crime, or crimes, of which he had been accused. It was whispered in his ear every evening that his one chance to save himself was to admit that his entire farm was the rightful property of the Farrash Bashi, who would then, as an act of generosity, give him freedom and enough money to make a pilgrimage to one of the holy shrines in Persia, where he could pass the rest of his life in peace and prayer. Finally the man confessed a series of imaginary crimes. The next morning, while he thanked God, he was led forth by the jailer and two farrashs, who said the Farrash Bashi had ordered his freedom and wished to see him. Two days later the man signed all his property over to this rascal before a mollah. He handed the document to his tormentor, at the same time receiving from him a paper which he believed to be a document granting him freedom to make the promised pilgrimage. But it proved, instead, to be a warrant for his death, for crimes of his own confession!

"Those who had done their uttermost to save him from prison, now tried to save his life, but with no success. It was said that his old mother went to a shrine to pray on the tomb of a martyr to help her son. Her lamentations were heard in Heaven; Akbar came to the rescue! Akbar happened to be in the shrine and (as he always happened to be where he was needed), had been moved by the sight of this woman. I do not need to tell you that he learned the story of her son and decided to save him."

Here Laleh stopped to reach in his hip pocket for his tobacco box!

"Will you please go on, Laleh, and tell me what Akbar did?"

"You must learn to be patient," he said. "For the last ten minutes you have shown great signs of nervousness and impatience. You must learn to calm yourself, sir!"

"But you must know Laleh, I am longing to hear how that innocent man was saved."

"That is all very well, but I do not care to have you get excited and fall into the basin."

I remembered now that I was sitting on the very edge of the stone-slabbed pool in our court and that my excitement might well have aroused his anxiety. I suffered his rolling a cigarette, and after a few puffs, which he seemed purposely to make long, he continued:

"Akbar sent the old woman away, promising that on the day set for his execution her son would join her at the very place where she was kneeling! What happened is quickly told: It was customary for the executioner to take his charge out early in the morning to the place of execution. This particular shrine was on the road to the ghapogh. At three o'clock, before the sun rose, when the death party passed near the gate of the shrine, a man crossed the street, and, in his hurry, stumbled against one of the farrashes, who, in turn, began to hurl insults. A hand-to-hand fight ensued. The other farrash, leaving the prisoner in the executioner's care, went to the help of his comrade. Then two other men, both mashdis, came forth and began to beat the latter. A general fight began, savage, terrible and murderous, on the side of the farrashes, and just, honourable and well staged on the part of the unknown fighters. The prisoner was, by now, in the shrine, where the Shah himself could not lay finger on him.

"In the late evening (the same hour when, three days before, the old woman had prayed at the tomb of the martyr for the life of her son), a man was seen kneeling, his head against the wrought silver grill of the sanctuary. Beside him an old woman knelt; her back bent with age, her wrinkled face flooded with tears, one trembling hand on the man's shoulder, the other outstretched toward the Holy Sepulchre. She was addressing a man standing at a corner of the Shrine. This man was Akbar!"

VIII

AKBAR'S HOME

AKBAR never stayed at our house at night. Once when I asked him where his home was he answered: "Dervish har Kodja ke shab ayad seraye oust."—"The home of a Dervish is where he finds himself in the evening."

"In that case, you should be sleeping in our house, that being the place where you found yourself every evening," I said.

"Unfortunately, I am not alone," he replied.

"But you are not married."

"No, not a woman. I am attached, body and soul, to an idea."

"What sort of idea?"

"Justice," he answered simply.

"Well, I should like to see your home," I said. "I have seen the homes of nearly all our servants who are married to women, and I should be interested to see the abode of a man who is married to an idea."

"Very well," he said, "to-morrow night you shall see it."

The next evening before dinner, I reminded him of his promise. With no reply to me, he called Laleh and said: "Our little master desires to be taken to see the place where I spend my nights. Shall we go?"

"Yes, by all means," said Laleh.

Three hours after sunset we three went out of the house into the dark streets, crossed the deserted tekkyeh and made our way toward the north of the city. I noticed we were taking the direction toward the district of Pesta Beyk

Garden, where my forefather was buried, but I kept walking silently between Laleh and Akbar. Curiosity was banned by Akbar as a bad habit.

Presently we came out from a covered street into the wide thoroughfare leading direct to the Pesta Beyk Garden. Far away, high up against the sky, the light which burned upon the dome of the Emam-Zadeh Zeid shrine shone like a star. The high gate of the shrine was closed and everything around it was shrouded in darkness. The dome with its two minarets made an impressive picture—dark, peaceful, majestic, and mysterious.

"We have arrived at my abode," announced Akbar.

"But this is the Shrine!"

"Exactly," replied Akbar.

"Do you live in it?"

"Whenever a change is necessary," he answered with a little laugh.

"You are certainly a strange man, Akbar! Fancy living in a shrine: Spirits of the dead come to life in the night and none but the guardians are allowed to live in the sanctuary except those people who find it necessary to take refuge from living creatures."

"Your Akbar, believe me, little master, is as tired of the living creatures as those who take refuge. My perfunctory relations with this world are only for an ambition; I must live to see that ambition fulfilled."

"May I venture to ask what ambition?" I inquired.

"The same as that of your great ancestor, Ahmed Mokhtar Saghaphi, the Avenger, the Emir of the Faithful and son of Emir Abu-Obeid Saghaphi, who fell in the Battle of the Bridge.

"Mokhtar—the benediction of God upon his soul—revenged the wrong done to the family of Hossein, the Divine Martyr," I replied proudly.

"In appearance, this is true; Mokhtar, the Avenger, did

avenge the innocent blood of the great martyr, but he was no relation to the martyr. He was not even a devout Mohammedan. His work and the khoroudj (act of calling the knight-warriors to arms) was to arouse the world against the tyranny of the usurper of the Caliphat. He himself was not a pretender to the Caliphat," exclaimed Akbar with the enthusiasm of a zealot.

"But all that was thirteen hundred years ago," I said. "There is no longer a blood-thirsty monster like the one who murdered Hossein."

"Not from that dynasty," replied Akbar. "Despotism still rules, but the spirit of Mokhtar is not dead," he replied.

I was about to make an answer when a voice called in the Turkish dialect of Azerbayedjan: "Guelam Kee?" which is to say, "Who goes there?"

"Did you hear that?" asked Akbar.

"That is the guard for the night; he is an Azerbayedjan Turk, and a soldier of the Shah," I answered.

"Guelam Kee?" cried the same voice more forcefully than before.

"Akbar!" said my strange bodyguard.

"Akbar is only one! There are others."

"Akbar's party," was the answer, impatiently shouted at him.

The guardian became silent at this. He did not even take the trouble to look and see what sort of a party Akbar had with him. We were now near the gate; Akbar stepped in front of it and tapped on its iron bar with a stone which he had picked from the road. He tapped once and waited for a second, then he tapped three consecutive times and waited again with his ear against the gate. "He is coming," he said.

Very slowly the gate opened wide enough for one man to go through. Akbar entered and asked us to follow. He closed the gate behind us himself, and addressed the man standing in the shadow of the wall.

"Anything?"

"Nothing," answered the man.

"Alone?"

"Together," was the reply.

"Asleep?"

"Reading."

The court of the shrine was completely deserted. The tall tchenars and the black forms of the cypresses standing out against the dark arches over the entrances to the shrine gave it a menacing aspect. The water in the large basin in the centre of the court looked like molten lead in the darkness. The mausoleums were in complete darkness and the shrubbery around the basin was black. I should have been frightened had I walked there alone, but between Laleh and Akbar, I felt as if I walked between an Emperor and a King. We crossed the court and when we came in front of the middle arch, I knelt in homage. The others followed my example, but none in such a pious manner as the man who came behind us. When we arose, he was still kneeling.

Akbar led us to a side door which opened into a court, in which in daytime small children picked white mulberries. Around the court were empty niches, as large as rooms, which were used as resting places when pilgrims came on Fridays to visit the shrine.

At the right hand angle of this court we stooped before a low heavy door, which the old man unlocked. Laleh had a box of sham-tche (matches covered with a coating of grease) and as we entered a long dark corridor he struck one and lighted the way. We came into another court, round and small, containing nothing but a pool, and after passing through another corridor we stood before a door decorated with silver bars. Very gently the old man swung it open and we entered a sort of chapel, lighted with silver ghandils (oil lamps used in shrines) which hung from the ceiling by silver chains.

Frames of sandalwood and ebony, some carved and others encrusted with gold and silver, hung from the ceiling in great numbers, enclosing pages of parchment, on which masters of calligraphy had written verses from the Koran, texts, prayers, and fragments of religious inscriptions— exquisitely penned and adorned with miniature paintings. Some of them were only ten inches above our heads.

On Fridays, after going around the shrine and the se- pulchre, it was a custom to go to this chapel to read the verses. The tablets hanging low were for children.

I took off my shoes before we entered the chapel. We stepped on an Ispahan carpet more than fifty feet in width and a hundred feet long. I always had the feeling, when walking on this carpet, that my feet were touching ancient velvet or the petals of Persian roses. We came before the silver door and knelt to pay homage to the Martyr. I kissed the threshold before rising again to my feet.

Akbar reverently pushed open the door and we entered the sublime and most sacred sanctuary of the Martyr. A flood of light from thousands of candles illuminated the place.

In the centre was the Holy Sepulchre, surrounded by a screen of wrought silver, ten feet square and ten feet high. The Sepulchre, a single piece of marble, was spread with a piece of ancient brocade, embroidered with fine pearls and precious stones. Gold and silver coins, trinkets, armbands, necklaces, bracelets, aigrettes, rings and thousands of other ornaments and jewels, thrown by the public and pilgrims through the grilles, lay heaped upon one another around the tomb in a pile three inches deep. The grille itself was covered with other silver and gold ornaments, mostly effi-

gies of eyes, hands, and hearts which had been attached to
it by the faithfuls who solicited cures from the Martyr.

I fell on my knees, my forehead against the grille, and
prayed as I had never prayed before, for the repose of the
spirit of my ancestors, and for the greatness of Iran and
its people.

When I rose to my feet I saw to my amazement and surprise the strange man I had met long ago at the grave of
my ancestor.

Laleh and Akbar stood before him as respectfully as they
would have stood in the presence of my father, and the old
doorman with the keys was bowing very humbly to him.
I also bowed. He motioned with his hand that we make
the rounds of the Sacred Sepulchre. I followed him, Laleh
came behind me, Akbar next, and the old man brought
up the rear. After going three times around, we stood in
line to make the last homage to the Martyr, and still keeping our bodies bowed in deference and our eyes fixed steadily
on the grille, walked backwards through one of the silver
doors, out into the arched hall.

As soon as the door was closed it seemed as though there
had never been any light. The cold air of the night and
the darkness of an hour ago, enveloped us again.

"Come, my soul" whispered Laleh, "we are going to
Akbar's place."

We walked on a soft carpet to the end of the hall, where
a space was reserved in daytime for the shoekeepers (who
received the shoes of visitors) and through a door which
opened into a small square room lighted by a wick burning
in a tiny bowl of castor oil. All the corners were in complete darkness. A simple covering of crushed bamboo reeds
was spread over the floor, a few books were heaped in one
corner, and a dervish bowl hung on the wall under a tabar
zin. This tabar zin, or hatchet, was a most terrible weapon
when used by skilled hands. Above it hung a crown like

those worn by the old Persian Kings, and later by the
dervishes, and beside this hung a simple Persian hat of felt
with words embroidered in black silk threads: "Hovas
Sultan el Montaghemel Haghyghy" which, translated, says:
"He, the God, is the real King and the Avenger." Now
this inscription, on a dervish royal crown, seemed to me
very strange. It was the motto of my family, belonging,
especially, to Mokhtar, the Avenger.

On the wall facing these heraldic arms hung two swords:
one of which I recognized as the double-edged short weapon
belonging to Akbar; the other was a long, single-edged
sword. This latter weapon was unsheathed and a gold inscription was visible on the blade: "To defend the rights
of the people and to uphold justice for the world."

There was nothing more in the room, not even a rug.
The tall man sat down, very straight on his bended knees;
Laleh motioned me to follow his example. Laleh, Akbar
and the old man stood respectfully in front of us.

"My son, you are welcome to our abode."

"Do you live, sir, in this place?" I inquired.

"This holy place"—indicating with his hand the Shrine
behind the door—"is my home, and this particular room is
my abode, or I should say, *our* abode, as Akbar is living with
me. We have divided the room into two hemispheres, as
we have divided also its wall; the south wall belongs to my
kingdom, and the north wall is Akbar's." He motioned
with his hand to indicate the respective armories on the
wall.

"And did you pray for our Country and our people?"
he inquired of me.

"I did, sir," I replied.

"We need prayers," he said. "I hear that you are to
travel with the Shah."

"I hope so," I said.

"And I hope so, too," he answered. "It will give you

occasion to see your country. Once outside this city of dust
and filth—field after field of golden wheat, orchard after
orchard—the richest under the sun—vineyards, gardens,
rivers, forests and mountains will delight your heart so
that you cannot help saying: 'This land of Iran is the richest
in all the world!' Then when you come to a village, be
it large or small, you will wonder at the wretched condition
under which our workmen drag out their miserable lives.
It is then you will realize that the reign of wickedness is
something against which no natural wealth in the world
can compete.

"You will soon understand that only one class is master,
the rest slaves. And the masters are savages. In the old
days, if a Beyk or a Khan or a member of the aristocracy
kept hundreds of servants and hundreds of tenants they
were taken care of as if they were his children. But to-day,
under the reign of alien people, the newly rich and newly
made nobility, have established under protection of the
tyrants a systematic servitude for the peasantry which day
by day is bringing the country to its ruin. I have been
told by those who have tramped the wide world that those
Christians whom mollahs call unclean are far cleaner and
more humane than we. We, as a nation, have forgotten the
traditions of our ancestors and the dignity of our land; our
children die before they are born, our crops are ruined by
our ignorance of the art of agriculture. Our Iran is mutilated
and pieces sold to strangers for paltry sums of money. Our
people are now backward and uncivilised—and we were
once the leaders of the civilised world! Our religion has
been diluted with alien supersitions. Our administration is
guided by omens, charms, star-gazers, and mollahs! Our
men are changing trousers for shaliteh (feminine attire),
our braves are becoming soft as halva (a sweet pudding)
and our ruling class is swimming in the filth of sensual life.

Our national health is being broken down by opium and hashish.

"To serve one's own country is a forgotten phrase among the Persians.   But the Faranguis have mastered it and will soon master the world, if we continue to live in such ignominy as this in which we are at present immersed.

The old man would have willingly gone on for hours, but courtesy to his guests made him end his speech, so he said:

"But do not lose confidence in our land or in our people; a hand from behind the mysterious curtain will strike the evil as I would strike the head of a viper.   The time is nearing and the hand is moving."

At this gruesome declaration I felt a chill creeping along my spine.   He spoke with such confidence that I almost thought a real hand was moving in the shadow of the room behind him.   I said, "I know about the unseen hand which will save the country, but who can be the evil?"

After a moment of silence, which seemed an hour, he said very gravely and slowly:

"You, one of the descendants of Mahmoud Khan, our Clan-Tar, you, the inheritor of his name, shall be given the privilege of beholding the evil and also of seeing the mysterious hand which shall strike in the hour written by destiny."

By now I really felt uneasy.   The room, dark except for the tiny flickering light, those three figures—Laleh, and Akbar standing quietly in the shadow, as before God, and the old man, bending his body forward, his eyes and mouth wide open, listening to every word spoken by this weird man—and, above all, the mention of a viper and of a mysterious hand, were sufficient to make me dream all night of horrible things!

"I believe it is time for you to go," the strange host said. "I feel that your Laleh thinks it is already too late."

"Yes, sir," said Laleh, speaking for the first time since he entered the room, "we had better take our leave."

The strange gentleman arose as nimbly as a boy. "You had better say good-bye to me."

"Am I not to see you any more?" I asked politely.

"I am afraid not."

"Are you going away?"

"Very far, oh, very far away," he said with a chuckle, as if he meant it for a joke. Then very gravely he added: "I am going to die."

"To die!" I exclaimed.

"Yes, my son, to die! Is there anything strange in dying?"

"No, of course not, everybody must die, but nobody knows when," I answered gravely.

"Perfectly true, but it happens that I do know when I am to die."

"When?"

"A few minutes after the evil is banished," he said. Seeing that this carried no meaning to me he added: "I am an old man, I do not know my hour, as you know not yours, but I can look back over my life such as I hope none of my fellow creatures will ever endure. I should have been dead long ago, but a spark has burned in me which will only be extinguished when the Unseen Hand strikes the evil, the lingering flicker of my life and that of the evil are so interwoven that when one is dead the other must soon die, too."

I found nothing to say to this; the old man held the door open.

"Good-bye," I bowed.

The strange man bent and kissed my forehead: "Good-bye, my son, and may God protect you!"

Laleh and I made our way home silently. Only once did I interrupt the stillness:

"Who is the gentleman?"

"Only a holy man," he replied. It was the same answer he had given me after my visit to the grave of my ancestor.

"And the old man with the bent back?"

"He is the man I was telling you about whom Akbar saved from the executioner."

PART III

I

I SET OUT FOR THE LAND OF THE WHITE MONSTER

I HAD thought that my brother and I would leave Teheran with the ordou, but instead my brother was ordered to accompany the Governor-General who went in advance of the Shah to see that everything was in good order on the frontier of the province of Mazenderan. The Shah was to move a few days afterward, but my brother decided that I should not start with him but travel, instead, with my own men. In this way I could become a full-fledged cavalier before I joined the imperial camp. My brother attached to me a native of Mazenderan, who would be useful as a guide.

This guide Abdol-Latif (the Slave of the Delicate!), was a young man whom I knew well. He had come some years ago the capital to learn to be a doctor. After three years of constant attendance on my brother, mostly as major-domo, while he learned to read and write, he thought himself already a doctor and, many times, prayed that my brother would ask a subsidy for him from the Shah so he could go back to his country and practice. He was greatly surprised when my brother told him he must study a while longer. He had already attended, in his medical capacity, a donkey belonging to one of the peasants at our summer place; two days after his visit, the donkey had died. Also a sick peasant who had been waylaid by this too enthusiastic physician had paid the same price the donkey had. To have spent a year with my brother, or with any man of his reputation, was equal to a certificate; and after such apprentice-

215

ship, these men could go throughout Persia as medical graduates. As a result, the undertakers' business flourished as in no other country.

My brother tried to persuade Abdol to remain in Teheran, but, failing in this, decided to take him along so he could watch him.

I believe my brother thought I could handle him. Anyhow, I was instructed to deliver him, safe and sound, into my brother's hands.

Two days after my brother left, Akbar thought it time for me to start. But to my great dismay he said that I was to go without him, accompanied by my men, and that he would join me at a day's journey from Yoush. All my arguments were waved aside and, stranger still Father and Laleh were of Akbar's opinion.

They told me that here was a chance to prove myself a man; money, horses, servants, power, reputation, name and knowledge, were at my disposal. Now was the time to put into practice the lessons of my teachers.

"Why," they all said to me, "if a boy of your family cannot manage to travel to the North, how can he be expected to travel with the imperial ordou and earn the dignity of walking under the Shadow of Allah?"

More strange, when I found opportunity to speak about this to Her Majesty, the Queen Ghamar-ed-Dowleh, she seemed very much pleased, and exclaimed, "How delightful for you, my boy! Oh, how I wish I were in your place!" The first day of our journey was very pleasant. Laleh and half a dozen servants accompanied us to the first halting place, called Dja-Djo-Roud.

The most thrilling event was my first adventure in crossing a river on horseback. At first, I thought our way lay over a bridge, which we had been told had been repaired for the Shah to cross, but Laleh pointed out rifts made by winter storms and cold. Large holes gaped in the floor and there were no side walls for protection against the dark, tumultuous water underneath, thundering against the dilapidated arches. I agreed readily with Laleh that we should cross as people did in the days of the Pharaohs.

We rode farther up, where the water seemed more propitious for the venture. Two of our horsemen encouraged their mounts to enter and behind them went the servant whose mule was laden with leather jars of drinking water and other supplies. After him went the third and fourth mules, laden with our small military tents and their accessories. I was anxious beyond words! I kept my heart quiet and took my courage in both hands. Abdol-Latif dismounted and announced that he was going to cross the bridge on foot, making excuse that he had valuable surgical instruments with him, which he could not trust to the water.

"But, you will be blown away by the wind!" Laleh said. "And besides, you ought to be ashamed of your fear to cross a tiny stream of water on horseback—you, a native of Mazenderan."

"My life as a future hakim," Abdol solemnly answered, "does not belong entirely to myself; it is valuable to the hundreds of poor, sick people who need my medical assistance. I have no right to endanger it."

"You must do as the others do," Laleh firmly announced. "There will be other rivers which have no bridges. If you want to take care of your precious medicines and instruments, keep the box in your arms and ride behind one of the men." Thereupon, Laleh called out to a man to make place for Abdol to sit behind him.

Abdol seemed undecided, whereupon, I noticed a "You-do-or-you-die!" expression come into Laleh's eyes. Yadollah noticed it, too, and, before Abdol had time to say another word, Yadollah raised him in his strong arms and tucked him behind the horseman like a neat bundle! The horseman, with no further ado, rushed into the torrent.

"Aye, aye, O Khedow! O Khedow!" "Oh, oh, God, help! Help!" yelled out Abdol. But in the next second his cries were silenced under the crushing waves. I thought they were drowned. But presently the first man's head and then the head of the horse appeared. Abdol was encircling the waist of the Gholam with both his arms, his head against his back, quiet as a pantry mouse! The horse (I could see only his ears) was swimming in the wave line traced by the horses in front. His rider knowing that quick execution of an order is proof of efficiency, had not waited to consider the right place to take the river and, therefore, had exposed our psuedo-doctor to a most undignified mishandling; both were drenched to the skin.

This was a good lesson for me. Before taking the river, Laleh chose carefully the point and, with stirrups, urged his horse in; I followed. A short fall which was enough to bring my heart into my mouth, and then a feeling of comfortably gliding through the water. I stood up in the stirrups as we do when galloping.

"Loose the reins, and do not look at the water," commanded Laleh.

This instruction was timely, for my head had begun to turn: I thought I was to be seasick! When Laleh saw that I could not resist glancing at the water, he took his rifle from his shoulder and began shooting into the air to divert my attention. Two of the Gholams, in front of us, followed his example and a merry bombardment followed. Getting out of the river seemed more difficult for the horses than swimming across it. My horse tried two or three times to get a foothold, and each time fell back against the waves as if giving up the struggle. Finally, he crawled for a few yards, with outstretched neck, nervous and shaking under me, and then, with a tremendous effort, sprang clear of the water to a safe landing. As I came out of the river, Laleh dismounted and swung me onto his powerful shoulders, shouting, "Here, you men, is a master for you! Every inch of him is Saghaphi. I wish I had had courage at his age to make this marvellous crossing for the first time in my life." His words nourished my pride, but I felt a secret shame that I had not had the courage, in the river, to ask the loan of his rifle to fire, as he had done.

The servants were already preparing camp for the night. A big fire had been made in the centre of the tent reserved for Laleh and me, and another fire was glowing outside to frighten away wild animals. We had a cold supper—chicken hashed meat and vegetable omelette, called koutou, with bread and hard-boiled eggs. For beverage, we drank clabbered milk mixed with water.

A small mattress and cushion, with a quilt, was made ready for me in the corner of the tent, while Laleh's and Abdol's beds were made down, next to one another, in front of the opening. Two Gholams kept watch over us during the night, and more especially over our horses, for these hills of Djadjoroud are infested with catamounts and leopards, which, when hungry, attack horses rather than men. From a great distance, they can scent horses, and crawl near the camps to kill and devour them. The Gholams were famous hunters and, had it not been that I was tired, our fires would, no doubt, have been extinguished, to encourage the approach of leopards for the sport of killing them!

When we were ready to start, Laleh said "good-bye" and went back to Teheran with the stable boys. It was a sad parting; he kissed me on the forehead many times before mounting his horse—the poor chap was crying. After he had given numerous instructions to my men, he took Abdol apart and spoke to him in a low voice; perhaps he was telling him to try to be a man. Then he left, reluctantly.

We watched them cross the river, Laleh and Yadollah in front, and the stable boys behind. When they arrived safely on the other side, they opened fire. We answered with all our rifles. Then we saw them gallop away; ten minutes later, they were at the top of a hill in a group; another volley of shots as a last good-bye, and they were seen no more. I was left alone—my own master.

My company had diminished in number. It was now composed of one abdar with his two apprentices and two tent-pitchers and one farrash, all riding mules. There were two Gholams, lent to me by my eldest brother to accompany us as far as Afdjeh, our next halting place, where I was to dismiss them, to go their own way or back to Teheran.

One of these gholams, by name Abol-Ghassem, the Katchal, was a notorious cavalier, belonging to the retenue of my brother. He was quite bald as a result of a disease called katchali, hence his nickname. Otherwise he was very good-looking—tall and athletic. His title, gholam, in reality, means slave, but it is, also the title of a regiment of riders belonging to the Shah, who allowed them to become body-guards of the different dignitaries of his court. This wild regiment was made up, almost entirely, of well-to-do provincial men who desired to earn the privileges of being attached to the government or to the court.

The Katchal was from a well known family of good and peaceful citizens, but he himself was wild and adventurous; therefore he enlisted in the aforsesaid regiment, in order to become a mounted guard of the empire. The advantages of belonging to this regiment were worth being called slave, as they raised the Katchal, for instance, from the life of a good-for-nothing to that of proprietor of a very rich land in Afdjeh.

How he had succeeded in procuring the land is typical of the way in which the new aristocracy of Persia achieved theirs. He had gone to Afdjeh as a warrior-rider, with a group of tax collectors. Having discovered that the burgomaster of the village was far too wealthy for a simple peasant, possessing a fine house, many servants and dependents, plenty of food, and a corral filled with cattle, Abol-Ghassem determined to relieve him of a part of it. Now Abol was gifted with a quality which is rare among Persians: he could make a decision quickly. As soon as dinner was over he asked the burgomaster for the hand of his daughter, without really knowing that the burgomaster had a daughter! He was lucky. The host did have a daughter, and the demand of the young adventurer seemed to him very flattering. To become father-in-law to a guard in the Shah's army would enhance his position as burgomaster, and he thought this son-in-law might prove useful in future dealings with tax collectors.

On the following morning, the village mollah was called, and the act of marriage, including the dowry of a small house with a good, but small, piece of land, deeded to Abol, was performed. After this the host gave a feast to celebrate.

When he showed a desire to make a really befitting marriage celebration which would incur great expense, the goodhearted Katchal swore, on the heads of all the prophets, that in his opinion, any money his father-in-law intended to spend on this occasion should be given to the son-in-law to buy a property, however small, to divert the tongues of the jealous neighbours who, otherwise, might say that the burgomaster's daughter had married a pauper. The father-in-law gladly consented and, in the evening, a simple dinner was served to a few intimates and, shortly afterward the newly married couple left for their own little house where a most fearful surprise awaited Abol!

The bride had been very shy, but, Katchal thought she was making gher-o-ghamze, that is to say, was coquetting for a show of affection. This feminine aloofness he recognised with due respect, and went so far as to give her his silver watch chain to induce her to remove the veil from her face. He even overlooked the part of the Persian marriage ceremony which forbids a husband to kiss his wife before she has given her consent by herself taking off her veil; the new bridegroom imprinted two kisses on the veil. But, all the tactics he had learned in his wanderings with his regiment failed to make an impression upon his bride, who seemed determined to be won in the usual manner, which is for the bride to be presented with a sum of money in gold. Katchal was forced to comply, though reluctantly. He took a few coins, which he had previously borrowed from his father-in-law, and grudgingly gave them to his bride. Then, the surprise!

"Allah have mercy on my soul!" cried the astounded cavalier. The unveiled bride was a spinster of some forty winters, with a face like a frost-bitten quince.

This unfortunate discovery was so staggering that Katchal snatched up the watch chain and rushed out from the happy abode of love. A stormy altercation ensued between him and his father-in-law. The latter, realising that his hopes of placating the tax collectors were shattered, decided to sacrifice his daughter to keep the friendship of the Shah's gholam. The outraged bridegroom dictated his terms and, the next morning the village mollah read the famous verse from the Koran which, with a snap, severs the sacred chain binding two loving hearts for eternity.

Moreover, the mollah declared that in view of the explicit desire of the virgin daughter of the burgomaster, he asked the husband to release the bride from the marital bond in exchange for the bestowal of her dowry upon the gholam. This done, he, the standard bearer of the Prophet, in accordance with the law of Holy Shariat, pronounced this divorce final and unalterable. A strange group, this retinue of mine! On the second day of our journey, one of my mounted guard asked me in a most casual voice if I would miss my doctor-guard, Abdol-Latif.

"Why?" I asked. "Does he want to go away?"

"No, Ghorban," said the man, "but I thought, if it would not be interfering with any of your arrangements, I might throw the doctor into one of the canyons, where he can join the departed spirits of the old, famous Platos!"

On another occasion, I found it necessary to ask the doctor not to deceive peasants and shepherds whom we met along our way. He had said to some of the men, from a near-by village, that his master and Agha, the son of the world-known Hadj Agha, was ready to distribute his wonderful and hereditary knowledge of drugs to all the sick in their village! The result was that, when we arrived in the village, we found fifty odd peasant women and children gathered in the little open space before the Mosque to beg me to cure them with drugs. They were looking up at me with such pathetic eyes that I had not the heart to tell them I was not a doctor!

Meanwhile, Abdol-Latif was at the height of his glory. He was delighted to see such a crowd around him, asking medical advice. The fact that I was the son of a great physician was so important a reason, in the minds of these peasants, for my being, also, a doctor, that I believe Abdol-Latif, himself, honestly, at that moment, thought I had been born capable of curing the sick!

They spread a rug for me to sit upon, and each patient, in turn, presented himself. I could not understand their dialect, and Abdol had to act as interpreter. I took their hands, felt their pulses and asked them to show me their tongues. Some of them had fever and others were chilled by the nowbe, which is a kind of intermittent fever, and causes the patient to shiver while burning with a high temperature, an ordinary disease, prevalent in that part of Persia.

On the whole, they seemed ailing from a lack of nourishment and a total absence of sanitary surroundings. For this I thought the best solution was to open my leather bag, which was wrapped around the waist of my treasurer, and divide its contents among the crowd. This would, at least, give them means to buy food and clothes.

But, not satisfied with this procedure, the crazy Abdol insisted upon writing, for each of them, a prescription, as was the usual way with doctors! When I protested one of the stable boys stepped to my side and whispered, "For God's sake, master, do not let the ass give them these prescriptions! He will kill them all, and their blood will be upon our necks."

"How can I stop him?"

"Tell him to give them the pills he has been rolling. The pills will not hurt them: I saw him rolling out thousands of them; they are made of nothing but the cooked rice which the shepherds gave us the other night."

Much relieved, I called Abdol to me. He fetched his pen box and sat opposite me, very much pleased at the great show he was making before the peasants. Very gravely, he took a pen in his hand and a slip of paper, and looked up at me for instructions. (This was the way he worked under my doctor-brother.) I knew what he wanted and gave him satisfaction:

"Write down, O you scrivener of our house and family, for each of these sick people, a long prescription of medical herbs, known to us as infallible against fever, which must be boiled in hot water and taken as tea. Write down, also, that I shall give to each a package which contains twenty pills, prepared of unnamable drugs under our supervision; that, for five days, they must keep inside their homes and take four pills at intervals of two hours by the sun; and that each patient will now receive two krans, in silver, with which they must buy these herbs and necessary food."

The last-mentioned medicine brought immediate relief to all present. And when I told Abdol to make small packages of his own pills his eyes glittered with pleasure. He bowed his head toward the patients, and, in his Mazenderan dialect addressed them a flowery speech which I could not understand and although I heard my own name mentioned many times.

This was the second day of our adventure.

On the third morning Abdol came to me, crossed his arms as before a Shah, bowed, and in flowery language asked whether my highness did not consider it too unpretentious to travel behind our procession of food and water, with our servants who rode on mules? He thought it was time for me to discard this system. It would be more, far more suitable to have the others travel before us, or follow, but no longer in our company!

This proposition, from the "slave of the delicate," met with the unanimous approval of all concerned. I was beginning to find it very tedious to trudge behind the heavily laden mules. When left to ourselves, we could gallop up and down the mountain slopes and through the deep valleys, as the ancient riders did.

The Katchal, in view of his anxiety to arrive as soon as possible at his estate, also approved the plan. Instructions were given to the servants to take the road at once and to meet us at Afdjeh, in the evening.

Half an hour later we started to gallop—one gholam in front, I, Abdol, and Katchal following. I was now riding my new horse, a beautiful four-year-old Abrash, half Arab and half Kurd, with reddish and grey hair. My saddle was covered with a fine, red felt, which was very fashionable in those days, and very becoming to my horse's ruddy coat! The harness was ornamented with silver and, around his neck, was a beautiful gold collar, from which hung a long, thick fringe of red silk threads. Two other fringes hung low from behind the saddle, and still shorter fringes hung at either side of his head. The stirrups were large and encrusted with gold and turquoises. My short rifle was on

my shoulder and two cartridge belts were strapped cross-
wise on my chest.

After some hours of riding we came to the famous path
of Afdjeh, called "the rocky stairway," one of the most difficult pathways in the Elburz chain. It is a real staircase,
in some places six feet long. No one knows how it was
formed. Perhaps the usage of this road for thousands of years
has been the only method of its building. The steps, at first
about six inches high, become higher, until they measure
ten or twelve inches at some points. The path, itself, is
fearfully steep. It takes a courageous man and a good horse
to risk it. A goat, a mule, or a donkey is much better than
a horse.

Katchal pushed his horse in front and led the ascent; I
followed and the other gholam and Abdol brought up the
rear. I loosened the reins to let my horse get a foothold
where he could; besides, I needed both hands to keep myself from slipping down over his tail. The stairway, in most
places, was narrow and served, at my right hand, as a brink
to the sharp and smooth cliff, descending straight down to
the dark canyon below. On my left, the imposing range of
the Elburz rose like a rampart, blazing in the sun, awe-inspiring and almost vertical. I did not dare to look about
me, lest I grow dizzy.

About three hundred feet up, the path became so steep
that Katchal thought it might be wiser for us to dismount.
This we did with pleasure. I led my horse and, at the same
time, found a foothold, as best I could, for myself. But I
felt more confident on foot than I had on horseback, and
could look, now, at the vast country before me. There were
only mountains and hills, as far as I could see in front, and
the cone of Demavend, white with snow, which towers over
the land of Iran as a symbol of her greatness. We continued our journey on foot, and only in the afternoon, when
we had reached the plateau behind the mountains, did we
mount again.

II

WE MOURN FOR THE GREAT MARTYR

ABOUT three hours after sunset, we arrived at the outskirts of Afdjeh, very tired and hungry. Before entering
the village we held a council to decide the line of procedure,
in view of the fact that any traveller belonging to the Shah
was an unwelcome guest, even to the provincial Persians,
who are proverbial for their hospitality to strangers.

Katchal's advice was that we ride into the house of the
new burgomaster (the one whose daughter he had married
was dead and so was the daughter) and make requisition
to him to provide us with food and a house to pass the
night. This, he insisted, was our right, and in case of refusal, we could force him to observe the customary obligations toward so important a member of the imperial suite
as myself. Katchal could not take us to his own house
because, first, he was paying an unexpected visit to see how
his property was being taken care of and, second, it would
be a blight upon my social position to pass through Afdjeh
unnoticed. He suggested that the other gholam be despatched, at once, to the head of the village. But Abdol said
that the man would probably be asleep and offered another
plan.

"We are in the month of Moharram and people must be,
at this hour, in the tekkyeh, where dinner is served to all
the population of the village. Besides, I know for sure,"
said he to me, "that the Agha Seyyed Mohammad Sarraf,
one of your relatives, is the great man in Afdjeh, and his
generosity, for the sake of Hossein, the Martyr, in the month

of mourning, is known all over Demavend and he is, at present, in Afdjeh."

"That saves us all the trouble," said I. "I know my relative and have no doubt of a welcome."

"Then let us to the tekkyeh," cried Katchal and we formed the appropriate procession: The other gholam rode in front, with instructions to inform the passers-by of our identity, and Katchal and Abdol rode behind.

Already we could hear the chanting of people and the sound of beating their chests, and in a little while could see the tekkyeh in front of us, covered with a huge tent. Near the gate, I dismounted, and my relative, who had been informed of my presence, rushed out to welcome me.

The tekkyeh was beflagged in black and illuminated with hundreds of oil lamps and crystal candelabra. An immense crowd of men and children were in the middle, beating their chests and calling to Hossein, and chanting in chorus the refrain sung by the Nouheh-Khon (head of the mourning singers). The banner of Afdjeh was attached to the central pole of the tent.

The chanters had come back from their nightly procession, and the band of trumpeters and drum-beaters were sitting in one corner, drinking tea. Every shop was filled with visitors and they were all being refreshed with sherbets, tea, coffee and water-pipes. Now, a halt was called and the young singer leapt down and came to us; the shopkeepers and notables of Afdjeh gathered around.

To do honour to their illumination, the seyyed asked me to go around the tekkyeh and look at the shops. We made a procession and visited each one of these in turn. I had to drink as many small cups of coffee as there were shops; to refuse one would have been a sacrilege. And it was not sweetened—black coffee must be drunk during the month of Moharram without sugar as a sign of mourning. Our tour finished, we sat again at the place of honour, which was a niche decorated and illuminated by my relative.

The clouds of smoke and the odour of the incense, burned before the shops in charcoal brasiers, the strong aroma of coffee and rose water, made me giddy. They brought me a plate with toasted grains of coffee, some of which, out of politeness, I had to taste; they were bitter and disagreeable, but immediately after they gave me a glass of sherbet.

Abdol was sitting with us, and Katchal and his companions were being entertained in like manner in the next niche. Our hosts asked me to remain in Afdjeh for the Ashoura, the greatest day in the month of mourning, when the assassination of Hossein was to be enacted. This I had to refuse, against my will, for I knew that I should be entertained like a king.

The singer went back to the platform to sing a part of the narrative about Hossein's martyrdom—evidently, in my honour. The sadness in his voice made us all weep. Tears came rolling down my face, and, when the singer indicated with his hands that we should accompany him, the whole multitude started beating their chests in cadence. Everybody was crying aloud—in fact, howling! And some were even beating themselves on their heads and faces. From one corner, the shrieks of women were heard.

This singing and weeping is most contagious. I have seen many Faranguis crying, in Teheran, when they were allowed to assist at one of the passion plays. I was beating my chest and crying at the same time, and the singer, seeing my praiseworthy attitude, swung around, with both arms outstretched, and sang in a frenzy. The next minute, he cried out to the assistants:

"O people! O my brothers, do you not know that Hossein, for the sake of the freedom of men and for national dignity, faced the notorious army of Yazid, the accursed usurper, with only seventy men and women and children of his family? Do you know that, when he was killed, the women and children, mostly wounded, were taken as prisoners to Damascus? Do you know that martyrdom for the sake of righteousness and for upholding universal justice is the heartiest and manliest ambition a man can harbour in his bosom? Do you know that suffering the rule of usurpers and tyrants is the lowest indignity to a man's pride? Do you know that, to expose our women to the corrupt hordes of aliens to our religion and traditions, is a worse crime than if we had murdered our own mothers and sisters with our own hands? Do you know that, to leave the rights of the people in the hands of unworthy leaders is as if we had turned our backs from the world's civilisation and forgotten that there is a God?"

His voice shook with emotion and tears were streaming down his face. Finally, he could go no further. He seemed choking; he was as white as death; he gasped for breath, and, getting no relief, threw up his hands under his chin and tore his shirt open to his waist.

Words cannot describe one hundredth part of the intensity of that scene, the heart-rending cry from the multitude, "Ya Hossein! Ya Hossein!" The tents began to shake with the shrieks of women and lamentations of men. The scene went black before my eyes. In my frenzy, I rushed to the platform and stood beside the singer, unbuttoned my coat and tore my shirt, crying:

"Freedom for man and justice for the world!"

I do not remember what happened after that; I felt myself falling from a seemingly great height, against a pillar. When I opened my eyes again and my ears began to hear the whole place was ringing with the words, "Freedom for man and justice for the world! Oh, Hossein! Oh, Hossein!" And the band had started playing the saddest music ever heard.

Oh, the cries and shrieks! It was maddening! It was

thundering! I was held in the arms of the seyyed, my relative, whose turban had become disarranged around his shoulders and whose clothes were torn. He helped me back to our place and a glass of sherbet was forced to my lips. My two gholams and Abdol were still crying; the latter was beating himself on the chest, notwithstanding the fact that the band had stopped and the singer had come down from the platform to calm the people.

A crowd of women—all peasants—and children, gathered before the niche in which we were sitting. Although their faces were covered with their black tchadors, I could see by their attitude that they were waiting to see if the scene was to continue.

But, the time for dinner was near. My relative insisted that we dine with them, but I felt a most terrific headache. My appetite was dead and my only desire was to be alone. I could not think of an excuse to offer, but Abdol came to my rescue by saying that his master and his men had had their evening meal before coming into the village, and gave an exaggerated description of our servants' foresight in the matter of food, adding that we had ordered them to continue their route while we sought a place for rest in the village. This made it possible for us to escape.

A house had been already prepared for us and we left our host; the whole crowd accompanied us to the gate of the tekkyeh.

The house was a small, village dwelling—three rooms and a garden with a basin in the centre. There were no doors to the rooms and no furniture inside; the floor, the walls and the ceilings were of mud. A carpet was spread on the floor and there were two beds in the first room and two more in the room beyond.

I washed my face and hands in the basin, and went to bed immediately. Abdol slept in the other bed and the two gholams in the next room. I slept at once, but an hour or so later I awoke with a most acute feeling of hunger. There was a strong odour of food coming in at the doorway. For more than twelve hours, I had been riding without food, except for the tea, black coffee, and sherbet we had taken at the tekkyeh. I wished I had not refused the dinner my relative had offered. I called Abdol, "Are you awake?"

"Yes, Ghorban," he answered. "It must be the spirit of mourning for Hossein which keeps me from sleeping."

None of us knew that coffee might be the cause of our insomnia.

I sat up and discovered that our garden had been chosen as the place to cook the food for the tekkyeh. I could distinctly see red flames under huge cauldrons, and cooks busy filling dishes which were to be carried on large wooden platters to the tekkyeh.

"Look, look," said I to Abdol. "Tell those men I am hungry."

"What, Ghorban!" he exclaimed, as though I had insulted him. "Are you, my own sire, not aware of the impossibility of such a thing?"

"What sort of thing?"

"Asking for food!" he hissed out.

"Well, what of it? Are you not hungry too?" I asked.

"Hunger is not the word for what I feel," he answered. "I am ready to chew the sole of your boots, but the idea alone of asking for food for my high-honoured and exalted master would kill me right here in my bed!"

"But, look here," said I, "anybody might be hungry. That is no disgrace, and besides, the food is given away by my own relative!"

"Abdol-Latif may be sacrificed, but it would be beyond the dignity of the son of the high-honoured Hadj-Agha to be found without the proper number of abdars and ghahvehtchis. Besides, I have already announced in public that we have dined."

"It was certainly unwise to have left our servants behind," I said.

"The fault is mine," said he, quite undisturbed.

"Why not look for them? They may arrive at any moment," I suggested.

"Katchal has left word with people in the tekkyeh to tell them where to find us, but I am sure they will not arrive during the night."

"See if Katchal is awake. He may find a solution," I said.

He returned to say that Katchal and his men were not in their beds.

"I am sure they have gone to supper!" I remarked.

"No doubt, but they are servants."

"Then what can I do? I am really very hungry."

"I advise that your high and honourable person try to forget it," said he.

"Then please tell those men not to pass so near; the odour is too tempting!"

"With pleasure," he said and immediately put his head out of the door space and whispered to one of the men to warn his colleagues that his master was sleeping and that they should not cross the yard so close to our door, as their footsteps were annoying.

Although the men complied with his instruction, I could still smell food. Abdol's compassion seemed touched because he put his head close to me and whispered, "Are you asleep, sire?"

"Not yet."

"Are you still hungry?"

"Very!"

"May I give you some wonderful pills to make you sleep and to give you the necessary force to overcome your hunger?"

"No!" I said decidedly.

"What about my ring?" he asked.

"I cannot eat a ring," I answered, wondering at my own patience and endurance.

"No, but, this special ring has a wonderful Aghigh"—bloodstone—"and if you put it in your mouth and suck it, your hunger and thirst will gradually disappear," he explained. "It has appeased my own hunger and I know it will benefit you in the same way."

I was about to ask him to give it to me, when I remembered that he must have had the stone in his own mouth all night. I decided to wait for the morning.

Very early we started on our journey. We were to ride to the high rock, four hours away from Afdjeh, and watch there for the Imperial Dragon, the Shah's ordou.

Akbar had told us exactly where to wait. Luckily for me, before we had gone far, we saw a shepherd who gave us food. It was Katchal who discovered him. Sighting a herd, he sang aloud the Persian peasant song, which says:

"When you see a shepherd, be sure there is also a goat, and where you find a goat, you may be sure of finding milk, and where there is milk, you may be sure of finding Persian hospitality."

We found all these at once. A herd of sheep and goats was grazing along the green slopes of the hillside, and high up on the summit a piece of cloth was pitched to form a rude tent. We galloped toward it and found a young man in a short, thick doublet and large, white, cloth trousers. His feet were bare and he came forward, with a long stick in his hand, watching us closely.

"Hey, Khoda Barekat!" exclaimed Katchal. "God give you plenty."

The boy threw his head up, looked at the sky and said, "For every mouth God has provided food, welcome to mine if you are travellers."

"We are travelling behind the Shah, lost our men and mules, slept a night of hunger and have many hours to journey," replied Katchal.

"The sun is gloriously shining and darting his arrows. Come under the shelter and rest; there is food for a regiment."

We dismounted; the horses immediately began to gaze with the sheep. The shepherd called out to one of his goats, who seemed to understand him, for she came to him at once. He unbuckled a sack which he carried on his shoulders and took out a wooden bowl, which he milked half full. Then he picked up a handful of stones, hot from the sun, and threw them into it. Next he took from his sack a few pieces of dried bread and a wooden spoon. He spread a cloth before me and set everything on it. We all sat around it. He crumbled a piece of bread between his palms and dropped it into the milk until the bowl was filled. When this was done, the meal was ready and he invited, "Please, strangers, partake of my food which, although poor in quality, is presented with all my heart."

He handed me the spoon and the others ate with their fingers. I never enjoyed a meal more. The bowl was soon empty, but our host filled it again by milking another goat and crumbling more bread. This time, we were all satisfied. He then brought a long-handled pipe, filled it with tobacco and lighted it. After drawing a puff to see that it worked well, he presented it to Abdol who, after myself, seemed the next in rank. Abdol thanked him for his courtesy and told him he would not smoke. Thereupon, he presented the pipe to Katchal, who took it and went behind the shade to smoke, since servants never smoked before their masters, nor, in fact, ate before them; but, when travelling, both servants and masters observed the laws of the highroads and allowed a less rigid display of formality in their relations. Katchal knew he could have smoked before me there, but he liked being punctilious and did not want to set a bad example for his companion, the other gholam.

The shepherd sat, as behooved the host, in front of me. He was a tall young man and very handsome, with the two characteristic features of his race plainly marking him, namely, a prominent chest between his square shoulders and a Persian nose, which closely resembled a battering ram.

He was very much interested when we told him that we were joining the Shah's ordou, and asked so many questions that Abdol took it upon himself to enlighten him.

"This present journey," said he, in condescending tone, as if he were about to disclose a secret of state, "is something more than the yearly camping of his majesty. Very soon, his majesty will celebrate the jubilee of his fiftieth anniversary[1] since he came to the throne, and so this year's ordou must surpass all the others. His travel through the jungle of Mazenderan will mark the beginning of his third cycle in life and the climax of his reign as the Shadow of Allah."

"What was the nature of his first and second cycles?" asked the boy.

"The first was when, as a young sovereign, he was attacked by a royal tiger, while hunting in Djadjoroud. But, his majesty's star being ascendant, his august person came out unhurt and the insolent beast was ripped open by the royal hands. The second cycle was when he was shot at by a group of men, in the clothes of women, supposed to have belonged to the religious sect of Babi."

The shepherd and I sat listening with great attention.

"What is to happen during the third cycle?" I asked.

"The third cycle, Ghorban, will pass as harmlessly as the two others: his majesty will issue, on the day of its beginning, universal amnesty, and grants of ten years'

---

[1] Counted according to the Mohammedan Calendar.

exemption from taxes, and will declare himself no more Master and Lord of the Country but Father to His Subjects."

"Let us hope," said the boy bitterly, "that the day will soon arrive."

At this moment, Katchal called out that it was time to start. While I was waiting for my horse, I asked Abdol if we could do anything for the boy or give him money.

"No, sire, a shepherd is a king on his hillside and a king cannot be paid back."

The horses were fetched and I got into the saddle. But, somehow, I felt that I owed this shepherd an extra politeness. "Our gholams will be leaving us this afternoon, going back to Afdjeh, and I hope they will meet you again and bring you our thanks for the noble hospitality which we have received at your hands," I said.

"I deserve no thanks; I have performed a duty," he replied. "Besides, your gholams will not find me here when they return."

"Are you moving?" I asked.

He smiled. "I have no other choice than to get myself and my herd as far as possible from the view of the returning camel drivers."

"But, why should their coming cause you to leave?"

"His majesty has not yet reached his third cycle. He has not yet declared himself the Father of His Subjects; therefore, neither my own life nor my herd are safe, once the Shah is on the other side of the mountain."

"You do not mean that these men would hurt you?" I asked.

"No, but they would carry away my herd to the last goat!"

I felt very sorry for the boy, but, I found myself at a loss for a reply. He read my discomfort, for he smiled again and said, "I must thank you for the kindness of your heart. And, be assured, I shall take care of myself and of my charge."

"I hope the day may come soon when the Shah will become the Father of his Subjects," I said, putting spurs to my horse.

"We have our Father *there*," he said, pointing to the heavens, "and the Unseen Hand will rid us from oppression." These were the last words I heard as we turned to make our way towards the rock from which we were to watch the ordou pass.

III

THE PASSING OF THE IMPERIAL ORDOU

THE ORDOU was threading its way in a long procession of men and beasts along the narrow paths of the Elburz Mountains, forming a caravan which rivalled those of the Caliph of Bagdad, Haroun-al-Raschid. Long before I could see them I could hear the hollow, deep notes of the caravan bells making fantastic music among the mountains. They had been moving night and day, halting only a few hours before dawn to rest the animals.

The whole troup was following a long string of camels, who slouched and climbed slowly behind the famous drunken camel, their leader, the proudest animal of the imperial ghetar. He was a Bactrian dromedary, as big as an elephant, with two humps and dark brown hair falling in thick, flat plaits on either side of his neck. He was caparisoned with purple embroideries and held his head high in the air while he climbed steadily, with measured and rhythmic step. Two bells hung from heavy silver chains at either side against his flanks, giving forth, with each step, deep, resonant notes of such volume that their echoes bellowed and roared like a horde of hungry lions. And this King of Camels was led by none other than the Supreme Marshall of the Imperial Camel-Drivers—a man of the same structure and figure as the dromedary himself, and as proud and grave as if the entire caravan belonged to him and to none else. The drunken camel behaved as if he were really drunk with alcohol. He was restless with his head, irritated and snap-

239

ping, uttering angry growls or a low-pitched moan from slathering jaws, white with froth.

Behind him came a train of Arabian camels with one hump, loaded with tents and accessories, looking, with their curved necks, like monstrous ghosts under the shadow of the dark slants of the mountains towering two thousand feet high.

It was well know that camels were not fit for travelling in the rugged mountains of Elburz but the Shah, intent upon making a great show, had ordered that they be used to make up the imperial gala. Some of the officials had planned to ask the Shah to let them go back to Teheran as soon as they were on the downward descent, but meanwhile the camel-drivers gave vent to their righteous complaints and raised Hell and Heaven against the tyranny of their imperial master, the Shah.

After the camels, more fantastic, more colourful and noisier came the royal mules. A mule almost hidden with embroideries, draperies and ornaments came into view. By his side walked the High Chief of the Shah's Mule-Drivers, a man notorious for his dare-deviltry. He was dressed in a long, blue coat, plaited in the back, which covered a white shirt, open under his short tunic of Ispahan ghalamakar, tightened at the waist by a red silk girdle with a short dagger pushed through its fold, a pair of trousers so short that they reached only to his knees, and a pair of guiveh on his feet. He wore on his head a Persian mashdi hat of lambskin. It was long and egg-shaped and he wore it at a rakish angle. His face was clean-shaven except for a fierce mustache which suggested two sharp, straight spear points. A long sword hung from his red silk sash by a pair of red silk fringes which touched the ground. As he came, he filled the air with terrible oaths, swearing indiscriminately at the sky and mountains, insulting the mules as well as all the members of the caravan, including the Shah!

"Damn the whole world! Curse the whole bunch of them! Go through this hell of mountains as if we were goats! No roads, not even a decent path for the beasts to take a foothold! Yes! Damn the whole world and damn the Kajars!"

But, this was no cause for alarm; the insults from the mule-drivers, addressed mostly to His Imperial Majesty, the Shah of Shahs, were the spice of the journey. His Majesty had heard them, time after time, and I believe really enjoyed the anger of these hardy people. Upon one occasion, when a mule-driver was cursing him almost under his nose, he exclaimed in sheer pleasure:

"Ho, pedar soukhte! Ho, pedar soukhte"—"Oh, son of a burned father. I should give his head to be cut off, but he is courageous! He is courageous! Indeed, he is our imperial mule-driver!"

It may be that the Shah, admired this lawless crowd so different from the cowardly members of his own corrupt entourage. A flutter of an eyelash or a high-pitched tone from the greatest among his dignitaries and viziers would have made him call the executioner, but these mule-drivers were different.

At sight of the mule-drivers, I became excited; my horse, reflecting my mood began to fret, and it took all the skill I possessed to keep him in hand. I was keenly watching a man who was walking beside the chief mule-driver, dressed exactly like him, with the difference that he wore his blue coat folded and thrown over his shoulder so that his face was half hidden from me and my men. He held in his hand a pipe two feet long, (the usual length for a mashdi's pipe) smoked and walked in silence. Although I could not, from this distance, recognise his face, I had no doubt the man was Akbar! Akbar, my bodyguard, in company with the chief of the Shah's mule-drivers! I said nothing of this discovery to my companions, but bent my attention upon the pageant.

Several hundred mules followed the first and, with them, hundreds of mule tenders. These animals were all charged with equipment and carrying bells of different size and sound, which pealed a symphony that the mountains echoed and repeated with exaggerated force and volume. The effect was stupendous! The ordou crowd followed—thousands of servants and attendants, old and young, on mules and horses, some sitting high on luggage and bags. After these, there was a breach, during which I marvelled at the string of camels and mules zigzagging, like a huge serpent, against the mountain slope.

"There they come again!" exclaimed Abdol and I looked to see a procession of riflemen advancing. They were dressed in coarse, black tunics and black riding boots, rifles slung on their shoulders, and each wearing two belts of cartridges. They were immediately followed by another regiment of warriors wearing huge, round hats (big as pumpkins) made of sheepskin, with long hairs drooping from the brims over their faces. They carried no arms except swords, which were tucked at the sides of their saddles under their legs; in their hands were long whips. These were the Shah's warriors, called Shah-Savans. I believe there were thousands of them.

A pause, then a procession of hundreds of riders, richly dressed and very colourful; these were the high officials, officers, equerries, and attendants belonging to the imperial harem. Behind these, a crowd of eunuchs, white and black, young and old, all richly dressed. The chargers of the group before them and their own were the most beautifully equipped of all the ordou. Their harnesses were either of solid gold or of silver. Here and there came other horsemen in saddle, leading other riderless horses with tails painted red. These horses with red tails were of purest Arab stock and, on this rough road, their presence was for show, not use. I was glad I had left mine behind in Teheran.

Here now, came the members of the harem! The women! Hundreds of them, riding astride, with their faces unveiled! Many had swords tucked at the sides of their saddles; a few had, actually, short, double-edged swords hanging from under their tchadors. Brave women—the bravest among the feminine members of the Shah's harem.

Behind them rode the Queen, Ghamar-ed-Dowleh, and the favourites, all young girls and young women. I knew that Tuberose was with her. Because of the earnest entreaties of the Queen the Princess Ezzat-ed-Dowleh had graciously allowed the girl to go on the northern trip. The women had discarded their long, white veils for short black ones, called neghabs. (These are like handkerchiefs, about five inches square and made of horsehair woven by hand.) Following the Queen and the favourites, came more eunuchs and more men and women; these last men were the pages and chamberlains of the harem and the attachés to the persons of the Queen and favourites. The women were the ladies-in-waiting and heads of departments, numbering about five or six hundred in all.

Now, another regiment of Shah-Savans. After them, a breach of nearly half an hour. This gave me time to keep my attention on the ladies who were riding skilfully through the narrow passages between the mountain peaks and the immense precipices, which separated them from the rock where I sat watching. Presently, other horsemen, riding tandem, two-by-two, at a distance of a hundred feet apart. These were high officials and dignitaries and Khans and chieftains from the North, in front of the imperial procession and behind the imperial harem. No servants rode in this group. When the last pair turned the corner and began the zigzagging ascent, a single horseman came into view.

His Imperial Majesty the Shah! The Shadow of Allah! He was dressed in a short sardari, with turned-back collar, a round military hat with no ornament and high, shining, black riding boots. His horse was a beautiful white Arab with red tail. The purple cloth under the saddle was embroidered heavily with fine pearls portraying the Persian emblem, the Lion and the Sun, embellished with precious stones which scintillated in the sunshine. The pommel of the saddle and the harness were of solid gold heavily bejewelled. A pair of pistols in holsters set with diamonds, emeralds and rubies, forming the Persian insignia, was slung on the front of the saddle. The Shah himself wore no jewels except a belt made of leather and covered with black velvet set with diamonds. A double-edged sword with handle and sheath set with jewels was hanging from his belt. On the forehead of the royal charger there flamed, like a burning coal, a diamond as dazzling and as large as the famous "Sea of Light," mate of the Kohinoor.

But that which really singled the Shah out among the hundreds of horsemen (their chargers glittering with gold and precious metals) was the purple parasol which his majesty carried, the insignia of the most dreaded monarch in the Orient and the most powerful Shah of Persia. I confess that he seemed to me the handsomest man I had ever seen.

The Shah rode alone. Only two footmen, in their ancient, purple costumes, funny red headgear, shaped like the crown of a prince, and white breeches, carrying gold and bejewelled sceptres, walked at the side of his stirrups.

Fifty yards behind him the courtiers were coming up. Among them two figures stood out prominently—a seyyed with large black turban and a black aba, riding a black mule, and immediately behind him the mollah bashi, with enormous white turban and white aba, riding a grey mule. Hundreds of men, composing the royal suite, brought up the rear, and after them came the bashi and their acolytes: abdars, for tea and water pipes, ghahveh-tchis, for coffee, sherbet-tchis, for sherbets and water, and others, for clothes, arms, rifles and so forth, each with his numerous subordinates, forming, in all, a group as large as any before them. Then came more warriors, more gholams and what-not!

From where I sat on my horse I could see the whole party stretched out on the serpentine path. The head of the ordou, which started with the drunken dromedary, was now high up, near the mountain peak; the huge animal looked, from where I sat, no larger than a chicken! The whole procession formed the legendary Chinese dragon, creeping up above the rugged rocks on the edge of deep canyons, looping and zigzagging for miles and miles. It took the ordou more than six hours to move over the mountain.

When we saw the last horseman turning the cliff, Abdol took a large watch from his pocket, and said: "We had better start at once. We must meet your Khan brother on the summit of the mountain."

IV

A NIGHT IN THE MOUNTAINS

KATCHAL guided us down to the base of the mountain, and then took leave of us. He saw to my rifle, and although he assured me that the ordou of the Shah must have frightened all the animals around, warned me that I might have occasion to use it.

We made haste then to climb as high as we could before the sun went down. Half way to the top Abdol halted and descended from his horse, murmuring all sorts of reproaches to himself.

"What is the matter?" I asked.

"I have forgotten my Koran," he said, taking out of his saddle bag a leather belt. To this was attached a small sack, also made of leather, in which he carried a copy of Koran. He took the Koran in both hands, kissed it with great respect and strapped the belt over his left shoulder. Then he seemed more at ease and sat comfortably on his horse.

"Now we can face the whole world and all the beasts and jinnees therein!" he declared triumphantly.

"Do you think there are jinnees in these mountains?" I asked.

"Plenty of them and very dangerous too!" he answered, adding that the day jinnees were more troublesome than those who wandered abroad during the night. "The night jinnees," he explained, "will strangle anybody who has the misfortune to step on their tails or hurt the baby jinnees. Happily," he said, "we know that the simple invocation of the first

246

verse of the Koran will frighten them away. But the day jinnee or ghoul, is by nature a fiend who delights in playing tricks on the lonely traveller either by appearing before his eyes in all his native monstrousness or else in the guise of a fellow traveller, so as to betray him by leading him into a part of the mountain from which he will never be able to find his way."

"It is fortunate that we know our way," I said, more to relieve my own mind than to comfort Abdol.

"Oh, decidedly," he answered, "The only trouble is that the ghouls may try to frighten our horses and make them throw us into the ravine."

I clutched at my bridle.

"There is no need to be uneasy," he assured me. "This Koran will show them that we are amply protected."

Of course I trusted the Koran, but nevertheless I touched my hat to make sure that the mysterious amulet my coloured governess had secretly sewn into the lining of my hat was still there. The amulet was a tiny sack of lion's skin containing a single front tooth of a Caspian tiger. She believed that it would make my flesh unpalatable to all the wild beasts except the wolf.

The sun was gradually setting on the other side of the mountains. This side was becoming dusky, and where the shadows fell thick it was dark as night.

We were descending toward the valley with a vast forest before us encircled by a mountain belt. Huge clouds, very thick, were hanging low over the forest, and in some places towers of vapour were shooting up into the air. Half way down we halted, to see if we could detect light below. The air was cold, damp, and heavy. My hands felt sticky and wet. The horses shivered.

I thought I saw a light in the forest and notified Abdol, who was scrutinising the valley.

"That is not the light we are after," he said. "What you see is a bonfire made by a wood-chopper or——"

He stopped short and made the Koranic invocation saying: "In the name of Allah the Merciful!"

"By whom?" I shouted in anxiety.

"It is better not to mention the name in this hour of the evening," he remonstrated quietly.

I felt goose flesh and invoked Allah's name as fast as I could. Could it be possible that the light I saw was a fire made up by the ghouls to lure us into their den and turn us into wanderers for the rest of our lives?

"Let us be going," I said. "Down in the valley we will be in a better position. We may even come across a wood-chopper."

"Allah spare us!" exclaimed Abdol earnestly. Then he raised his voice to a high pitch and cried: "No, we do not desire to meet any wood-chopper! We are carrying our Koran and let all those concerned at this minute about us, or watching us, hear me saying: 'Allah is great and merciful!' "

I realized what he meant, and gave him a helping hand.

"Yes, we are protected by our Koran!" I shouted keeping my eyes on the gloomy air around. I thought our faithful chargers must be quite aware of our pluck, because mine had his ears cocked like a pair of daggers. I had been told that animals were the first to discover the presence of jinnees and ghouls. I kept my eyes on the direction in which the ears pointed, but saw nothing except the narrow path which descended the mountain, and lost itself under the shrubs where the forest began.

Finally Abdol decided to advance, but when he noticed that the path was not large enough for both of us riding abreast he urged his horse to take the road first. Evidently he was afraid to ride behind, where a ghoul might snatch him off without my knowing it.

This was not so much of a surprise to me, as the fact that I, myself, felt also a most terrible dread of riding behind! Although I did not say a word to Abdol, I urged my horse to keep pace with his. Jostling them together this way was sufficient to upset our horses who, until now, had behaved admirably. We discovered then, that they too objected to advance. Their feet were unsteady and they began to stumble at every step. And no wonder! The path was only an opening made by wood-choppers who had cut the trees four or five inches above the ground; the stumps, sharp as knives, covered on the ground and made it look like the floor of a torture chamber.

"We must go back," I said to Abdol, "this road is not practicable."

"This is certainly no road," he answered emphatically. Very dejected, he added: "I wish I knew where the good roads were!"

"What! Do you mean you do not know the roads?" I cried out.

"Yes, yes, I know the roads," he drawled (implying that he did not mean what he said), and then began to growl to himself: "Let us to the open. There I can think better," he finally said.

We returned in silence and Abdol pushed his horse against mine and whispered into my ear: "For God's sake, keep the secret which I shall impart to your honoured person: will you?"

"What is it, Abdol?"

"Well, Ghorban, we are lost!" he whispered.

It was strange that even in that extremity I did not lose my patience. I did not even feel angry. I only remarked: "It is very unpleasant to be lost at this place, and I could really never believe you capable of losing yourself!"

"But I never lose myself, Ghorban," he said, "and even now I claim that we are not lost."

"What are we then?"

"We are played upon and tricked by—by—you know what I mean. I do not mention their names."

"What a fool he is!" I thought to myself. I had almost forgotten the existence of those nightly and daily jinnees and ghouls until he reminded me of them!

"Look here," I said to him, "you have said so much about them that I am sure you must have attracted their attention to us. The only thing for us now is to say as many besmellahs as we can and proceed to find the road. Follow me."

I took the lead. After a few hundred yards again I noticed a light coming from the centre of the forest.

"There must be a road to that place," I remarked to Abdol, and turned the head of my horse toward the place where the trees and bushes seemed sparse. Abdol followed without protest. It was easier to see the ground here than in the open. The forest became thinner and at some places large spaces were free from growth. Presently I saw an open field covered with huge trunks of felled trees. The light was just in front of us. My horse became more willing.

"That must be an aghol," remarked Abdol.

"What is an aghol?" I asked.

"Where the cattle herder keeps his cattle during the night. We may find refuge," he replied.

"You see now the Koran is protecting us and God guiding us," I murmured reverently.

The black shape of a low-roofed dwelling was before us and a meagre bonfire flashed invitingly from inside. The ground was soggy. It was evident that it had been raining. There was not a sound. The cattle herders in Mazenderan were not in the habit of having watchdogs otherwise I was sure a dog would have welcomed us by barking. Into the doorless entrance Abdol pushed his head, calling:

"Hey! father, is there anyone here?" He received no answer.

He called again and again. All in vain.

There was another compound behind the first which served as stable and storehouse.

"We better remain here," I said as I dismounted. "There must be plenty of forage in the shack for our horses."

"The man who made this fire must have noticed our approach and concealed himself," remarked Abdol.

"Strange people," I commented, "to run away before two peaceful travellers who come to them for refuge."

"Do not misjudge them, Ghorban," replied Abdol. "They believe us to be horsemen of the Shah or his suite."

"We shall leave money for what we get," I said.

"And I shall willingly give them my medical service," Abdol murmured.

I was leading my horse to the second compound when Abdol stopped me.

"No!" he cried. "The fire is a proof that the jungle is infested by beasts of prey. We had better keep our horses with us."

We took them into our own compound, where they began eating dried hay. Their saddles we used as cushions to lie upon. I had taken off my thick coat but not the heavy cartridge belts. Laleh had stressed upon my mind that under no circumstance should I relieve myself of them while I was on the road. I put my firearm at my side. Abdol felt rather sad that he could not imitate me, but he had only a funny old flintlock and it was wet and useless. I remarked: "I am going to sleep; take my gun and use it if necessary."

"I had rather use my own, if you do not mind. I am more familiar with it."

"But yours is wet and has to be charged again."

"I shall discharge it first," he replied, taking up the old gun. A minute after, a terrible sound, resembling that made by the explosion of a bomb, filled the forest. Abdol came back, exclaiming: "I am so happy! Now I can load it with real bullets!"

Then searching the place he found a wooden plate with a cake of kateh, (boiled rice) dried and hard as a brick. Kateh was the only food these people had. It was made of the cheapest kind of rice, very coarse and unfit for food. The landlord and the tax collector got every single grain of the famous Persian rice cultivated in Mazenderan and the peasants who raised it had to feed on the kateh which now and then they ate with raw onions. I began to discover how ignorant I had been about the life of the peasants! I had thought they lived wholesomely and had even thought they were better off than the average dwellers of the big cities. "They have all the lands, all the cattle, and all the fruits," I had always said to myself, "while we have to buy them!"

"Do you think you can find some milk or water to drink?" I asked Abdol.

"We are not accustomed to the Mazenderan water yet," he replied. "The only water we may drink without risk is spring water which I doubt very much to find here. But I may find some milk." He went around the cabin and brought back an empty skin used as a water bag.

"This had been filled with doug—"clabbered milk"—and water. It is still wet, but not a drop of doug!" he said dejectedly.

I asked Abdol if this hard cake of rice and clabbered milk was all the food these people in the forest lived upon.

"In most cases they have only the cake. The clabbered milk is a luxury," he said.

"And yet they have all the cattle?" I remarked astonished.

"Yes they have them to attend to!" he said sadly, "But every drop of milk will go to make butter, cheese, mast and kashk—"curd and whey"—for the landlord or to sell in the market to pay the rent and taxes."

"So this is the way people live under the Shadow of Allah!" I cried in disgust.

"It is the truth," answered Abdol.

"Give me another piece of cake," I demanded, and bit it as if it were the head of the Shah. "I shall tell this to the Queen and to the Princess Ezzat-ed-Dowleh, and to the Shah. See if I do not!"

"I have no doubt you will, but I doubt very much if it will help," he answered, avoiding my eyes.

"I hope the inhabitants of this place will not bear us grudge for having invaded their home," I said.

"They will feel grateful that we have not burned the place for spite! That is what has been done by some of the government officials ——" Abdol was about to say more when the report of a rifle shot came to our ears.

"Did you hear that?" I asked. "Do these cattle herders use firearms?"

"Very seldom. They do not know how to fire them, but there is no cause for worry. We have our guns."

Thereupon I placed my head on the saddle to sleep. Abdol covered my shoulder with my coat and tucked my legs under the saddle cloth.

As a rule I slept soundly during the trip, but that night I dreamed I was attacked by a tiger, and when I tried to fire at it my gun refused to work. I dreamed I was lost in the jungle and surrounded by four highwaymen who were threatening me with daggers and swords. I tried to defend myself only to find that I had taken Abdol's worthless rifle by mistake. The most terrible dream, which made me cry for help, was when I dreamed the cabin was on fire and I and my horse caught in the flames. I shouted so loudly that my own cries awoke me. I looked up and saw that the fire was burning high and that there were two other men with Abdol conversing in low tones. Their backs were to me.

To my great surprise the man nearest turned to me and said:

"Well, my dear little brother, who ever thought of finding you in this place!"

It was my brother, the doctor. I arose immediately and began to rub my eyes.

"You are not dreaming and we are not ghouls! Come dear," said my brother, "permit me to introduce you to the Mirza Seyyed Abdollah, the High Scrivener of his excellency Nasr-es-Sultaneh."

I bowed to the High Scrivener and said that I was absolutely delighted to find him with us. He laughed and answered that he was a thousand times more pleased to find me and my companion safe. "The good and faithful Abdol-Latif has given us the details of your adventure," he said "We expected you at the little village a few miles away where we had posted men to guide you to us. After sunset we waited for some hours and finally came to the conclusion that you had lost your way. We left the house of the village chief to search for you and passed half way the good old man and his son in whose home we are now gathered."

"Do you mean the people who live in these shacks?" I asked.

"Yes, they had sighted you long before you entered the forest. Taking you for unruly guests they ran away to report the presence of dangerous night marauders to the chief of the village. Happily the firing of the gun gave us the right direction. You can guess the rest. Your brother is a great friend of these people. There is not a cabin, where he will not be received with open arms. But here comes our host."

I turned back and beheld a genial old man smiling at me. He had a thick coat, and trousers made of tchoukha, a woollen fabric which is manufactured in Mazenderan and is famous for its waterproof quality—most appropriate for the part of the country where it rains all the year around. My brother asked him to come near.

"Here is my little brother whom you took for a dangerous highwayman!" said the doctor to him in the dialect of the north.

"Ema tera Gherban berem," he said to me, which means "I shall be sacrificed to you," and many other phrases in the same spirit. While he was talking I noticed a little fellow not taller than myself, dressed exactly like his father, peeping at me through the opening at the back of the shack.

I motioned him to come to me. He looked like a little man on account of his dress, but was still very shy and childlike. I tried to speak to him but he was unable to understand me. He knew only the northern dialect. He was called Riga, which in the northern dialect means a boy.

"Poor little chap!" I said to my brother, "he must have a very monotonous life here."

"My dear boy," answered my brother, "this little scamp was the one who sighted you first and warned his father. He can hear a footstep miles away. He can see during the night just as we can in the day. He can smell a wild beast three hundred yards off and can fight and overcome him at close quarters."

"Do you mean that he really fights wild beasts?" I asked.

My brother spoke to the old man, who went out and returned with a beautiful bearskin.

"This is the last victim of this little child," said my brother.

The boy was growing red in the face.

"How did he do it?" I asked.

"He tried to catch the bear alive to play with, but he fought so strenuously that the boy struck him with his hatchet on the head, then strangled him."

"I wish I could have him to be my servant," I said.

"I am afraid his father cannot spare him," my brother said pleasantly.

"Let us ask him." I suggested.

Yes, he was unwilling to let his son go away, but if I decided to remain in Mazenderan longer than the summer season, his father would allow him to come to me wherever I happened to be, on the condition that I bring him back when leaving the country. The boy seemed pleased and insisted upon giving me the skin. This I had to decline. We had no way to take care of it. Then he brought a sack, with which, he told me, I could catch a young bear alive. I accepted with thanks, though very doubtful of my success with it, but when I tried to make him take some money his father protested.

"We are poor Mazenderany, but we are the lords of our hut," he said proudly.

At dawn we saddled our horses. The little boy insisted upon helping me and made sure that I took the sack for the bears. He accompanied us to the entrance of the mountain corridor keeping step with my horse and laughing at my suggestion that he ride behind Abdol. With the help of Abdol I was able now to understand him and asked him if he were not afraid to go back all alone to his father. He assured me that nothing would frighten him. He had nothing but contempt for all the divs and ghouls and jinnees; as for robbers, he had nothing worth taking. He and his father were afraid of nothing but government officials. These, in his opinion, were the worst creatures among the inhabitants of the world of darkness. They had no morals or pity. They would cause the death of men, women and children for the sake of money. They would burn their homes and take away their daughters to confine them in their harem or give them to their servants. In answer to my question as to why the jungle people did not kill them, the boy said that these cruel men would not present themselves as fighters, although they were armed with rifles and swords. "Besides," he confided to me, "if you protest or make complaint to the

Chief of the District, he will never trouble himself to protect you. He is very much afraid of the Shah. The Governor may take away all our help and young boys as soldiers and starve them to death."

The boy's interpretation of Persia's government was very exact, and I wondered in what school he had been brought up to know so much!

Shortly he pointed to a chain of mountains saying we were nearing the corridor. The road passed between two chains of jagged peaks, so high that the entrance looked like the opening of a monstrous grotto.

At this point we bade Riga farewell, turned around a high cliff, climbed up a narrow crag, and entered into the dark and yawning chasm.

V

CROSSING THE FAMOUS MOUNTAIN
CORRIDOR

AT FIRST we climbed a narrow serpentine path which was badly damaged and at some places quite worn off and dangerous. Half way up the corridor became very dark. The mountain peaks from both chains approached one another from opposite sides and fitted here and there so closely one might think we were inside a huge skeleton with its hideous skull and bare teeth set tightly against each other. The thundering of the river below, came to us in a terrific uproar. It took all my courage to glance over the side of the precipice, where I could see only a few hundred yards of sharp and precipitous rock. After that was nothing but a black pit from which a damp breath as of steam was floating and hovering over the chasm like phantoms of ugly monsters.

I am sure we too looked like phantoms. We rode in a column; Abdol was in front, I after him, my brother behind me, and the seyyed the last. No wonder the ordou had taken another road. It would need a year to cross this one. Now I could understand why people living in this part of the country feared no enemies. A single man sitting on the top of one of the crags could send a whole army into the pit below. He would have only to push each horseman over with his hand or a stick. The famous Persian hero Rostam had passed through this corridor to attack the notorious White Monster, who at the time was the only living monster defying the power of the Persian monarch.

After my eyes became more accustomed to the gloom, I

could see a wealth of wild growth far below in the ravine, where clouds of steam rolled and unrolled.   Among these monstrous plants I noticed one called gol-par, which is very much like cowslip and of the same family as rhubarb; its fleshy stalk was used for pickles, its seed dried and pulverized used as spice.   Here these plants were so immense that I thought I was deceived by the darkness and the long distance, but the Seyyed remarked that this was the land of divs; creatures hundreds of feet in length with the structure of prehistoric monsters and proportionately long horns and arms.   "Wait until you see geranium trees on the height of the Elburz mountain!"

"Look at that dark green roof and tell me what it is," he said to me behind my back.   But I would not try.   What I could already see was sufficiently terrifying.   I thought it wise to look straight before me at Abdol's back.   I wished also that my horse would keep close to the rocky wall at my right instead of to the left, but somehow he seemed to prefer the dangerous edge.   I wondered if he had any idea of what he was doing, but I did not disturb him.

"Did you look at the green roof?" called the seyyed again.

"Oh, it is wonderful!   By the way, what is it?" I answered, excusing myself to God for the untruth.

"That is only a leaf," the seyyed informed me.

"Probably a clover leaf," I remarked.

"Decidedly an up-to-date knowledge and quite appropriate for the occasion," he replied, "but it happens to be only a leaf of Bargueh-Baba-Adam"—Father Adam's leaf.

"Yes, Ghorban," came from Abdol, who had been listening to the conversation, "his highness Adam, who, we are told, was so large it took some minutes for a man to travel around him, could not have had a smaller leaf than this."

"Watch your step," my brother said to Abdol, "you are coming to the curve."

To my horror I saw the path completely disappear fifty

feet ahead of us—a sharp point dashing into the unknown with a sort of fence of wooden logs at its edge to form a barrier between the path and the precipice. Within a few yards of this place the path became a little wider.

"Halt!" my brother commanded Abdol.

Abdol dismounted and I with a beating heart let myself slip down at the side of the saddle. Oh, how happy I felt! The touch of the earth made me feel like a new born baby. I thought how pleasant it would be if my brother would let me walk to Yoush.

Now I could look behind. Both my brother and the seyyed were on foot leading their horses. This corner, called "The Curving Nose," seemed to be a platform hanging over the air. The wooden fence was in pieces; there was no sign to show that beyond it was nothing but empty air.

Three times I invoked the prophets and said: "In the name of Allah the Merciful," and then blew my breath, thus saturated with the invocation, at my horse, to make him calm and steady. Abdol passed first and disappeared with his horse. I followed very carefully, shaving closely the rocky wall of the mountain and keeping my eyes away from the Nose. Soon I found myself safe on the other side. Two seconds after, my horse appeared at the end of the bridle in my hand. Not a muscle of his face moved. The same expression of trust and faith was manifest in his dear eyes.

"You are the soul of my soul," I told him, "and I have no doubt that you, like myself, prefer to walk unhindered. Do you not?"

"I am sure all our horses do," my brother answered coming in view. "We will walk for a while; it will do us good."

Now that I was sure of walking, my courage came back, and I looked around. The growth of weird trees and plants formed an uncanny vista. The Adam's leaves were the largest I ever had seen or ever saw again. Some of these plants bore blossoms like a large platter, but they had no colour. Doctor explained that this was because of the darkness.

"What a pity we cannot see the dragons which must be crawling underneath," remarked Abdol.

"I am glad they cannot come up," said the seyyed. "There you contemplate the wisdom of Allah who allows the monsters to live and die yet creates a wall they cannot move beyond. Thus we understand that Allah is great and his prophet Mohammad is the last of his messengers!"

"Bellah ke tcheninast,"—"To God that it is so," commented Abdol.

"Allah will be more pleased if we walk with some speed," my brother said. "We have the other half of the corridor to go."

I was feeling already as if I had enough. I preferred the beauty of the garden in the harem and the palace of Sultanat-Abad to these majestic mountains and this abnormal growth. I would not, even now, give a single petal of the Mohammadi rose for a collection of these Adam's leaves. Nor did my idea of the greatness of Allah grow bigger through the sight of these fantastic creations.

I had been walking and thinking for some time when Abdol drew my attention to the place where a well known sculptor had carved in the rock the image of the Shah and his ministers. The artist had chosen a place where the path is a little wider and travellers are able to stand before the picture. My brother and the seyyed halted with us.

"A masterpiece," remarked the Scrivener.

"Very imposing!" agreed my brother.

"What a pity the artist did not take time to represent his majesty with his whole court," was Abdol's remark.

But what interested me most was that the right eye of the Shah was badly injured.

"What has been the matter with that eye?" I asked.

No one made an answer and I repeated my question again, but to my great surprise none ventured any comment. It seemed as if none of them knew anything about it. I turned to my brother.

"I think I knew the story, but somehow I do not recollect the details," he answered tactfully, and that was all I could learn.

There was another interesting scene farther along the road. At a certain place where the mountains brought their summits so closely together that the corridor seemed really like a long grotto, my brother ordered a halt and asked me to look up where the light entered.

Above our heads, near the mountain skylight, something was hanging to a point of a projecting rock.

"What do you suppose that is?" asked the seyyed.

"To me it seems to be a bow," I answered.

He laughed and urged me to take a second look. The skylight was so far above my head that it was necessary to support the back of my head against the mountain to obtain a good view.

"It certainly looks like a bow," was my answer.

"No, sire, it is a firearm, like the one Abdol has on his shoulder. If you look well you will see it moving. It has been hanging there for hundreds of years."

I looked again, but I could not see it moving.

"It is an enchanted flintlock," the seyyed continued. "Centuries ago a hunter pursued a mountain gazelle until he came to the summit near the skylight where no human being had ever set foot before, nor ever will. The gazelle was in reality the daughter of a pary king, who still lives on the top of this wonderful mountain, just as the King of the divs and jinnees is living at this very moment down below the precipice. The gazelle disappeared and the unfortunate hunter was lost forever. He hung his flintlock on that stone before his death to warn other hunters against his fate.

The skylight is made by the King's order; that part of the mountain summit is his watchtower and the hole a lookout for his spies, who keep watch on the monsters below."

Our way was now steeper than ever, and my brother thought it wise to keep on walking.

Another hour and the path began to grow wider, and there was more light. The opening above our heads was becoming broader and our path was gradually receding from the precipice.

"We are getting out of the devil's jaws," the seyyed said with a sigh of relief. "We shall be in our tents before night."

A short time after this we came upon a vast country covered with forest and shrubbery; expansive fields, green and delightful, were stretching before my eyes. The scenery was so enchanting that we decided to rest and have some food. Large and small streams of water were running in all directions, and far, very far away, the black shadows of the jungles were in view.

Oh! It was simply delightful to gallop on the soft green carpet! I was skimming through the air! Nothing in our way except clumps of small bushes, which we avoided easily. My horse seemed to know the road and also that from here on the country was a paradise, at the end of which he would get a long rest and forage.

We mounted a hilly field before us in a gallop and slacked down when we came to Yoush. This was the first village of the Province of Nour and Kodjour and a place which had some interest for me, for I knew that it had once been the home of the Queen Ayesha Khanom. Her brother—the same to whom my brother was attached—became the Governor General of the Province of Mazenderan. We were to be with him during our stay in the north. We had, of course, no time to stop now, but rode on to Neytal, which we hoped to reach before dark.

I had been told by my brother of the natural beauty of

Neytal but no words could describe the loveliness I found in this enchanted country when finally I beheld it. We rode through lovely valleys and green fields, among forests as beautiful as the Shah's gardens. We saw thousands of wild birds flying among the trees; hundreds of streams—some trickling into a creek, others gushing from recesses in the rocks, falling in cascades into streamlets—which my brother said were mineral waters; wild flowers, more colourful and more lovely than all the flowers I had seen before; fruit trees which, although their fruits were not for men to eat, were nevertheless delightful to see; small trees bearing the duplicates of the domestic flowers in clusters; and hundreds of vines laden with grapes. But I thought the flowers were the most attractive. Sometimes a whole stretch of land was literally covered with wild tulips, all mauve. Other spaces between the trees were covered with the same flowers, all white. More fields were coverd with hyacinths, with flowers as blue as the sky. It was in fact a paryland, with all its legendary attributes. My horse was enjoying himself as much as I; he was sniffing the perfumed air and throwing his head up like a king. At first he was shy when a bird as large as a duck flew under his nose, but later he seemed rather amused. Once a royal pheasant bird flew from under my horse's hoof, planed into the air without beating its wings and alighted on a tree. A gorgeous sight! Its plumage was of a thousand colours, its tail, nearly a yard long, was spread like a king's aigrette and on its head was a princely crown of purple.

From the top of a hill they pointed to me the djolgueh of Neytal. This was an extensive veldt of green, surrounded by jungles and crossed by a wide river. The water of this stream, under the glow of the setting sun, gleamed like quicksilver. It zigzagged and crawled the whole length of the veldt as far as my eyes could see. On the other side of it the points of some of the larger tents were visible.

"That is our home for the summer," said my brother.

VI

THE IMPERIAL CAMP

SINCE it would be at least an hour after our arrival before we could see the Governor, we lay down to rest.

When I awoke I found the tent completely dark and my brother not with me. Two men, quite unknown to me, came in and bowed in a very formal manner. One of them placed a candle before me and now both stood with crossed arms. They were husky fellows and by their accent I recognized them as natives of Mazenderan, very tall and strong. One of them had a dark face with prominent features; black eyes flashing under long lashes, heavy black brows, thick lips, white teeth and a square chin. The impression he made upon me was not favourable, but I could not determine at that time why he repelled me. The other was of the same structure and figure, but his eyes were gentle. He wore a short beard.

"I hope your highness slept well," said the first one.

"Very well indeed," I replied. "Who are you?"

"Your humble slaves, the domestics of your high brother, our dear master," was the reply.

"But I have never seen you before," I said.

"We are his servants when he comes to this land," said the first.

"We are his slaves," said the man with the beard. "We owe him all we have in the world."

"What is your name?" I asked.

"Your humble slave, Guel-Babou," said the man with the beard.

"And you?" I addressed the other.

"Your humble slave, Vali-Ollah."

They always had amusing names in that country. The first man's name meant "smell the flower," in his dialect. The other was more pretentious; it means "The Lieutenant of Allah."

"Where is the Khan Dadash?"—my Khan brother.

"He is with the Sardar and we are waiting to accompany your lordship to his tent."

They went out and when I appeared a few minutes later both were waiting at the entrance. Guel-Babou fetched the candelabrum and walked before me with Vali-Ollah behind.

From every tent lights shone. The river was more like silver than ever. Everything was quiet. Now and then a horse neighed, but that was all. The jungles looked black except for some bonfires here and there which the herd-drivers and wood-choppers had made to frighten wild animals away. There were thousands in the jungles, the worst of them being wild boars, of which I shall have more to say later.

Near the Governor's tents two men came out to meet me. One was the Governor's treasure-keeper and master of clothes. A fine old man, very religious and kind, although I have been told that he was most cunning at hoarding money. This did not bother me in the least. Very seldom had I heard of a servant otherwise.

"My eyes will be illuminated!" he cried when he saw me. He was so happy to see me that I feared he might have a fit of happiness and pass away.

"Oh, Ghorban, O, my soul of soul, O, my generous young Khan, how very, very happy I am to see you! Come, please come, everybody is actually dying to see you! My, what a bearing! My, what a tall figure! God is indeed wonderful to some of his creatures!" he exclaimed.

He was a very small man with shrinking face and grizzly

beard and hair.   He generally wore a black hat of imitation
lambskin, egg-shaped and unusually tall.   This was probably
to make him appear taller.   Other servants and attendants
joined him by and by and all seemed delighted to see me!
I was really pleased with the idea that I had evidently saved
their lives by coming to them with my brother.   Of course,
my brother was a great Hakim-Bashi and had saved the
lives of many of them, but in my case their emotion seemed
purely a reflection of the inner sentiments of their hearts.

I stepped in the gallery of the first tents and approached
the entrance of the one which was the sanctuary of the
Sardar.   An attendant drew the curtain, I entered and made
a very elaborate bow to the Governor, who was sitting; I
stood in attendance.   A dozen high officials and the
Governor's two sons were sitting in a circle before him.
Candelabra of single branch and many with five or ten
branches were lighting the place, and some very rare and
rich carpets and rugs were spread on the felt ground-
covering.   Before him a tablecloth was spread on the floor,
covered with fruits and candies and all sorts of nuts, also
small dishes of delicate food, such as fresh khaviar and
different salted and dried fish roe and various kinds of cheese;
dried biscuits and fresh bread.   Other small bowls contained relishes made of cucumber, watermelon skin, walnuts,
mangoes, tiny limes, and small egg plants, and others pickles
entirely made of aromatic herbs.   Everything was sour
except the few candies, which no one cared to touch.

At the Governor's right hand was a wealthy Khan and
statesman, Nasr-es-Sultaneh, the master of the seyyed scrivener, who owned two-thirds of this whole country from
the west to the east border of the Caspian Sea.   He was one
of the wealthiest landlords in Persia.   The Shah would have
appointed him Governor instead of the present Sardor, if it
had not been for his affection for the Sardar's sister, Ayesha
Khanom.   The tale of jealousy between these two grandees

owing to their wealth, (one acquired by the toil of the peasants, the other by the grace of his sister's marriage to the Shah), was on all tongues. Political parties were exploiting both of them. The whole northern country was inbued with the intrique of people scheming how to get the most possible out of each of them. Yet to see them meet one would take them for loving brothers who had come together after a life of separation, while in reality each would readily have given half his wealth to bite off the other's head! In spite of this I liked both.

My brother was at the Governor's left hand. When he drew the attention of Sardar to me, the Sardar said, with his face all smiles, "Why! It is our little khan, the light of his father's eyes and the soul of his brother's heart. Come, come, welcome to our home. Sit down my boy, sit down, my boy!"

He motioned to me to sit next to his youngest son, Esmail Khan, whom I later loved as a brother. I bowed in answer to the nods from the officials, and was presented by Sadar to Nasr-es-Sultaneh. Many times I had to raise myself half way on my knees to make the same movements of salutation to the other officials. A tedious work! But my Laleh used to enact these Persian mannerisms ten times a day. Sometimes he was the greater lord and I the lesser; often it was the other way around. I could have beaten almost any one in Persia in competition in bowing and jumping and smiling.

The Governor's son and I had the same idea about various things and the same tastes. We were still exchanging confidences when Mohammad-Hassan came in with decanters of Arag. The Governor and the guests were given each a glass, and soon after, they began on the delicacies in front of them.

After an hour the Governor proposed to my brother a game of tric-trac, and the servant brought in a beautiful

mosaic board and placed it before them. Everybody now
went near and made a circle around the players. The game
was for a piece of gold, and often doubled and redoubled.
Each time the Governor won he gave a gold piece either
to his youngest son or to me, as a gift of honour of his
good play. After a few games and the loss of a few gold
coins by my brother, the Governor challenged another
gentleman and won the games again. Nasr-es-Sultaneh was
watching with indifference, not because it did not interest
him but because to him the betting seemed too trifling.
However, he did not hesitate to ask the Governor to play
against him. All at once everybody seemed much more
agitated. I had never played for more than a Kran, one-
tenth of a Toman. I thought even to bet a gold coin was
too much. But these two great friends started with five
pieces of gold and each doubled and redoubled until the
game finished for some twenty or thirty gold coins. When
the Governor began to lose he called to the treasurer to
bring more money. Esmail Khan turned to me with a smile
and whispered, "Wait a little. This is only the beginning."

When money was brought, the Governor proposed twenty
gold pieces for score. Nasr-es-Sultaneh laughed and said:
"Why not make it fifty?" The challenge was accepted and
the game when doubled and redoubled reached each time
one hundred or one hundred and fifty gold coins. Esmail
Khan and myself received now and then one or two of them.
Fortune was against Nasr and he lost heavily. Presently
he called one of his servants.

"Bring Ali Khan at once!" he commanded the man.

In ten minutes a young man, looking like an army officer,
came in and bowed to him.

"Bring money!"

But when the officer was about to leave, his master called
him back and said:

"Do not bring loose coins, they are troublesome to count. Do you hear me?"

"Yes, Ghorban," said the man and disappeared. In another ten minutes the officer came back with a plate with a hundred small sacks of real silk piled on it which he placed before his master.

"Remain outside!" said Nasr-es-Sultaneh. "I may call you again."

Immediately the Governor's treasurer, the grizzly-bearded Hassan, put before the Governor a plate with sacks very much like those of his friend, only this plate was larger and the number of sacks doubled those of his rival. Nasr-es-Sultaneh looked a bit disconcerted, but said nothing and started the game at once. The game began for one of these sacks and doubled and redoubled each time for another sack. Each contained fifty to one hundred coins. Nasr-es-Sultaneh lost heavily, and when he saw that only a dozen of the sacks were left he bet the whole in one game, which he lost. He was about to call for more money when the head servant announced dinner. The game was immediately stopped, and the servants came in with silver ewers and basins for us to wash our hands.

This done, we walked under the tent and out into another where the dinner was spread on a large tablecloth, which was literally covered with dishes. The ghazy, or head clergyman, was standing at the head of the tablecloth. Everybody greeted him with great respect. Beside the usual dishes, there were a few special ones. A large china plate covered with a silver lid, which a servant presently came to remove, was placed in front of the Governor. A most delicious odour permeated the room as a big white fish in the form of a ring covered with spices, immerced in a giblet sauce mixed with finely hashed aromatic herbs, came into view. With a pair of silver spoons the Governor, with his own hands, cut a piece, put it gently on a dish, and placed it before his guest of honour, Nasr-es-Sultaneh. He then served in the same manner every one of his guests, except that the other dishes were presented by servants. I thought the fish must be full of fine bones and was very careful eating mine. But, to my astonishment, there was not a single bone to be found. Later my brother explained that the fish was fresh salmon caught two days before at a place three days' ride from Neytal, and sent by messenger to the Governor. Such messengers were dispatched from one corner of the country to another when speed was essential. Fresh horses were at their disposal and officialdom was ready to give them all necessary help. The fish, when caught, was directly cleaned and packed in a reed basket, which the messenger carried in his saddle bag. In this way it was delivered to the cook within twenty-four hours, and it took another twenty-four hours for its preparation. The unusual thing about the preparation was that the fish remained whole and yet all its bones had been dissolved mysteriously by a secret process of the chief cook. My brother also explained that the giblet came from a small, wild duck, not bigger than a pigeon and very hard to get a shot at, called naft-kin. Its flesh is not sought after, because the bird is too small and because its tail smells like petroleum. Hence, its name, "naft," which means petroleum, and "kin," meaning tail, in the northern dialect. But its giblets are most delicate.

*   *   *

A young poet, who was attached to one of the Shah's officers, and who came often to play chess with my brother, said that he found it marvellous the way his majesty changed his sumptuous life in Teheran for the comparatively simple life in Neytal. He believed that this was due to the natural beauty which surrounded him. The high mountains, the mysterious jungles, the torrential rivers and majestic scenery were such that no human being could remain indifferent

to their charms. Under their influence, even a Shah could soften and treat his subjects with more kindness. Here, anyone could look at his majesty, with both eyes, without fearing that the executioner would take those eyes out of their sockets. Here, anyone could present him a petition, without having his head cut off.

These ideas of the young poet were in my mind two days after Akbar's arrival when I was riding in the company of the Governor and fifty or more of his escort toward the imperial camp. We met the Shah at the outskirts of the camp, returning from the jungles, where he had been riding to maintain his good health. The sign which informed us, from afar, that the group was headed by the Shah was the purple parasol, which his majesty carried in his hand, ostensibly to protect him from the sun, but in reality to call attention to his imperial person.

His majesty spurred his horse, advancing alone, leaving his companions behind. He halted in front of us, seemingly very much pleased and—almost smiling!

The Governor presented my brother.

"One of your majesty's most faithful attendants, a gentleman who will not flinch in giving his life for his sovereign. A famous Plato of his age. A poet, a philosopher, a thinker, a writer and, above all, a life-giver to the dead! A real Messih!"—Messiah—"He has saved thousands of your majesty's subjects from the grip of the angel of death. He has saved the country from many terrible calamities and infections!"

After the Governor's oration, his majesty swelled his chest, threw his head back, and stared like a tiger at my brother. Then, he roared out in "the imperial growl,": "Ha, ha, ha, hoh, haoho, humhom!"—"Great, great, good, good, good! You are, you are, he, he, he!"

My brother bowed to him very respectfully, without making an answer.

"Ho, ho, ho," growled the Shah. "We make him a general, a general, a great general!"

Every one bowed at this appointment.

Having presented other dignitaries in their proper order, the Governor motioned me to advance.

"The little brother of your majesty's general!"—my brother was already a general!—"The son of the great Hadj-Agha, who needs no introduction, your majesty's loyal little servitor, ready to sacrifice his life. A hakim-bashi"—doctor—"and, already, at his tender age, a poet, a philosopher and a writer. He has saved many of your majesty's servants and slaves from the grip of death, while travelling to kiss the dust of your majesty's feet!"

This time, the Shah roared like a lion! "Bur, bur, bur, hem, hem, hem. Hum, hum, hum!" "We—we—we—we know him, we know him, the little rascal!"

Thereupon, everybody's face broke into smiles. The Shah laughed a little and then passed to other gentlemen waiting to be introduced. This finished, he turned his horse toward the camp and we all followed him like a bodyguard.

Twenty minutes later, we found ourselves before the imperial camp. It was a sight unlike anything I had seen before—a green veldt, cut into two sections by a mighty river, and planted with thousands and thousands of tents. It looked like a forest. Try as I would, I could not make out where the camp began or where it ended. Long alleys and roads crossed in and out in every direction. All I could see was that it was divided into three different groups.

One, belonging to the Shah and his immediate suite, was pitched on a slope of hilly ground, half a mile from the main camp. The imperial tent, of vivid purple, stood high above the rest, the top of its poles, made of solid gold, glittering like fires under the setting sun. I knew that under that huge purple tent was the second smaller tent, called the Shah's sanctuary, where he lived in the daytime.

Other gorgeous tents, all of rich materials, were pitched near it. All these were reserved exclusively for the Shah.

Still farther on the south, immediately below the one belonging to the Shah, were the two hundred tents of the harem, more gorgeous even than those in the Shah's section.

Halfway between the two, we left the Shah and headed for the main camp, which was a picturesque copy of the ancient camps of the Caliph, Haroun-Al-Raschid. The section situated on the north of the river belonged to the thousands of khans, officials, ministers, dignitaries of court and country, provincial nobles, chieftains, heads of tribes and different governors, with their thousands of attendants.

The other half, on the opposite side, was like a large town, with hundreds of shops and a bazaar! The clamour was incredible. One heard the neighs from the thousands of horses and mules, the braying of donkeys and the cries of vendors and shopkeepers. Hundreds of people had joined the camp for business. In fact, it was Teheran, minus the city people, but plus the mule-drivers and officials who would not have been in evidence there as they were here.

Outside this camp, farther down the river, we came upon another section which was reserved for the stables and warriors and horsemen.

This first visit made a great impression upon me, but real insight into the people who formed the ordou came gradually. I found that nearly every man had come with a hope of gaining something. Aside from the shopkeepers, who secured fabulous prices for their goods, there were mollahs who charged double for making pilgrimages to the holy places as substitutes for the religious-minded persons, who were too busy making money to undertake the pilgrimages themselves, haberdashers who sold leather belts for ten times more than they could get in Teheran, and fortune readers who for an exhorbitant fee told everyone that he would become a high dignitary in the service of the Shah.

There was the world of officialdom, from the cabinet minister to the last insignificant servant, each with the same hope and the same ambition.

It was interesting to note the different types of men who tried all the year to get an invitation to the camp. Once invited, they must assume an appearance of wealth whether they had it or not.

The parvenus of low birth, who had been accumulating money by graft, were the only men who came to camp as paupers! They had nothing to lose, and moreover, having hoarded money by exploiting the peasants and the unprotected landowners, they had every reason to masquerade as poor men who had lost their belongings in serving the country.

There was one man whose life in the camp amused everybody. His intrigues earned him the post of governor and, by his systematic extortions, he had become one of the wealthiest men in Persia. He had come to the camp with two wretched-looking servants, a horse, a mule and a donkey. He lived under a dilapidated tent and took his meals at the tents of different khans. He lived the life of a parasite and complained always before the Sardar, and others, of the bad treatment he had endured from the Government. He had bought his first governorship in one of the small towns in the north. Ten times he had been dismissed for dishonesty, and each time he had succeeded in bribing other dishonest officials to help him reëstablish himself in a new post. He had been actually thrown out of his last office by the public, and now he was in search of a new one!

It was obvious that very seldom did anybody in Persia, especially at the court, gain a position by sheer merit. One great source of trouble lay in the fact that various occupations became the property of a family, like the heritage of a title. For instance, the mostowfi who accompanied my brother was registered as mostowfi, simply because his father had been one. The son of hakim-bashi was believed to possess the mystery of medicine before he was born. The son of an army officer was registered before his birth as a captain and sometimes if his father knew how to handle a mostowfi, this latter could put the unborn son of the officer on the payroll for old age pension! The son of a governor, no matter how much the governor had robbed the people, was eligible for the position of his father, after the latter's death, even if he were under the age of ten. The son of a Mohammaden clergyman, a mollah, was believed to receive every night the visit of the angel Djebrail, to inspire him with the mystery of religion as he had inspired the Prophet. If the child belonged to a modjtahed, the high clergyman of first degree, his nurse had a right to pretend, his evening suckling over, that the baby was transported to heaven on the wings of some of the many angels who commute between heaven and earth every twenty-four hours. The son of a mostowfi, who kept the old age pension record, could, while still a child, fill his father's place immediately after his death and scratch baby hieroglyphics on a paper which could be translated by minor scribes to mean the death of such and such person who received a pension from the Shah, notwithstanding the defunct pensioner's presence in flesh and blood to rectify the error. In fact, in Persia the only people whose children could not make any pretension to their father's professions or posts, were the children of those who did manual work, like the sons of camel-drivers, mule-drivers, kitchen hands, and stable boys. But as Allah is gracious, always to his creatures, it was quite possible for these offsprings to become governors, princes and ministers under the auspices of the sovereign, the Shadow of Allah. The Sardar, or Governor-General, was naturally the one to whom the disappointed schemers brought their sorrows, praying him to hand their petitions to the Shah. Some of them had been dismissed by the Sardar himself! After the Sardar, they could apply to Nasr-es-Sultaneh. These two men were considered the mightiest in the Shah's suite. One can easily understand the privileges of those who were attached to one or the other. The general respect shown to my brother and myself, and other members of the Sardar's suite, was most exaggerated. Hundreds of people bowed to us whenever we passed through the camp. The simple joke of the Shah, calling me a "little rascal" was added a hundred-fold to my importance and caused many to pay me compliments.

It took me only a short time to discover the value of the Shah's joke, and Akbar and I exploited it to the very maximum.

Money was plentiful. Everybody seemed to have great sums of cash in silver and gold. We had no banknotes, and very few knew that such a thing existed in Persia. My own best source of revenue was the coins the youngest son of the Governor and I received nearly every evening from Sardar and Nasr-es-Sultaneh, when they gambled. My brother also allowed me a liberal sum to defray my expenses, which consisted only of tipping numerous servants or peasants who directed me to places of interest in the mountains or the forests. Otherwise, all the monetary obligations were paid by the Governor who, in turn, received all the money he wanted from the revenues collected from the province.

In other words, everybody, from the Shah down, was supported by the peasants, the only class who toiled incessantly and were, at the same time, the poorest among the Persian people. At first I did not understand their condition, but gradually, under the tutorship of Akbar, I learned that the peasants were in no better condition than the slaves who worked in ancient kingdoms of the world.

The grandee, Nasr-es-Sultaneh, had a revenue of hundreds

of thousands of tomans a year; yet his peasants had just enough boiled rice and hard bread to keep them alive. Their dwellings were miserable; they had no doctors, no sanitation. Hundreds of peasants all over Persia perished yearly of diseases which could have been cured if they had been living in a more sanitary country. Others were flogged to death or seriously disabled by the landlords and overseers.

One day when we were riding on the outskirts of the jungle, where a few wooden shacks were in view, Akbar asked if I had been impressed by the wealth of the Shah's camp. When I answered "Yes," he pointed out a miserable-looking cabin, near which twelve wretched persons—men, women and children—were working in the fields.

"If those peasants were to perish, or stop working," he said, "the imperial camp would collapse and the Shah, himself, would tumble from his throne, like a wooden monkey on a single leg!"

"Then, why do they not stop working?" I asked.

"Human beings cannot forever endure the torture of bastinadoes," he replied in an angry tone. "The landlords force them to keep on."

"Why do they submit to it? After all, the Shah's officialdom is only a small part of Persia," I retorted.

"It is not only the continual beating which turns them into animals. They suffer from a greater misfortune— ignorance!" he answered. "Their deliverance will begin when they become enlightened enough to know they are abused."

"I wish the day would hurry!" I exclaimed.

"It will not come until at least ten per cent. of our people are allowed some kind of education, and that will not come until after this Shah is gone. He is the most ignorant of the Persians. Our only hope is in men like your brothers."

"What can they do without his majesty's help?" I asked.

"They are already helping as professors in the Imperial College. As for the Shah, we have hope of relief by the 'Unseen Hand'!" Akbar declared.

"What is this 'Unseen Hand' you are all talking about?" I asked. "I believe in the jinnees and the angels and parys, but I shall not believe in the 'Unseen Hand' until I see it with my own eyes. Is it a man's hand or the hand of one of our prophets?"

"It is a man's hand, and a mighty one," he replied. "Every Persian is expecting it but none is familiar with the time and manner in which it will fall. But you, Ghorban, and I may both live to see justice done." Very pensively and yet deliberately, Akbar gave his answer, which was like a death sentence for the Evil, whatever it might be. Presently he gave me a searching glance and whispered, "Do you remember, Ghorban, the story of the Emir Hodj-djaj, son of the Emir Yousef Saghaphi?"

"Yes," I answered, "I know that he was a most cruel man and that, during his reign, tens of thousands were massacred, especially among the Arabs, who suffered so that, even to-day, when his name is mentioned before an Arab, he invokes the malediction of Allah upon him! Is that what you wanted to remind me of?"

"Not exactly," he said. "I am sorry to have caused you to talk unfavourably of a great man who was of your own blood and flesh. But of the story of his humour. . ."

Then he told me a story of an Arab who met the Emir in the Sahara, when the latter was alone on horseback, waiting for his retinue, which he had outdistanced.

"Do you know the Hodj-djaj?" he asked the Arab.

The Arab threw his hands above his head and said, "May Allah curse the man whose cruelty has become a byword among the nations."

"Is he so bad as all that?" asked the Emir.

"May Allah take him away and burn him in hell!" repeated the Arab.

While he was cursing Hodj-djaj, the group of warriors, accompanying the Emir, appeared in the distance. At the sight of the purple banner carried before the horsemen, the poor Arab began to doubt the wisdom of his utterance. He knew that his last minute had come but he bravely faced the Emir and said to him, "May I, O Stranger, make a demand upon your discretion?"

"You may," replied the Emir.

"Then, please consider our conversation about Hodj-djaj as a secret between ourselves!"

The Emir laughed aloud, and ordered one hundred pieces of gold to be given the Arab for his resourcefulness and wit.

This story made me laugh and, to Akbar, I said, "I see the point. You want me to keep our conversation about the 'Unseen Hand' and the Evil between ourselves?"

"Yes, Ghorban," he answered quickly, "and the hundred pieces of gold, to wit!"

"I do not believe I have so much gold but, if silver will do, I am ready to act like my ancestor," I replied.

"Thank you, my own little master. The crowd in that poor little cabin will be happier tomorrow than ever they have been before!"

VII

DETERMINING A CHESS CHAMPION

THE TWO noted rivals, the Sardar and Nasr-es-Sultaneh, thought it worth their while to use me as a means for furthering their personal interests with the Shah. Nasr-es-Sultaneh was the first to take advantage of the situation.

One evening, my brother, a most notable chess player, was urged to play a game with a gentleman who was anything but a good player. My brother excused himself, and they asked me to play instead. I accepted reluctantly, for I thought my playing would interrupt the flow of money coming to me and the Governor's son. But I had no choice, and tried to lose the game as soon as possible, in order to make the gentlemen resume their gambling. Fate, however, was against my opponent, who, in spite of my stupid moves, which grieved my brother, lost the game. Both the Governor and the grandee had bet on me. They won heavily and the whole crowd admired my wonderful game!

As a matter of fact, my playing had been so bad that my brother, in all honesty, began to defend the man who lost, but nobody would listen. They shouted him down and proclaimed me the champion of the evening. I received a part of the winnings and paid no further attention to the discussions till I found that the outcome of their clamour was that the grandee himself had now been challenged by Sardar to play against me! As a polite man, he laughingly accepted the challenge. Seeing that whether I came out loser or winner a part of the money was sure to

281

come to me, I threw my lot with the Sardar and played. To my astonishment, he lost sooner than the other man!

A short time after this he drew the attention of the Shah to my game, by telling him that he thought I could beat anyone in the camp!

His majesty was very much interested and, being in the habit of using any means of amusing himself, especially when it was at the expense of his people, laughed beyond the prescribed decorum for his divine personality, which fact aroused the ire of the grandee, who asked his majesty to name a player to pitch against me and play the game for any sum, from one toman to a thousand, he himself being ready to back my game.   He had a way of exaggerating things, and on this occasion so enormously misrepresented my ability before the Shah that half the court officials were ready to stake money on my game.

Many of them suggested my playing against my brother, but the grandee was wise enough to cry for a less renowned player.

The funniest part of it all was the faith of the Governor, who went one step farther than the grandee and declared he was willing to bet double any amount mentioned by Nasr-es-Sultaneh.

My poor brother became terribly excited and, fearing my failure, tried to tell everybody that I was no more a player than was the grandee himself.   This made the said gentleman more stubborn than ever.

The Shah had been pleased to allow the match, and the day was decided upon.   I was to play before his majesty. My brother set a course of games, in the afternoons, to coach me, and was wholly unhappy when he saw that I lost every single game played with him.   Meanwhile, my sponsors were searching for an opponent.

Shortly afterward, news was brought that none of the adults was willing to play against me and it was decided

that I should play against another boy who was with his
father in the Shahs camp.   The boy's father was a remarkable statesman by reason of his long beard, which he painted
regularly with henna.   He was, moreover, very well known
for his religious sentiments.   Although playing for money
was distasteful to him, he was glad to see his son coming
into prominence before the Shadow of Allah.

The Governor, to whose person I was attached, thought
himself justified in resenting the grandee's way of attributing to himself all the credit for advertising me to the Shah.
My brother in turn resented all excitement and said no one
should be hailed as champion who had not played at least
twenty years.

I was, to be truthful, at first more concerned with the
cash than with the game itself.   Akbar had drawn my
attention to the fact that, since his arrival, the treasure box,
which I had entrusted into his hands, was becoming light.
But as the day approached I found myself as excited as the
rest.   Try as I would, I could not help feeling nervous.   But
the more frightened I became the more determined I was
to win; and when we were on our way to the camp I was
so sure of myself that I wished to cry out, "I am going
to win!"

I was received at the Shah's tent by Nasr-es-Sultaneh.
The tent was open on all sides.   The Shah was standing at
the farther end, surrounded by courtiers.   Near the entrance
was another group of officials, who, I guessed, were to watch
and bet on the game.   My opponent was very grave and
serious, like his father, but very much upset at being near
the Shah.   I guessed it was the first time in his life.

We greeted each other and were asked by Nasr-es-Sultaneh,
who seemed to have assumed the rôle of captain, to sit
down and start.   The chess board was his own.   He would
not have trusted another!

"Have you been playing a good deal since your arrival?" asked the boy.

"Nearly every evening," I told him.

"Then I am sure I shall lose to you. The High Agha (meaning his father) knows nothing about this game and rarely leaves me alone to play. He takes all my time to recite poetry or practice calligraphy. But I have played a great deal in town, and I do not think it will be uninteresting for you to play with me."

I liked the boy very much.

When the game started, the captain stood halfway between us and the waiting gentlemen. My opponent played a good game, which would have been far better had he not been completely impressed by his surroundings. Every now and then he looked in the Shah's direction. It was evident he was not comfortable.

At the very beginning, he played rather badly. My impression was that he had no plan, but as the game continued his play became more steady and I began to doubt the outcome. "Has he been fooling me?" I thought to myself. He was perfectly calm now and paid no attention to anything but the board before him.

I was trying my best when, to my horror, the captain whispered, very loudly, "Where are you now? Hurry up!"

The boy looked up as if awakened from sleep and from that minute fell back, playing as he did in the beginning. His subsequent moves lost all the advantages he had and within ten minutes I had his game under my control.

Our captain came on tip-toe, looked over our heads, and went back, shouting, "I will bet any amount as extra! I am sure of the champion!"

Hearing this, the boy said, "My game is lost, no matter how long you take to give the check," and seizing the piece belonging to me, played the last move intended to checkmate him, saying, "My game is lost!" as if he was relieved from a great responsibility.

The whole crowd rushed to us. The captain ran to the other end of the tent and presently came back with the boy's father and my brother and many others.

Very gravely they looked at the game, and my brother said, "You both have played well. My congratulations to both of you."

The grandee seized my shoulder and hurried me to the Shah. His majesty at first seemed to have forgotten the match, but gradually realised the fact and, looking at me as if I were the most peculiar-looking thing he ever had seen, growled, "Huh, huh, huh, great champion, our champion, good, good champion!"

I made a bow and went back to the scene of battle. Soon the whole matter subsided and everybody went to his duties. I rode home with Akbar very happy yet rather disappointed. I expected a more fitting end to my victory, but when evening came and I went to the Sardar for dinner, Nasr-es-Sultaneh immediately took me by the shoulder and exhibited me to all present.

There were about fifty extra guests who had won on my game and each was trying to be first to present me with money. My brother, who had taken no part, either in the game or in the betting, handed me two ashrefi (Persian gold coins) and saying, "Try to play with me as you did to-day and I shall bet money on your game as willingly as their Highnesses, the Sardar and Nasr-es-Sultaneh!"

Throughout the evening I was royally treated, and when we were back in our tent, Akbar, at the sight of the money said, "What a wonderful game is chess—just as good as the holding of a caravan on the highroad!"

VIII

HUNTING IN THE JUNGLES
OF MAZENDERAN

EARLY in the fourth night after my arrival in Neytal I was awakened by a terrible noise from outside. Numbers of people were howling as if in distress and while I listened the howling changed into wild shouts.

I jumped out of bed and awoke my brother, saying, "I believe people are fighting outside. I am going to awake Akbar!"

My brother laughed and told me to go to sleep again, that the noise was made by peasant "field watchers." "They have to sit all night in a tower made of wood, covered with branches, to frighten the wild boars away from the rice fields," he said. "Field after field has been destroyed by them, and the only way to save the rice is to frighten them away."

"Why don't they shoot them?" I asked.

"The price of a firearm is a fortune to a peasant, and moreover each shot costs money."

I covered my ears under the blanket to shut out the noise, and took an oath that, if I should live long enough and stay long enough in the country, I should kill every wild boar in the jungle.

Next morning I told Akbar, who of course was greatly interested, and luckily we found the Governor's son, Esmail Khan, a ready confederate. Unfortunately, our first battle finished in complete defeat.

Akbar told me how to follow the tazis (hounds), who

were used as boar-trackers, and warned me to be ready in case I should be attacked unexpectedly, or miss my shot. The boars, he said, are apt, if only wounded, to charge, and in most cases with dire result to the hunters.   He told me that the ugly beast took good care to keep his tusks sharp by rubbing them against a rock, testing the edges afterward by charging a heavy branch.   If he easily cuts it in two the tusks are ready.   Akbar advised me not to be frightened, and above all things not to run away.   Very calmly he told me that if I missed my shot, which would be followed by the boar charging at me I must hurl my gun away and throw myself flat on the ground, on my face, assuring me that if I did this nothing would happen.   The worst I should get would be a kick or two, as the boar leaped over me.

"What about his tusks?" I inquired.

"This is the only way to escape them.   A boar charges at you with his tusks, which are curved outside and, having a stiff neck which he cannot bend downward, he will at the most brush your back with the flat part of his tusks."

"Right!" I said bravely, but with a sinking heart.

"Is there any other way to escape?" I queried.

"None!" he said shortly.

The beautiful hounds were full of anticipation and so were we—Esmail, his man, Akbar, and myself.   We chose the late hours of the afternoon, when the boars would be coming down toward the fields, and were soon lost in the depths of the jungle.

To my surprise I found, before we had gone far, twelve wood-choppers waiting for us, each with a murderous-looking axe on his shoulder.   I asked my friend, Esmail Khan, who these men were.

"We need some help for this hunt," he said.   "They are our beaters."

Presently they disbanded, each going in a different direction. We, too, were ordered to scatter. The dogs were darting under the bushes, sniffing and wagging their tails.

For a long time nothing happened. Then suddenly a shattering sound came to my ears, as if a storm had swept over the bushes, followed by a shot and a long whine from one of the dogs. At the same time, the clump of shrubbery before my eyes was torn asunder and, to my horror, a dusky-looking monster hurled itself out of the thicket like a bullet. The gun flew from my hand and, in a flash, I was stretched headlong on the ground! I felt the beast rushing over my body and thought myself finished. I was still under this impression, when a second monster, as swift as the first, passed over my body and, this time, by all the prophets, I felt something brushing the back of my head. A cold shiver went to the very marrow of my bones. At the same time, a shot rang out simultaneously with the voice of Akbar, shouting, "I got it!"

I jumped to my feet and saw Akbar standing a few yards away with his gun, which was still smoking.

"You did it wonderfully," he said to me. "Upon my soul, the narrowest escape I ever saw!"

It all happened so quickly that I could not believe my eyes. The second black monster was huddled up, dead, ten feet from where I stood. Akbar's bullet had caught him in the neck. Esmail Khan and his man now came out from the thicket the former flushed and agitated, cursing his fate and crying aloud, "Devil will be damned! The very first time I missed my shot, like a fool! And the wretch has chopped off the tail of our best dog!"

While he was cursing, the dog with missing tail rushed at him, apparently quite indifferent to his misfortune.

Esmail Khan's anger had more than one reason; having missed his shot, he had thrown the gun away and rushed behind a tree instead of falling on his face. We sent half of the beaters to find the gun, while others placed the dead boar on the shoulders of one of their comrades, a wood-chopper famous for his strength.

We returned dejected. To have come back with only one boar was considered a defeat, not to mention the missing gun and the tailless dog. We decided to keep the incident to ourselves but we found that both our camp and that of Nasr-es-Sultaneh were alive with the details of our unfortunate plight. A false rumour had spread that the boar had been killed by me, the little khan from Teheran! I told them that the boar was killed by Akbar, but not one of them would believe me. Strangest of all, Esmail Khan and I each received, from his father, the customary gold coin in honour of the day, and were hailed as the youngest and bravest hunters of the season.

When the Governor handed us the coins, Esmail whispered to me, "Mine for having lost my gun and yours for not having fired yours!"

The following day the hunt was described to His Majesty, the Shah, by Nasr-es-Sultaneh, who accredited me with the killing of two boars!

The false rumours made me a hero. Of course, no one knew better than I the untruth in them and it began to worry me. I recalled a proverb told me by my Laleh to the effect that a man who accepts false credit runs the risk of becoming, in the long run, the laughing stock of his friends and foes. I tried to deny the credit given me, but little by little I felt that the denial was growing less forceful.

This was most distasteful to me, and I tried to find a way out. I had to decide upon an action which would guarantee the stability of my futre life among the crowd who to-day would flatter as only Orientals can, and to-morrow ridicule, again as only Orientals can.

The chess game before the Shah had added greatly to my wisdom. I was aware that the boy lost more through nervousness than lack of knowledge, and that probably a second match with him would result quite differently, in which case the same people who hailed me as champion before the Shah would laugh at me. I finally settled upon a plan which I believed would dispel my apprehension. It was simple: I decided to become a hero, a real hero. I would wage war against the boars. War to the death.

Akbar fell in with my scheme, and under the guidance of that admirable knight I plunged into the battle. I was no more the timid boy who threw himself on his face at the sight of an ugly hog; I was no longer afraid to face one standing. Every penny that came to my treasure box was spent to get new beaters and new confederates. If I had any doubts as to the utility of my crusade they were soon dispelled by the gifts that were brought to my tent by the peasants and rice cultivators. They consisted of baskets filled with oranges, pots of preserved fruits, fresh fish, small handmade bags, or simply verbal messages of gratitude.

As the massacre proceeded I grew more ambitious and asked Akbar if we could find a lion or two to kill. He said there were no lions in this part of the country, but we might get a chance at a Caspian tiger, although we should probably have to wait for the month of August. Then I remembered the bag that the son of the wood-chopper had given me and asked Akbar if he thought we could catch a live bear. The idea pleased him so much that he dismissed the beaters for the time being, and we started on the new project, which was to be carried on in great secrecy.

Next morning we set out very early for the jungle. There was no need to take a gun. Each of us carried a stick and Akbar had his long dagger tucked under his sash. We were not going far. All we had to do, Akbar explained, was to find where the wild fruit grew.

Akbar first inspected the bushes to estimate the amount of fruit. Next day he could tell if any bear had taken any.

If he had, all that was necessary for us to do was to find the right track and follow it, or simply wait for our prey. We chose the latter.

One morning, between eight and nine, after hours of waiting in ambush, our patience was rewarded by a strange noise in a bush about thirty feet away. On two former occasions we had been mistaken, but the third time Akbar was so sure that the noise was made by a bear that he stood up, beating with his stick the undergrowth around him, and jumping from one bush to another like a crazy man. Then sharply he turned back and rushed in the direction from which he had heard the noise. Two dusky hulks fled before him, always keeping under cover. One was large, the other small.

"Chase them," Akbar whispered to me, "but do not rush them. Follow steadily."

The big fellow was calmly but clumsily running away, without looking backward, but the little one was nervous, now lagging behind, now ducking under a bush, now turning to look at us.

"The big one is his father," Akbar remarked to me in a whisper.

"How can you tell?" I whispered.

"A mother would take better care of him."

Presently the little one hid under a bush. Akbar motioned to me to keep watch on him while he chased the father away.

I saw two little black eyes peeping furtively out of the bush, but when they caught sight of me they disappeared. Akbar came back after ten minutes smiling.

"Is the little fellow still there?"

"It has not moved since you went away," I replied.

"Now careful. We must not frighten him."

He gently pushed the branches aside to get a view of the bear. But there was no bear!

"By all the devils!" he swore. "The little wretch has fooled us. I was sure he would!"

I was greatly surprised and very much ashamed of myself. I was sure I had him there, I said.

"They are very cunning," said Akbar to console me. "I have been fooled more than once myself. Besides," he continued, "we need not worry, to-morrow he'll be here again. The only two things which keep a bear from coming back to his haunt are the report of a gun and the shout of a man. That is why I did not bring a gun with me or speak aloud to you."

The following morning we found the little bear alone, and when we chased him he behaved in such a cunning way that we could not help laughing. He actually played hide and seek with us and really seemed to enjoy the game. More than ten times he ducked under a bush only to dash out again and under another. Again and again he peeped at us from under the thick bushes to make sure that we were after him, each time fooling us by escaping in a different way. He played with us an hour before he was cornered in a cluster of shrubbery. Akbar tried first to catch him with bare hands, but each time the bear backed away, and once, in an unguarded moment, he rushed out into the open space and ran for dear life.

In a flash Akbar was after him like a deer, with the bag in his hands. Once he fell down on the fugitive, but missed him. A second time I saw him going down, actually falling again on top of the little fellow. When I arrived on the spot I saw him gathering the mouth of the bag. We sat on the ground for a while, as Akbar desired a minute or two for rest; but in reality the rest was needed by our prisoner, who, Akbar said, must be very tired, for he was only a baby.

Akbar brought him home on his shoulder. I insisted on carrying him for a while on mine, but the policy of nonresistance which he had adopted for the occasion made him too heavy for me.

We attached him to a rope outside Akbar's tent and hundreds came to look at him. The same evening, after dinner, the Governor insisted on seeing him, and Nasr-es-Sultaneh ordered that I bring him personally and make him shake hands with everyone.

He was a most cunning little fellow, completely black except for a little white spot on his forehead, which was unanimously declared a sign of good luck. My brother said the white spot was the mark of Firuz-Bakht, meaning good luck for myself and everyone who looked at him first thing in the morning. The Governor thought we should start a subscription for the bear to enable him to live in luxury when we got back to Teheran, but I refused, saying I intended to take care of him myself as long as he lived. Everyone was enthusiastic about him, but he refused food and seemed rather bashful about making friends. Instinctively he pushed himself against me as if he knew I would protect him.

Next morning, while I was still in bed, Akbar came in with the news that the bear had gone. The rope was still there but the bear had run away.

The lucky white spot on his forehead incited the interest of the whole camp, and a group of stable boys started to scout the jungle in search of the fugitive.

Akbar was unwilling to go with them. "The bear will never be caught by a party of fifty persons, shouting and yelling as they do!" he said, and sure enough, very late in the afternoon they came back, reporting no success. I should have cried if I had not been afraid of being mocked. I had already begun to love the cunning little rascal. I was so dejected that the Governor told me that he would have a dozen bears caught for me the following day. Unfortunately, I did not want a dozen bears. I wanted only this bear and no other. The Governor rightly interpreted my polite silence, for, raising his voice that the servants might hear, he declared very solemnly, "Whoever brings back that same little bear shall receive ample reward from me."

This meant that hundreds would start for the jungle next morning. When I told Akbar, he said, "If you want the bear, you should prevent this noisy crowd from going after him."

Directly, I sent word to the chief of the stable that I preferred to search for the bear myself, adding that, if I came gack with him, each boy would receive a tip to commemorate the truant's return.

Very early the following morning Akbar and I set out for the forest where, as Akbar had predicted, we found the little scamp at his old haunt, hiding in a thicket. To our amazement he remained calm and watchful. Akbar called him endearing names, and went slowly toward him. The baby bear put up his little snout and waited. In the very moment when Akbar reached out to catch him, he started backward and tried to run away. But we caught him after a little while and I took him in my arms. I was overjoyed, and begged Akbar not to put him in the bag. So he carried him home in his arms.

The Governor received us like conquerors. The bear was petted and admired, and the Governor ordered a Cashmere shawl to be brought for Akbar. To me he gave twenty pieces of gold with his own hands, and also a promise that my bear was soon to be presented to His Majesty, the Shah.

Two days later, I was requested to get ready for the presentation, and after luncheon we started for the Shah's camp, Akbar sitting on a mule with the bear on the saddle in front of him.

It was a great day! The story of the bear had been told to the Shah with all the rattle-tattle of Oriental exaggeration. Everybody expected to see a huge savage beast, and

I believe they were disappointed when they saw the baby bear on Akbar's saddle, like a child. But his majesty was not at all disappointed. His attention was at once arrested by the white mark on the bear's forehead, and he paid no attention to his size. He had already been told about this mark by Nasr-es-Sultaneh and was anxious to look at it, as he was a staunch believer in bad omens and good luck.

At the entrance to the imperial tent I took charge of the bear, bringing him myself before the Shah, who at once took a liking to him.

"Hum, hum, hum, hum, very lucky, very lucky, he, he, he, he! What name, what name, what name?" he growled aloud.

My brother bowed and said, "Ghorban, this is the most lucky mascot I have ever seen. Methinks Firuz-Bakht"—Lucky Destiny—"will be a befitting name for him."

"He, he, he, hum, hum, good, good, good name. Firuz, Firuz, Firuz Bakht, a good name," he said.

Everybody bowed in assent.

"We shall also call you Firuz, Firuz, a good name, a good name," he said to me. And I bowed in my turn.

"A lucky name for your majesty's future little doctor," said the Governor.

"Very good, very good, hum, hum, hum; we gave him also the title of Firuz-ol-Attebba!" he roared out at the Governor.

"Yes Ghorban, yes, Ghorban," replied the Governor, bowing to his majesty.

Immediately, the Court Poet stepped forward and asked permission to recite a spontaneous quatrain to commemorate the change of my name and the conferring of the title. His majesty made a sign for him to commence. The poet coughed a few times, drew the edges of his long robe together, crossed his arms on his chest and began:

"Bovat Firuz ra bar bande mennat,
Ke manra pishe mardom Moftakhar kard.
Begardanid namamra molaghab,
Be Firuz-ol-Attebba motabar kard!"

"I am grateful to Firuz-the-bear, who caused the change
of my name and the honour of such a lofty title as Firuz-
ol-Attebba."

"Ahsant, Ahsant"—"Bravo, bravo," cried the group of
courtiers.

His Majesty seemed pleased, and turning to me said,
"Firuz Khan, you will keep the bear for our majesty."

I bowed very respectfully and took the bear back, amid
the general admiration of the company.

After we left the Shah we saw the eunuch Djouhar Khan
running toward us and shouting:

"Oh, how happy I am to meet you on such a wonderful
day when you have been so graciously received by his majesty! I have been despatched by Her Majesty, the Queen,
who desires to see you. You must bring the bear with you.
The whole harem is waiting to see it!"

We mounted our horses, with the bear riding once more
in front of Akbar, and made for the harem camp. Her
majesty was as happy as a child as she kissed the bear and
patted him, and the little rascal seemed to like all this
attention and behaved very creditably, now and then rubbing his snout affectionately against their hands.

"How did you bring the darling with you?" asked the
Queen.

I told her that Akbar, my man, had taken charge of him.

"Do you mean the terrible Akbar, the notorious swordsman?"

"Yes, Majesty. He is my bodyguard and a man whom
I love and respect!"

"They tell me that he would really give up his life for his little master," she replied. "Is that true?"

"And I also would give mine for him," I said sincerely.

"Like master, like servant," she smiled, and, turning to Djouhar, said, "Please tell Akbar to show the bear to the other ladies. I know they are dying to see him!"

Now that the Queen and I were alone a long conversation followed.

"And so you are no longer Mahmoud Khan," she said, "but Firuz Khan. Are you pleased?"

"Of course I am. Only the other day when his majesty made my brother a General he gave him also a pension!"

"You are quite right," she said. "You shall receive a pension, for I will see to it."

"I should like to have a sword too," I said.

"Wonderful memory!" said the Queen. "You have remembered his majesty's half promise, and I shall see that it is kept. No one here has provided as much fun for his majesty as you have. Your chess playing, your war against the boars, and now the little bear! Yes, you certainly deserve both a pension and a sword."

"Your majesty is right. I deserve both," I said in a matter-of-fact tone, and we laughed.

"Oh, you funny, funny boy! If it were not for your father, I would never let you go home when we return to Teheran." Here she looked at me and smiled.

When I left the Queen I talked for a while with Tuberose.

"Did you know," she asked me after we had told each other what we had been doing, "that the Queen saw Akbar, years ago, when she was living with her father?"

"Did she?" I asked, very much surprised.

"She does not remember his name as Akbar, but she is sure he is the same man. She says that once when the whole population rose in rebellion against the Governor of Shiraz he caught the ringleader of the rebels, a young man

of about twenty years, and sent him immediately to jail
to await the day of his execution. But before that day the
young man broke out of jail, fought against six armed men
with a sword he had snatched from one of them, killed two,
wounded the rest, and disappeared. A year after this, while
travelling to Kerbela with her father, the old grandee
Khan, her majesty met the same man on the highway, between Kermanshah and Khaneghein. He was keeping a
roadhouse, where travellers rested for the night. What
struck her majesty as most strange, was the familiarity
between him and her father. It seemed as if they knew
each other well."

This story interested me so much that I failed to hear
her majesty's voice calling Tuberose. But, she heard it and
said, "Let us go to her majesty. She is calling."

I followed her to the tent and stood at attention.

"I felt so lonely," said the Queen. "Come here, both
of you, and entertain me a little, before you go away."

We talked for half an hour, and then Djouhar came back
with the bear, saying, "Oh, my poor head! Allah, Bellah,
I cannot tell which of us two, the bear or your slave, is
more worn out. My! I am so happy that this little soul
of a bear is not going to live in the harem. So many kisses
have been showered on his head and so many lips and so
many palms have been rubbed on his white spot, that I
am afraid he will grow bald.

Later, Akbar asked if I was pleased with the Shah's changing my name.

"Rather. But I liked my own name quite as well," was
my indifferent reply.

"But the Shah never liked it!"

"Why?"

"It reminded him of the Clan-Tar, the great Mahmoud
Khan, whom he murdered! You must have noticed that
you have been always mentioned to him as 'the Doctor's

brother' or as the 'son of Hadj-Agha,' but never as 'Mahmoud Khan.' But change or no change, Mahmoud Khan
or Firuz Khan, it shall have no effect on the Shah's destiny.
His fate is in the hand that governs the world. He may
believe in lucky and unlucky names and numbers, but Fate
knows no law except that written by Destiny."

IX

RIDING WITH THE SHAH

Because his majesty had said that, "Firuz Khan should be waiting at the imperial stirrup," the Governor often took me with him when he accompanied the Shah on his expeditions into surrounding mountains and forests.

Akbar believed the favouritism shown me by the Shah was due to my capture of the little bear with the white spot on his forehead. My brother's idea of calling it Firuz-Bakht and the subsequent changing of my name was, in his opinion, the real reason for the Shah's having me near at hand. The very sound of a lucky name, or the sight of a lucky face, was considered by the Shah to possess a magic to protect his life.

He did need protection, it is true, not from outside danger, but from his own hot-headed person. The perils that he created for himself and his followers could only give the impression that he was crazy! None of his courtiers could equal him as a hunter. It was with justice that he was acknowledged the imperial hunter of his time, nor had his title, "The First Sportsman of the World," ever been challenged.

My own wild dreams to become a great hunter were diminishing in face of the stories I was told about the Shah. I had come to consider him beyond any comparison. His rifle-bearer said he never accompanied his master without having first kissed his wife and children good-bye and made a settlement of his fortune!

Laleh, who had many times hunted with him, told me

300

that once, when in the Imperial Reserve, outside Teheran, his majesty ordered his companions to smoke out a royal leopard. The Shah dashed at him on horseback, cutting his way through the wilds with no other weapon but a hunting dagger. My Laleh witnessed the terrific combat. The splendid beast leaped like an arrow into the air and hurled himself against the Shah, landing with all four feet on the charger's haunches. The horse broke down like a Chinese lantern, and the Shah and the beast rolled on the ground as one body. A wild cry went up from the onlookers, all hunters, all warriors, yet none dared fire lest the Shah be killed. This lasted only a minute before the huge cat leaped again into the air and came down with a thud, its belly ripped wide open from one end to the other! The Shah, in a flash, was on his feet, his dagger, dripping blood, in his hand. He forced his foot, encased in a high boot, into the jaws of the dying beast and stood looking down at him. Not a word had been uttered by the Shah from the beginning of this scene to its end.

I never went so far in my imagination as to wish for a like scene in my own hunting, but I remember well that I prayed, night after night, to Khoda, that I might have the privilege of witnessing such a one with the Shah in the rôle of hunter.

His lust for thrilling and bloody encounter—either with beasts or human beings—was a part of his enjoyment of life. Even a simple ride for fresh air had become a sort of "going to meet death" to his entourage.

Of this particular phase of a courtier's life, I had already been given a taste. Riding one day behind him, with twenty or so of the best horsemen among the Khans, with the Sardar and Nasr-es-Sultaneh at each side of the Shah, we arrived upon a rocky hill, about a thousand feet high. He admired the panorama and then, instead of choosing the path by which we had come, turned his horse toward

Neytal, where the hill descended in a sharp slope strewn with cobbles and stones. Nobody thought he meant to go down that way, but his majesty clapped to his horse and led the way for the rest. We followed immediately. Halfway down, he put his horse to a gallop, sending a volley of sharp stones and cobbles before him. I tried, in vain, to keep my horse from galloping too. I do not know exactly how I was carried down but when my horse was at the base of the hill he turned a somersault and threw me over his head. I rolled for a few seconds, and then went sliding down, with my face on the ground, slashed by the fall on the sharp stones.

"Who is it?" growled the Shah.

"Firuz Khan, Ghorban," answered a man. "His horse has failed!"

"What of it?" came a second harsh growl. "Get up," he ordered, very curt and sharp. "Get up, and show your horse you are a man!"

In a flash, I was helped onto my horse and went riding away as if nothing had happened. My hands and face were bleeding, and some of the tiny pebbles, lodged in my flesh, were burning my palms. The Shah did not look up and nobody made a remark about the accident.

Back in camp, I was taken into a tent, where a stable-man wiped my face and hands clean with a cloth and took out the stones. Later, in my own camp, my brother treated my wounds in a more proper way, saying, however, that they were nothing to speak of. "In a day or so you may ride again with his majesty."

This incident, although so small in comparison with hundreds of others that happened almost daily to the Shah's suite, worried me for a day or two, for I thought it might disqualify me as a horseman and bar me from the pleasure of riding with the Shah. But I was mistaken. It turned out that, according to the general belief of the imperial suite, an accident which was reserved for the Shah, on that day, had been parried by my lucky presence!

Well pleased with this interpretation of what had happened, his majesty took pleasure in having me, more frequently than ever, among his suite. In Akbar's belief, there was another reason for the Shah's surrounding himself with people whom he believed lucky. There was a belief fixed in his mind that he was not to die a natural death, unless saved by a miracle or by a lucky man or woman who would shield him by taking the penalty of his fate instead! This weakness in a man like the Shah was not known to his entourage. The only others, besides himself, who knew it, were my father, the Shah's sister, the Princess Ezzat-ed-Dowleh, the Jewess, Sarah, and my own man and bodyguard, Akbar.

Akbar was positive about the fate of the Shah; he was not to die either by natural death or by accident. A *hand was to kill him!* All my demands on Akbar to tell me whose was the destined hand were in vain. But he was perfectly willing to tell me that the Fates had reserved such a death for the Shah because the Clan-Tar, in his last breath, had cursed him, saying, "As you murder me, without giving me a chance to fight, so shall you, in your turn, be murdered without warning!"

The Shah, hearing this from the lips of a dying man, had become so nervous that he ordered all the murderers beheaded, while he took an oath before the Almighty that never again, so long as he lived, would he cause the death of another member of the Clan-Tar's family.

Moreover, Akbar told me, his majesty had tried to defy the curse of the Clan-Tar by charity and by sending mollahs and seyyeds to holy places in Persia and Arabia, and by paying scores of Mohammedan clergymen to pray and to fast for him. All the sacred Shrines in Persia received imperial gifts of money and jewelry to atone for his crime, that he might escape the dead man's curse. Persians believed that every prayer and pilgrimage a person paid for would count in his favour before Allah and the angels. One of the men sent to Mecca by the Shah was my own father. For who better could pray for the Shah than a relative of the Clan-Tar? He charged his very intimate eunuch, the same Hadja-Rabi, to accompany him and bring him safely back to Teheran.

Thus the malediction of a dying man had become the curse of the Shah's life.

Another phase of his life with which he was often reproached was his attitude towards women. He loved them, cared for them, respected them, but would expose them to the same dangers as those to which he exposed men. He expected them to ride and even to fight, if necessary, like men. If they failed to equal men, he reproached and disgraced them. This was one reason why all women who accompanied him on his summer travel were especially picked from among the rest.

To change his daily routine, he ordered one morning a part of his suite and his harem for an expedition around the Nour and Kodjour. The Governor decided to send his elder son as his representative, and I insisted upon going with him. My brother did not especially like the idea, but Akbar, who was going with me, made him relent. The expedition was to last only four days. I was to be my own master and live in my own tent. Akbar arranged for the necessary servants, and it was decided that I should ride with the Queen Ghamar-ed-Dowleh and the Governor's son with his aunt, Ayesha Khanom. My friend, Abol-Fath, was still with her. I had met Abol on different occasions, but always for only a few minutes.

I had not been ten minutes in my tent on the first night of our journey when I heard Akbar's voice just outside.

Ten more minutes passed before he came in, flushed and worried.

"I found the extra servant of your Khan brother, here in the camp," he explained. "He discovered that we had left our rifles behind and, thinking we had forgotten them, he asked the Khan to let him bring them to us."

"Very stupid, and a waste of his time," I said.

"Let us hope that he is stupid," said Akbar. "He is going back to-morrow. I do not want him here!"

"You really do not like that man, do you?" I asked.

"I dislike him immensely," he replied with emphasis. "I do not trust him. I cannot make out why, but I hope to God to find out as soon as we go back to Neytal."

After that, I thought no more about the man, but I noticed that Akbar continued to sleep outside my tent every night.

The next morning we were on our way to the Shah's camp. His Majesty had already gone hunting. I spent my time playing chess with the Queen and Tuberose. In the afternoon, I paid a visit to Abol-Fath, who introduced me, for the first time, to his Queen, the beautiful Ayesha Khanom.

His majesty arrived in camp late in the evening, with half a dozen wild rams which he had killed himself, and with Galesh, a cattle-herder whom he had found in the jungle fighting a bear that had taken him by surprise. This man, after an exciting struggle, had succeeded in strangling the bear with his hands! The Shah was so pleased with the exhibition that he ordered the man to come with him, intending to send him back to the imperial camp as a stable man.

My evening was spent quietly with the Governor's son and his mollah Bashi, who was the teacher of Arabic in the service of the Governor, the latter having sent him to take charge of his son's study while away from the camp.

Next morning we were all ordered to the Shah. It was the day chosen for general cavalcade. I was included in the group following his majesty, with Akbar behind me. The harem was also on horseback, a quarter of a mile behind us. At noon we arrived at a place where a picnic had been arranged by one of the Khans, who had invited the Shah. A great fire had been made on the top of a mountain, for the purpose of roasting some wild bulls. No ceremony was observed and our meal was served to us in the open. A single tent had been pitched for the Shah, where he sat at his meal with his host and a few others.

The meal over, we rested an hour or two, then started riding still farther up. We soon fell into a narrow, zigzag mountain path. Halfway up this ascent, his majesty became impatient. He said something to those near him. Instantly everybody began to spur his horse to keep up with the Shah, who was now fast climbing up. He turned a sharp corner and soon we found ourselves on a long platform where the Shah halted until the whole crowd, including the harem, came into view. When he saw that the last eunuch had reached the platform, he ordered a gallop for the top of the hill, himself choosing a most dangerous pathway, called "Goat Road."

I began to push my horse to the front. Akbar murmured under his breath, "Careful, my soul, careful. We are no longer on the platform. It is zigzag again!"

But I hardly paid any attention to him. I thought of my accident and a mad idea came into my mind. Instead of following the zigzag, I turned my charger's head toward what seemed to be a wall. Loosening my grip on the reins, I pushed my body forward and said to my dear horse, "Come on, my soul of souls, take the wall!"

In a flash he was off, half trotting, half galloping, like a bird.

"Wrong! Wrong!" shouted the man behind me, but it was too late.

I had no choice now, even if I had wanted to stop. Every stone that was touched rolled down in front of the other riders and after a struggle which seemed very long to me, I arrived on the top. At this instant, I saw another horse give the last jump, arriving also at the top, then a third one landed just behind me. I do not know how I got there. But I do know that I was the first on the top of the hill. His majesty was on one side and Akbar on the other. My horse was panting laboriously, and perspiration was running down my face. I did not know whether to go to the Shah or to stay where I was. Presently, when everybody was safe on the top, his majesty rode toward me, with the rest behind him.

"Well done, well done, Firuz," he growled.

"Ghorban," said one of the courtiers, "he might have been killed! It was the wrong place for a dash!"

"Not he," said Nasr-es-Sultaneh. "He is the lucky Firuz of his majesty!"

The Shah seemed very much pleased to hear this. Was it with me, or with Nasr-es-Sultaneh? I could not say. But from that moment, henceforth, I was recognized as a man! And as a horseman! This became more evident when I noticed, going back, that every rider, without exception, made place for me to ride nearer to the Shah.

For a reason which I did not then understand, his majesty was led to descend by another road.

In the evening Akbar asked me if I knew the result of that madcap order of the Shah.

"What result?" I asked. "Everybody arrived safely at the top."

"Not all," he answered. "More than ten went down the hill—half of them women!"

Next day I was summoned by the Queen, who presented me with a short, double-edged sword, from his majesty to "the luckiest rascal in his Empire."

These, she told me, were the very words spoken by the Shah!

X

OPIUM SMOKERS

THERE was one phase of life in Teheran which was not so apparent here as at home. I mean the smoking of opium. From childhood I had been witness to this degrading habit among common people in Teheran. I am not aware at what time of our history it was introduced from far Asia, but poppies had been one of the dominant crops in Persia for centuries. Most of the people who persisted in this kind of smoking were, as a rule, among stable boys, camel and mule-drivers, beggars, and loafers, but by and by I found that the evil had spread to different groups of people, such as the petty government officials and the Persian army, which was thoroughly infected. The Cossack regiments—men and officers all, except a few—were opium addicts.

The government did nothing to stop the spread of this evil, nor did the Moslem clergy. In fact, there were turbaned heads which bent over the pipe in the intimacy of their homes and offices.

Some ingenious person among the addicts collected the burned residue which remained in the bowl attached to the pipe after the opium had been smoked, boiled it, and made it into a paste which was called shireh. This was sold to be smoked for the second time by those who could not afford prepared opium. The poorest of the poor could buy it. Shireh did the same damage as opium. For less than a cent a man could purchase enough of it to poison his health. Under its influence strong young men were losing their manhood, athletes were reduced to bones covered with skins yellow as old parchment. Parents lost their sons or were themselves lost to their children. And addicts were endowing the country with imbeciles and morons.

My father had forbidden the use of opium among his servants. He thought its use a national crime against the country, and an international felony against the civilised world. The first time I passed before one of the coffee houses where the proprietor allowed men to smoke, the smell made me sick. Later I developed a dislike for those who smoked opium which became so violent that I could hardly bear to see anyone smoking without an almost irresistible desire to inflict physical punishment upon him.

My Laleh, being aware of this, took great trouble in choosing servants to accompany me to the north. Happily none of our men was addicted to opium and I had no occasion or right to interfere with other people's servants. Akbar once told me that those who had come to imperial camps were mostly accompanied by a better class of servants and among those in higher ranks there were hardly any addicts, owing to the fact that the Shah Nasser-ed-Din hated anyone who smoked opium. Another man who disliked the addicts was none other than our high Sardar, the Governor General of Mazenderan! I heard that he was such a fanatic in his dislike that he actually ordered the dilenquents to be flogged. Akbar said they were flogged outside the camp and the fact kept secret.

Things were at this point when one evening, I was on a visit to the secretary of Nasr-es-Sultaneh, something happened which put me on the track of the Governor!

We were invited to play chess with our host and a few of his guests. My brother was playing with the host while the rest of us were sitting around to watch. We had a rainstorm in the morning followed by a moonless night, dark and damp. All our people had to remain inside their tents, instead of taking a walk before dinner. All of a sudden a strange feeling came over me which Akbar had explained on another occasion, as catching "the breath of the jungle." Living in the jungles one has to depend a great deal more upon this strange feeling than on any other weapon. Akbar had made me walk in the jungles during the early part of nearly every evening, to develop my eyesight and sharpen my instinct. These walks had rewarded me by stringing my nerves, at times, to such high tension that my whole body became as sensitive as the chords of a musical instrument.

In this condition I could dispose of my eyesight completely, however dark the place. I could avoid a branch at a yard distance. My hand, without any conscious control from me, would dash before me to shield my eyes and at the same time to strike away the branch which would have been impossible to see in a thicket as dark as ink. Often Akbar and I, playing a match, dashed through a thicket in complete darkness, to see which one came out sooner and without a single scratch. The same sensitiveness was true about our feet. They would avoid a small ditch or a piece of wood or trunks of trees lying on the ground, as naturally as if they could see and understand.

To resume—while comfortably watching the game, my eyes, slowly but very surely, of themselves, were raised toward the front of the tent, where the entrance had been closed with a rope running through different holes. The feeling lasted only a second! "Someone must have been looking inside," I thought to myself. Remembering an alarm which had been given some nights before about a thief, I left the circle quietly, opened enough space in the curtain to peer out in the dark and saw a man going toward a tent twenty yards away. He was moving slowly and seemed careful not to disturb anyone. I followed, saw him trying to look inside that tent, and decided he must be a thief. I drew my short sword, which, since I received it from the Shah, never left my belt, with the intention of taking him by surprise. He turned back at once. He had heard me coming, in spite of the fact that I had held my breath for a minute not to disturb even the air! "A clever man," I said to myself, "just like my Akbar!"

"Hu-u-u-sh," I heard from his lips while with his finger he was signaling to me not to move or say anything. He came slowly toward me and when he was quite near I recognized the Governor!

"Here," he said to me, "give me your hands."

He took my hand and lead me away, without giving me a second to apologize for having followed him.

"You had better tell Akbar to oil the blade of your sword. It did not come out as easily as it should, I heard it!"

Then talking to himself he murmured: "Firuz is a clever rascal. He had seen me looking inside the tent. He is a devil too! Fancy drawing his sword to attack a man four times his size! But of course he has all the time to learn how to use a short sword when the man is as big and tall as I am. To attack a man bigger than himself he has to use the sword as a spear and throw it at the man! But, as I said, he has a long time to learn. He is a good boy too!"

Now he said with a curt laugh, "He will never tell anybody that he has seen me haunting the place, and I, to reward him for his silence, will show him how to take care of his camp and his servants, who must be saved from infections and bad company.

"Do you understand me?" he asked, pressing my hand.

"Yes, Ghorban," I replied.

"There is a dear boy and a discreet little Khan."

Presently we neared one of the servants' tents. He halted and asked me if I scented a peculiar odour.

"Oh," I said, "I do smell it."

"You are just as I am," he answered pleasantly.

He looked about the entrance curtain through the small aperture. I was too small to reach the place. Then he hurried me away saying:

"Is it not terrible!"

"Akbar told me none would dare to do such a thing in the camp," I remarked.

"We shall see, presently, if anyone will dare to challenge our orders after this evening," continued the Governor.

Here he stopped speaking, and going to the edge of the river, stood on the bank and said, "Now anyone can see me," and then he whistled twice.

Two men sprang to their feet in the distance and began walking toward us. In one I recognised Hassan, the Governor's confidential servant and treasurer, in the other, a young attendant.

"In the second tent on your right," the Governor said sharply to the men, adding in the same tone: "Bring both of them!"

We were too far away to see how the servants proceeded to execute their master's order, but in a short time I saw them coming back with two other men. They passed before us like ghosts and halted near by. Then one of the men was thrown on the ground and forced to stretch his body flat, with his face on the wet grass. Hassan sat, keeping the man's head down, while the other attendant snatched one of the poles from the tent and began slashing the back of the prostrated man. At each blow the man groaned and begged for mercy. At a sign from the Governor the beating was stopped and the second man was stretched next to the first. He began to cry, taking God as witness that it was the first time in his life he touched the miserable pipe.

"For that reason you should be beaten to death," said Hassan.

"But I shall never touch the accursed thing again as long as I live!"

"This beating will remind you to keep your promise," sneered the young man, bringing the heavy staff down on the man's back with all his force.

My heart was growing sick. I turned to the Governor to ask mercy for the man, when he lowered his voice and said: "Better kill a man than to let him live as a contagious disease amid his kin and countrymen." But he motioned to the man, who stopped beating at once. The two prostrated men now rolled on the ground and moaned from extreme suffering.

I heard the young man saying: "This suffering is nothing to what you will endure a month from now, if your head is not chopped off before that time!"

"Would you, Ghorban, kill them if they smoked again?" I asked the Governor in spite of myself, knowing it incorrect of me to question a man like him.

"To save other hundreds, yes," he answered very gravely.

"I am sorry for them," I said, more to myself than to him.

"So am I, my boy," he answered in a melancholy voice. "You may go now," he said to me. "Akbar is waiting for you."

I kept the incident secret and waited for the Governor to renew our search whenever the night was dark. He found a valuable confederate in me, for I was able to scent the sickly odour from far away. Every time we caught new addicts and every time the same punishment was meted out. This went on until one night a man was caught smoking not in the tent, but out in the open. I found him sitting below the edge of the river where no one would ever think of going during the night. He was ordered to come up. Fifty feet from the Governor I recognised his voice as that of my brother's extra servant, "Allah's Lieutenant."

"Who is this man?" asked the Governor.

"This is, Ghorban, the new servant of Doctor," I answered.

"Send him away!" ordered the Governor to his men. "No one should be out of camp at this time of the night. Should this man be caught again he will be flogged like a dog!"

The man, when led away by the attendant, began to protest in a loud voice that he was innocent, repeating his words instead of hurrying away until the attendant became angry, saying: "Hold your wretched tongue and strangle your voice!"

The Governor encouraged me to search for anyone who dared to smoke opium, and in case of his absence, to administer punishment. I carried on the war to such an extent, that many of the servants began to fear me more than they feared the Governor. This brought my brother to talk to me one evening when we were alone in our tent.

"Do you know to what extent I love you?" he said without any preamble.

"I can fathom its weight by my own love and respect for you, my brother."

"I never allow myself to doubt yours, but in order to prove mine I should ask you to share the love you bear me with some of our unfortunate people."

"I should be too glad to do so, if it will please you."

"It surely will please God!"

"Who are the unfortunate ones?" I asked.

"Those in the grip of opium," he replied.

"The wretches who endanger the life of our nation and degrade the name of our country?" I asked, indignation in my voice.

"Even so."

"Please explain. The Governor tells me I am doing good work. I punish everyone I catch and the punishment will certainly cure the evil in them."

"In theory your idea is excellent, but when put into execution, it weakens some of the human qualities—especially love—which are most desirable in man. A man should share his love equally among all men."

"Do you mean in theory or practice?" I asked.

"In practice," he answered.

"It seems impossible!" I exclaimed.

"You can begin by trying to feel for them with another divine sentiment, pity! which is akin to love," my brother said gravely.

"You mean that instead of—"

"Beating them," my brother interrupted me, "have pity for them! They are to be considered as patients which we have to try to help. Opium has them in its grip because they have been weak and ignorant."

The guiding spirit of my brother changed me altogether. I went on no more nightly expeditions and there were no more floggings. I gave them all the money which came into my hands to help them get medical treatment. My brother was even able to change the Governor's ideas; and he helped by giving money whenever I asked for it.

Not many days after my brother first talked with me I found myself before the tent where Abdol-Latif was receiving a group of addicts whom my brother had placed under medical observation. Among them was "Allah's Lieutenant."

XI

A SHAM SEYYED

AKBAR thought that this "missionary work" among the addicts was very well and good, but a young boy should be doing something more vital. "My little master," he said, "should always be lively," which in his opinion meant riding, hunting, or fighting. "Besides," he told me, "we are forgetting that the bear must be trained to salute his majesty like a soldier." This consisted in making the bear sit up and place his paw against his head. We had no trouble in making him do the first, but had some difficulty with the second. I asked Akbar if a scene of bastinading before the eyes of the bear would help bring home to him our intention. Akbar said it might and summoned one of the stable boys, speaking very harshly to him and calling on him to salute with his hand. The boy had to pretend to be stupid and unable to understand. Thereupon he was stretched on the ground with his feet in a noose attached in the middle of a staff, each end in the hand of a farrash, while a third beat on the soles with a branch. Of course the beating was not actually done, but the boy had to cry and moan. All this the little bear watched with interest and, according to Akbar, with much understanding. In his turn he was stretched on the ground his paws in the noose. To our great astonishment he made terrible noises when the farrash began to hit, not at his paws but on the staff. The little comedian moaned and cried as if we were hurting him! People came out of their tents to see what was the matter and the Governor, roused from his nap, sent a man to find out who was making such terrible noise. When he was told that Firuz Khan was bastinading the bear to salute, he laughed so much that my brother was called to go to him in case a vein might burst, and I was summoned to explain my action.

"You rascal!" he shouted at me, "when do you take a rest?"

"A man like me, Ghorban, has no time for rest," I answered, "my time is spent in the service of his majesty. I am executing his order! The bear must learn to salute and I must teach him."

The Governor was suppressing his laughter. "I know what you can do," he said. He took one of my ears, brought it near to his lips, and whispered, "Why do you not take your bear behind the tent of Nasr-es-Sultaneh for training? There is plenty of room and I will see to it that you get plenty of funds for your addicts."

Next afternoon, Akbar, the bear, the two farrashes, the stable boy and I hurried near the tent of the grandee Nasr-es-Sultaneh just when he was in the middle of his nap. We commenced directly by bastinading the little bear. In a minute the fat secretary of his highness came out like a wild man, both hands in the air, without hat and shoes. "O, my God! O my Prophets! O my Holies! Why are you making all these noises? His highness is asleep and you are waking him up! Do please stop the racket!" he pleaded in earnest voice, imploring me to save the whole camp from his master's wrath. But I was just as serious as he and begged him to go back and let me do my duty unto his majesty the Shah!

"But—but—" he ejaculated in terror, "you will wake him up—you will wake him up!"

"What of it?" I asked sharply. "His highness is the last man to interfere with the wishes of his majesty."

The poor man shuffled hurriedly back to the tent, shaking his hands and looking at heaven to see if it was going to fall on his head. Presently the guardian of the wardrobe of his highness came out of the tent and said that his highness wished to speak to me. Akbar winked at me, and I followed the worthy messenger to his highness who was lying on a thick mokhatteh blinking his eyes.

"What is it, my soul, what is all this noise for? Do you never rest, you!" I told him all I had to say and waited like a man weary of always doing his duty and meeting interference.

"Yes," he murmured gently, "I know life is difficult but orders are orders! I do not blame you in the least either for the uproar close to our tent or for your being bent on doing your duty. I must help you as much as I can. Let me see . . . if . . . Oh, yes, I have it!"

He made me sit near and in a low voice said, "Look my soul, you know how much I boast of you before the world, but the place you have chosen for training of his majesty's bear is not the right one. He is accustomed to your own tent and the change of scenery makes him hard to train. I suggest you take him around the Governor's tent and beat him hard. You certainly will be surprised at the result." Now I was at a loss what to say. My silence lasted so long he whispered: "There is another thing. I know that this sort of work must cost lots of money, in the tips to the farrashes, then a honorarium to the stable boy and so on."

He sighed, "Ah, verily, the discharge of any duty costs money to the faithful and I should like to give you a helping hand. I think twenty tomans, to begin with, and I will relieve your burden with another twenty the next time you train the bear behind the tent of his highness the Governor. Now, do tell me what you think."

"I think, Ghorban, you are really a most wonderful man! In fact, Akbar always tells me that ten men and gentlemen like your wonderful self will be enough to make Persia the greatest country in the world!"

"And now," he said, "that the whole thing is settled, I am going to ask you to go away and let me go back to sleep."

Some days later when all our money was gone I summoned the bear and walked along undecided whether to stay in our own camp or go to that of the grandee. My brother, coming out of Governor's tent, caught sight of me and asked where I was going. "To train the bear," I answered.

"Leave him alone to-day," he said. When we were alone in the tent he turned to me with a weary face and said: "I did not want you to disturb Nasr-es-Sultaneh to-day. He was in a bad mood when I left him just now and with reason. A fool has been insolent to him."

"Which fool?" I exclaimed.

My brother chuckled. "A good remark 'which fool?' —we have so many around us!" he said. "A seyyed has sprung up from God knows where who pretends to become crazy when someone mentions the word 'kashk' "—a sort of dried sour milk. "His eyes bulge out of his head and foam issues from his lips. He insults everybody and since he is a seyyed, a descendant of the Prophet, no one dares oppose him. An insolent brute. This morning some of the courtiers asked Nasr-es-Sultaneh, if he would like some egg plants for lunch and with what flavor? The good grandee mentions the word 'kashk' and immediately the seyyed attacks him like a savage and slaps his face before the whole court. Nasr-es-Sultaneh gets into a rage and orders the man to be caught, when the whole Court, amid laughter, intercedes warning that he was a seyyed and a crazy one."

"He ought to be in a madhouse!" I said, indignantly. "Fancy slapping a man like Nasr-es-Sultaneh."

"Now I want you to promise me one thing," said my brother.

"At your command," I answered.

"Please do not get yourself into trouble with that man."

I promised and I went to Akbar. As always he knew already more about the man than anyone else.

"Your khan brother is right," he said, "not that a fool is anything to be afraid of, but his being a seyyed gives him the odds over the other fools."

The eccentricities of many of the official fools were very trying. The chief fool of the Shah, Sheik Sheipour, used to blow like a trumpet, unexpectedly, in the ears of various people, or make fun of the high officers of the court, especially those from the provinces to the delight of the Shah, who always encouraged him. There was another who roared like a lion behind people's backs and uttered obscenity in their faces. Both men were coarse, indecent and thoroughly obnoxious.

The last named fool, used to call very politely on my brothers in Teheran at the first day of each month and receive a small salary from each of them which he was sensible enough to understand would stop if he tried any tricks upon them. The other, more prominent at court, had reason to remember my father as long as he lived and therefore was very careful not to trespass beyond the limit of propriety with any of my father's family. In the beginning of his career at court he had been once, only once, impolite to Father, who kept his temper and waited for an occasion to punish him. A day when the Shah was receiving guests and a feast was arranged in their honour, this fool was commanded to be present to make fun. This gave him a wonderful opportunity to earn honours and money. Unfortunately for his plans he begged my father for something to cure a headache. Father took out a box and handed him a few pills. The sheik swallowed them and very soon began to feel a horrible pain in his stomach, which not only deprived him of a unique day in which he could have made a fortune, but kept him in bed with atrocious pains and suffering for weeks!

I had met these worthy fools at the imperial camp, where they lived a luxurious and indolent life at the expense of the Shah. Both pretended always to be delighted to meet me and paid me many compliments which they would not tender even to the Shah. The reason was that they knew that a boy like me not only could do a lot of harm to them, including physical mischief, but also might injure their prestige as well. The fact that I was always on horseback when I met them, made them very considerate toward me. At the first improper remark, they knew I might snatch the sacred turbans from their heads and gallop away! Such an act would have ended their careers as his majesty's fools right there and then.

Therefore, "seyyed or no seyyed, I am not afraid of that man," I said to Akbar.

"But, Ghorban," pleaded Akbar, "they say he has a black palate like a mad dog, which means that if ever he prays to Allah or his ancestors the Saints and Prophets against any-one, his wishes will be granted. That is why not one, not even the Shah, dares stir a finger against him! His black robe and black turban are sufficient to frighten anyone among the crowd."

"Black robe and black turban do not frighten me!" I said.

Akbar sat up and said in sheer delight: "There again is the real spirit of Mahmoud Khan the Clan-Tar!"

Next evening we were sitting with the Governor when a servant announced the mad seyyed had come to remain as the Governor's guest for the night. Before the Governor had time to answer, a man came in striding and said: "Salaam to you all and benediction or malediction of my

. . . . Oh, how stupid of me not to remember the name . . . . Tell me, Doctor, what is its name?"

Instantly the seyyed sat up and grabbed his staff. The doctor smiled and said," I really do not remember the name, unless you mean the thing, the white stuff called—"

"Yes, yes, I mean that!" urged the grandee, hungry for excitement. "The name begins with K, A, and—"

"S," interrupted my brother.

In a flash the seyyed smashed the glasses on the tray and pounced upon my brother. A terrible confusion ensued. I rushed at the seyyed with the naked blade of my sword in hand.

"Firuz!" the Governor snapped out, halting my dash, and in another second ten persons were between my brother and the madman begging them to be calm.

"You son of a———Prophet," cried the grandee at the seyyed, "why all this fuss? What do you mean by attacking the good doctor?"

"I thought, I thought, he was going to say—'the word,'" cried the seyyed, shouting like a mule-driver but realizing that he had no reason to become mad, as no one had mentioned the word "kashk," he sat down. Then turning to me with a horrible look in his bulging eyes shouted: "And you wanted to kill a son of Mohammad! You, a young boy and yet a sinner! Shall I curse you now?"

"Calm yourself, honourable seyyed," entreated the Governor, "Firuz Khan thought you were going to harm the doctor."

Thereupon he declared that the gathering was at an end. "We shall give ourselves the pleasure of your company,"— to the seyyed—"to-morrow evening and continue our very interesting conversation," he added in his most charming manner.

That night I weighed the seyyed in my mind and could not help doubting him. The seyyeds as a rule behaved themselves properly, especially in public. Further, very few seyyeds would willingly give themselves up as fools or mad-men, knowing that not only their own interest but the interest of religion would be jeopardized. This man was an imposter. Besides, the idea that he would have injured my brother tortured my mind so violently that sleep became impossible. The whole night I tossed in my bed, and I was happy when the dawn came.

I arose and went quietly behind the partition to wash and dress. My brother and I used to throw our underwear on the same trunk and while taking mine I saw a handkerchief that belonged to him, spattered with blood. I went back and looked at my brother. The first finger of his right hand was wrapped with a handkerchief coloured by blood which was now dried. I hurried to find Akbar who was strolling outside near the river.

"Good morning, my soul!" he said cheerfully. "I had no time, the evening before, to ask how you were hindered by our dear Governor from killing the insolent upstart."

"Akbar!" I said, "that Seyyed must be punished, he is dangerous! I am going to shout the word 'Kashk' at him and I do not care what happens after! I have decided, so please do not say anything unless you want to say when and where will best suit my intention."

"I do not care when and where," he replied. "Give me a day to see to some details necessary to bring about a good result."

Everybody was disgusted with the seyyed. He had attacked many of the servants outside and inside the tents, had spoiled the evening parties for the Governor and his guests, and had made himself in every way objectionable. The servants especially were tired of him. His presence prevented the gambling and therefore no tips were given to them. The head attendant of the Governor, a good friend of mine, confided to me that he was ready to catch the seyyed by his neck and throw him into the river, only he was afraid of the Governor. He had no fear of the Prophet nor the last day of Judgement. He entreated me to do something.

"I know the little khan, with his Akbar, can do anything," he said.

"All right, my good and wonderful friend," I told him, "you may be sure I shall look after you, only give me one day to see to some details necessary for the desired result!" Akbar's words.

Another bit of encouragement came from Nasr-es-Sultaneh, whom I went to thank for some money he had given Akbar toward the expense required for training the bear. While talking I made a reference to the seyyed, which he took as a good opening to tell me the man was a rogue and deserved to be flogged. "Did you see him that evening how savagely he behaved to your brother? Now, your brother is the only man who thinks only of the welfare of others and the comfort of poor people. A good seyyed has to appreciate such a man and make at least an exception of him."

"Well, I am going to kill him with the word 'Kashk,' if that word will be sufficient for the killing!" I said, keeping my head high and rocking my chest the way Akbar did. He laughed like a boy, tapped my shoulder and said: "There is the boy of my own heart. I shall celebrate the day the seyyed hears the word and turns crazy!"

On the fourth day of the seyyed's visit Akbar came to me looking very solemn. He cleared his throat with ostentation and cried: "I am ready!"

His cry would have been enough to destroy my courage if it had not been for the other information which he yielded to me.

"Everything is arranged," he said. "The enemy is ignorant of the calamity hovering over his turban, and our victory

will come cheaply because we have the sentiment of everyone behind us. We shall attack to-night in the tent of
the Governor, and retire immediately to a line of defence
some hundred yards in the heart of the jungle, where the
enemy, in his pursuit, will fall into our hands without blood-
shed. The population of our camp is wholly on our side.
There was no need for expenditure nor was it necessary for
me to waste time or words to persuade them."

Evening arrived and my courage began to rise gradually
with the dark. There was nothing more reassuring to me
than the sight of the jungle, dark and mysterious to the
ordinary man from town, but so familiar to me that once
within it, I felt capable of challenging even the Shah. According to Akbar's suggestion I left my sword in his keeping and went to the Governor unarmed. I noticed that
some of the members of the Governor's retinue were unusually glad to see me. Their reception was fully spiced with
friendly smiles and signs of understanding. Inside the tent
I found everyone looking stupidly at everyone else and
resigned to a dull and dreary evening. No games, no drinking wine, and no laughing. The few jokes by Nasr-es-
Sultaneh, whose joviality was far stronger than his pretence to Oriental dignity, fell like cold water on a winter
night. Now and then the seyyed would sit up straight
and plant his staff before him with a threatening gesture,
pretending to have heard someone whispering the word
"Kashk," but even this manouvre had worn itself out and
no one took any notice. Dinner was finished, and once
more we went into the Governor's room and waited for
him to give the signal for our retirement to our tents.

The seyyed, finding us quiet, seemed quiet too, but his
desire for notoriety was so strong that he began to look
around like a man waking from a heavy slumber. His
eyes fell on me, and after some minutes he exclaimed: "Aha,
I see, the little khan has thought it wise to leave his weapon

at home! Very good, very good, and a highly wise line
of conduct. A sword in the hand of a boy is more dangerous for himself than for anyone else. Aha, Aha, Aha!"
These words brought smiles on the faces of all present
including my own.

"A sword is not the only weapon used by men of his
calibre," remarked Nasr-es-Sultaneh. "In hands such as
his a pen will do the same work."

"From what I have heard I gather that this gentleman
spends very little time using the pen," said the seyyed
insolently.

"Ha, ha, seyyed, be careful," said the grandee, "you are
treading on thin ice. There are two persons—one of whom
is our Firuz Khan, the other shall be nameless—we do not
talk about lest our words be interpreted as profanity; besides we have found by experience that in speaking of one
of those two, one is apt to speak of the other, and as far
as I am concerned I shall take care first not to speak of
them except in a most respectful manner!"

The Governor and my brother and the rest could not
help laughing at Nasr-es-Sultaneh's remark, which of course,
was only a pleasantry, but the seyyed sullenly replied: "I
shall not speak of anyone with respect except of Allah and
his Prophets."

The Governor's son, Esmail Khan, who seldom spoke in
the presence of his father, now sighed loudly and said in
a low voice and only for me to hear: "How can one know
a real seyyed from the faked ones? Black aba and black
turban does not mean anything to us."

The seyyed instantly turned to us, saying: "Be careful,
you two, I am not deaf!"

The Governor, who really had not even heard his son,
now feared an altercation between the two, for the seyyed
was shouting at the top of his voice: "Oho, Oho, be careful

or I may use my staff as my ancestor, Mohammad, used his sword."

This was really too much even for the Governor, who had the patience of an angel. "Be quiet, seyyed, will you?" he ordered. The seyyed's mouth remained wide open in amazement, but instead of restraining himself he threatened to rise and fight Esmail if he did not apologise. Poor Esmail grew red and was at a loss what to do when I arose and addressed the seyyed:

"It is my duty to resent your insolence toward the honourable Esmail Khan. Listen, you faked seyyed, you deserve to be fed with kashk, do you hear me with *kashk, kashk, kashk!*"

In a second he was rushing at me with staff high above his head. I rushed out of the tent into the damp cold night. I heard the shouts and cries of the seyyed behind me snarling like a mad dog. I jumped over a creek on the path which lead to the bushy part of the jungle, while shouting back *"Kashk, Kashk!"* to the seyyed, who was behind me like a bloodhound. I never expected him to be so light on his feet. We were now six hundred feet from the tent, and he was sure of catching me when a dog began to bark. I had just time to look back to see seyyed crashing headlong to the ground with a terrible oath!

The barking dog, who was none other than Akbar, and another man were stooping over him. His feet were caught in a noose. The trick was easy and one that is known to every Persian. A long noose like a circle is spread on the ground with the end of the rope in the hand of a man hidden behind a tree. All he has to do is to draw the rope toward him as soon as the victim's feet are inside the circle, at the same time drawing his attention to make him look backward; the man in the ambush imitates the sound of an animal and that is all. A bowl of liquid kashk was on the ground, which was to play the tragic part in the seyyed's plight.

Akbar turned him on his back and said: "Now, faked seyyed, shout and you get my dagger in your throat, remain calm and you drink the delicious kashk especially prepared for your honour."

Seeing that he would not open his mouth, Akbar pressed his cheeks with his fingers, forcing it to open itself, and thrust the end of the seyyed's staff between his teeth. Then he poured the liquid into his mouth.

"You have to swallow kashk or be choked to death," he told the seyyed, and there was nothing for him to do but swallow the kashk as quickly as it was poured in his mouth. When the bowl was empty the seyyed burst into tears and began to moan.

"Shut up you scoundrel!" Akbar commanded. "And come say your prayers like a good boy. Come, say after me. 'I, the son of a dog,' "——but when he saw the seyyed was stubborn he pressed the point of his dagger against his throat.

"Let us then start again," said Akbar. " 'I, son of a dog, a peasant from Barfurush—a dishonest man, who had been kicked out of his village by the authorities—pretending to be a seyyed, pray to God to forgive me for the lie which I have told, and declare in all solemnity that I love kashk— that my father and mother loved kashk and ate kashk— that I shall eat and drink kashk before everyone in the camp when Akbar gives it to me, and shall never tell a lie again as long as I live.' "

Seyyed repeated word for word without faltering. When the ceremony was at an end his feet were loosened, the remainder of the liquid was smeared on his face, and he was left on the ground.

When we told the Governor the story he deemed it wise to bring the seyyed back, to balm his wounded pride by giving him some money. Some men went where we left him but after an hour they came back declaring there was no trace of the seyyed, nor was anything heard of him during the rest of our stay in Neytal! He had disappeared completely.

XII

WE COME TO THE END
OF THE SUMMER

THERE was nothing of great interest in the days toward the end of the summer except a review of the two famous regiments of cavalry, one called "the Warriors of Kurd-o-Turk," and the other "the Warriors of Khadje-Vand." The head of this army was my own relation, Zolfeghar Khan, who for a reason I shall explain had not been summoned to the imperial camp as had the rest of the Khans. However, he was called upon to arrange a review for the end of the season, so that the Persian officials could see with their own eyes the power which stood behind His Majesty the Shah for the defence of the country.

The reason the Shah kept Zolfeghar Khan at a distance was that the latter believed that the Empire belonged by right to him and not to the Kajar Shah. The famous Clan-Tar whom the Shah murdered was accused of being a pretender to the throne of Persia. This young man not only pretended to the throne but actually had shown his mettle on an eventful occasion which had nearly cost his life. I have already told that one of the eyes of the sculptured representation of the Shah on the Mountain Corridor had been scratched out as if a bullet had hit the stone. Akbar had told me how this happened: Zolfeghar Khan was the perpetrator! Some years ago when he came before the picture on the rock, the scene of Mahmoud Khan's murder flashed into his mind, he took his gun and sent a bullet right at the eyes of the Shah, saying: "A Shah who is not only an usurper of the throne but a coward and a murderer!" This remark was at once reported to the Shah who in the same year, when reviewing the regiments of Zolfeghar Khan's cavalry, called him into the tent and asked if he was the insolent one who had dared to profane the imperial effigy of the mighty Shadow of Allah! The hot-headed Khan replied in the affirmative. The infuriated Shah insulted the Khan, who instantly drew his sword and rushed at him. That day would have been the last day of the Kajar dynasty if some of the courtiers had not been quick to interfere. Zolfeghar Khan was disarmed and the Shah summoned his executioner to behead him then and there.

While they were waiting the Prime Minister, who had a better knowledge of the power of the Khan over his warriors, implored the Shah to have a look through the aperture of the tent, where three thousand men, sturdy, vigorous, armed to the teeth, half of them on white horses, the other half on black charged alternately, formed a spectacular scene. A sight sufficient in those days to unnerve a host of Shahs!

His Majesty turned to his Prime Minister, saying: "Well, what of it? Why did you wish me to look at our warriors?"

The Prime Minister replied: "Every one of those men is as solidly attached to the Khan as a son is attached to his father." Without giving time to the Shah to answer he added: "Your majesty, the executioner is ready, awaiting orders!"

The Shah was not a fool! "Send him to hell! and bring the Khan before me," he said to the astonished but relieved minister. Zolfeghar Khan courageously stepped before him, believing that he was to be handed to the executioner. His majesty ordered his sword to be given back to him, took off his own fur coat and threw it on the shoulders of the Khan as a token of admiration.

The review of the warriors was gorgeous beyond my expectation! Six thousand horsemen were arrayed before my eyes with gold and silver harnesses glittering in the sun. At the head of them, Zolfeghar Khan, my kinsman! A short man, not more than forty years of age, with his famous sword, longer than himself. His white horse was caparisoned with gold harness studded with jewels. The review lasted five hours. When it was over the Shah evinced his pleasure by inviting the Khan to his tent. Shortly he came out wearing on his shoulders a magnificent robe of Cashmere lined with sable, and a new decoration on his breast. A great feast in the evening was given in his honour and next day he received all the officials in his own camp. When I was presented he took me in his arms and made me sit on his lap. "It is one pleasure to see a kinsman but another to meet a younger son of your great father," he said to me. Next day he sent me a beautiful horse and three wonderful saddles made by master craftsmen in his native town.

Two days after, he left the imperial camp with his regiments. My brother and I and a number of other officials and dignitaries rode with him for an hour, lunched with him in the jungle and kissed him good-bye.

Shortly after this I was given occasion to use my sword. It was one night when my brother, very tired, having remained long in the company of the Governor, slept heavily. Akbar and I had been busy the whole day, arranging for our departure. He was dismissing the extra servants, natives of the country, and paying their wages. This was the usual occupation of everybody at the end of the season. We had to be more careful of our own safety and that of our worldly belongings. Many thieves had been caught during the last few days and everybody was more careful during the night.

It was in the middle of the night when the "breath of

the jungles" caught me and my eyes were opened in spite
of me. It was absolutely dark and yet a shadow more black
than the darkness was gliding toward the partition where
we kept our possessions. The apparition made no sound
and it was difficult to hear a breath. To make sure whether
it was a man or a shadow, I waited to see what it was
going to do, first because the experience was so new, and
second because I had the blade of my sword naked, next
to my pillow, as Akbar had instructed me to have it always
when in bed. The shadow disappeared behind the partition and after a few minutes came out slyly and stopped
short about twelve feet from our beds. In the next second
I saw it approaching us with a hand high, holding something. Not that I could see anything in the hand, but its
position was sufficient indication to me that the shadow had
a dagger in its hand. Immediately I was up with my blade
in hand. In a flash the shadow threw itself on the ground
and quick as a serpent crawled to the aperture of the tent.
It was half through when my short blade whizzed into the
air and hit the shadow with a sound which one hears when
a piece of meat is thrown into a frying pan. All this had
been done in less than the time to tell it and in dead silence.
Then a second sound, this time that of splashing water, and
then again complete silence.

I kept awake the rest of the night but nothing more
happened, and with the first break of dawn Akbar came in.

"No need to speak about it to anyone, not even to your
Khan brother," he whispered to me, when he understood
what had happened.

"It seemed more of a shadow than a man," I said.

"Shadow or man, none will escape Akbar!" he replied
between his teeth.

*   *   *

Another interesting episode of my life in Neytal was
meeting a man who later was to play a strong and tragic

part in the history of Persia. He seemed to be quite above the ordinary crowd in the imperial camp and especially interesting to me because he seemed so unusual and his trade was so queer. Akbar, according to his promise to let me see the notorious chief mule-driver of his majesty, with whom he was in a brotherly relation, took me to his camp before leaving Neytal. We found him a typical knight errant and a notorious mashdi, sitting on a rug before a string of thousands of mules, watching the stable boys feeding them. He was without a hat and in his shirt sleeves, smoking a pipe as long as a walking stick. His sword lay on the ground and thirty knights errant stood respectfully before him as if the man were a Shah. He behaved like one! His speech, which he growled out like his majesty, and the way he carried his head and looked at the people, were a studied impersonation of royalty.

When he saw me riding towards him, Akbar on foot beside me, he arose and strolled to us with perfect ease and grace, waving his hand to the waiting stable boys to leave us. "Welcome, Ghorban, to our stable," was the first greeting. Then bowing his head and raising his hand dramatically toward us he declaimed: "This is indeed a lucky day for us to receive the honour of a visit from Firuz Khan, the Nawtcheh—"youngling"—knight errant and worthy little master of our brother and life friend, Akbar. But, verily, we are at a loss whether to be pleased at you, Ghorban, or angry! We are completely deprived of the company of our dear brother. He devotes himself body and soul to your good self. What shall we do, Ghorban?" he said laughingly.

I replied that being a young boy I needed Akbar's guidance and added that I had heard such wonderful things about him from Akbar that I could not go away without saying a salaam to him.

He heaved his enormous chest and looked like a King.

"We are indeed honoured!" he said. "May I offer you a cup of tea?"

I drank my tea in the saddle, and after more talking said good-bye to our host and went farther to inspect the place, which was supposed to be the town square and the hub of activities of the common camp. It really looked like one of the crowded squares in Teheran, with all the familiar types of the bazaars; the odour of foods, the swarming flies, shouting people, crying vendors, even to the man called rammal, who threw dice on the face of an old astrolabe, reading fortunes and prophesying events.

Presently Akbar recalled that he had forgotten to say something important to his friend, the mule-driver, and hurried away while I made myself comfortable in the saddle, watching the crowd. Deeply interested in the sight before me and preoccupied with my thoughts, I had not noticed that someone was standing near the horse, looking at me, until the man spoke:

"Good day to you, little master of Akbar, would you like me to show you this wonderful 'Mizan-ol-Harareh' and see if your blood circulation is in order?" He showed me a glass bulb with two tubes communicating. The tubes were half filled with red liquid and in each a little effigy of a man going up and down as the liquid rose or subsided. The man who held this instrument was of medium size, wore an aba and a small scarf wrapped around his head, had a most striking face, clear skin, and short pointed beard, with handsome features enhanced by his calm bearing and the excellence of his speech and manner. But the most striking were his eyes, very clear gray with dark pupils, casting glances which pierced one's body like a blade of steel—otherwise his countenance portrayed inward sorrow.

"Please wait, my good man," I said to him, "Akbar will be here shortly and give you some money; you seem to be poor."

"I am one who does not need money. I have been for many weeks seeking an occasion to see what sort of young gentleman was keeping Akbar away from his friends. I know your most honourable father, father of the poor, and your brother, whom may God protect, but the pleasure of meeting a boy like your good self is one that only a father who has lost all his children can feel."

"Have you lost all your children?" I said to him.

"Yes . . . . May God help other fathers not to lose theirs in the way I lost mine." Tears began to roll down his face.

"Oh, do not cry. Let me do something for you, please," I said to him, very much upset.

"Your voice is sufficient proof for me to credit all I have heard of you. I know now who is Akbar's master and why! I thank you for your sympathy. If you want to know the pressure of your blood take this bulb in your hand." I took the bulb, and immediately the two little figures began to go up and down inside the tubes.

"A young blood," he remarked, "and a good one."

I smiled, and fearing the man might talk again about his children I ventured to ask him some questions to distract him from the sad topic.

"Are you a learned man and a mollah?"

"I have learned the drudgery of life with all its bitter taste, but thank God I am not a mollah," he said bitterly.

"Did they rob or play tricks—falsely clothed with the robe of justice—upon you and yours?"

The man was silent for a time and then looking with his piercing eyes at me said very low: "The mollahs are not to blame for their dishonesty and the yoke of iniquity and injustice under which our people are suffering is not due to that class or this class. It is the source of our national river which is full of filth and mud! Our suffering comes from

one source and the tortures are inflicted upon the unprotected children of Iran by a single evil, but we hope soon
—very soon—the evil will be destroyed."

PART IV

I

ON THE ROAD AGAIN

ON THE first part of the way back home I rode with the Queen Ghamar-ed-Dowleh and her court. In the day-time we galloped and played along the roads on horseback and in the evenings we sat under a tent before the Queen, with the eunuchs and the girls telling stories.

We were told that when we arrived at Paradise Bridge, my brother and the Governor would turn back toward the mountain, on their way to Sari, the capital of Mazenderan. My brother, as his doctor and head of the medical depart-ment of the province, had to go with him. I was to go back to Teheran with Akbar and the imperial harem.

Although feeling very happy to return home and relate my adventures, I felt sad to leave my brother. When the Governor heard me expressing my regret he cried out, "Who ever told you that you were to leave us?"

"I thought that was the arrangement," answered my brother for me.

"Not at all, not at all!" said the Governor. "His majesty is taking the bear and I am not going to let him take our Firuz too! Too many lucky things are not good for any-one. Do you want to come with us, Firuz?" he asked me.

"I should like to," I replied.

"Good, my little soul," he said, much pleased. "You will see our life in Barfurush, then in Sari, and you will obtain an idea of this vast and wonderful country. We shall enjoy a warm and pleasant winter and then return to Teheran at the beginning of spring."

343

When we reached Paradise Bridge there was a grand review of all the camp. A hundred officials were honoured by the Shah, with the gift of a khalat, or a title or some other favour. I received a pension, as the luckiest of all the physicians in the empire with promises for the future full of honour and felicity.

Taking leave of the little bear was difficult. I kissed him on his head and am ashamed to confess that I began to cry. He was to be lodged in the Shah's garden, outside of Teheran, which later became known as the Zoo Garden. He was the first animal, either tame or wild, that ever set paw in that garden.

Our farewells said, we turned back to a place which I believe was called Aliabad, where we were the guests of a wealthy Khan. The next morning we split our party into separate groups, each group travelling alone to different parts of the country to inform the governors, who had been appointed by the Sardar, of the latter's arrival. They were anxious to receive him with great ceremony and pomp. On such occasions, the whole population of a town, headed by the local governor and his officials, would form a cavalcade and ride out to meet his highness the Governor General. Sometimes this cavalcade would travel a day's distance and encamp for the night to be ready to receive him in the morning. Meanwhile arrangements would be made for a display of the army, a glorious sight for the women and children to watch.

It came about that my brother and the chief banker of the Governor, with an officer by name Mostafa Khan (whom I now introduce for the first time in this book) and myself were chosen to go to Amol, the first town on the schedule. This officer was a far relation of mine and I was instructed by my brother to call him uncle. He was a most charming man, and from the first day I liked him. He resembled

Akbar in his speech and manner, which were simple, free, and thoroughly independent.

Akbar, by the way, was delighted in the change of our program. He had taken leave of his friend, the head mule-driver of the Shah, and in his own words "the good-byes were very heartrending and tearful."

We had sent away all our servants with the exception of the native man, "Allah's Lieutenant," who had begged us to take him. Akbar, although I knew he disliked the man, decided to allow him to go, while Abdol-Latif was charged to look after my brother and the dispensary. The opium addicts were sent to Teheran with instructions to various doctors to take care of them. I left everything in Akbar's hands. The only thing I could not understand was his willingness to let "Allah's Lieutenant," who he knew was an opium addict, accompany us. What seemed strangest of all was that, while he gave him complete freedom and access to our possessions, he cautioned me not to leave anything valuable around.

"Are you distrusting the man?" I asked him.

"No, Ghorban," he answered, "I want him here to help me with a problem which I hope to solve with his aid. When the problem is solved we shall send him away. That is, if he lives long enough," he added cryptically.

"Do you mean he is to die?" I asked.

"That all depends on him," was the enigmatical response.

I was so happy about starting that I forgot the man and paid no attention to Akbar's plans for other matters.

Next morning, feeling fresh after our rest and the feast which had been served us by the burgomaster of Aliabad, we took leave of the Governor and started for Amol. My brother decided that we were now free to do as we liked, so we travelled slowly and took our time.

Akbar remarked that, in the afternoon of the next day, we should be passing through the part of the country where on our way up to the camp, I had met the wood-chopper boy.

"How I should love to have him," I said. "I promised to send for him if we decided to remain in the country."

"That has already been done," Akbar said, smiling like a mischievous boy. "I sent word by a mule-driver to his father to send the boy. He may meet us on the road now at any place and any time."

I could have kissed Akbar. He was the kindest and the most thoughful man in the world.

We found a peasant cabin in the jungle and decided to remain there for the night. Now that I knew the wood-chopper boy was to join us I felt less desire to advance toward our destination, lest I miss him.

"Do not worry about him," said Uncle Mostafa Khan. "That boy would find you even if you should hide yourself in some remote part of this vast empire. As sure as I know these people he is now making his way through the jungle or bounding nimbly through the mountain passes like a goat to meet us on the road. He will be here by night."

The cabin was a square shack with a partition on the other side in which the jungle man and his wife kept their cattle. We sat on the stone floor and slept in our clothes. A big fire was in the centre of the compound to keep us warm. After a conversation between the old jungle man and my brother in the dialect of Mazenderan, Uncle Mostafa, who had been listening very attentively, whistled aloud and shook his head at me saying:

"Boy, boy! You may get the thrill of your life to-night."

"How?" I inquired.

"By looking a tiger in the eyes. That is if you are as lucky as we all believe you to be." He laughed jovially.

"He may," remarked my brother. Then turning to the old man he asked: "When was the last one seen?"

"Last night," was the man's reply.

They told me that the most likely place for a tiger to attack would be across a single timber bridge which lay across the narrowest part of the muddy ditch which surrounded the shack and its annex. The only door to the shack was the open space before which the fire was made. We sat with our rifles ready. The thick smoky atmosphere made me sleepy. And after a while I lay back against a saddle with my brother's overcoat thrown over me like a blanket. They promised to call me if a tiger was detected, even if I was fast asleep.

I do not know how long I had been sleeping when suddenly I felt a hand shaking me and a voice whispering to me to keep very still but to look outside.

At first I could hardly open my eyes, because of the heavy smoke. Everyone was sitting behind the fire in the shadow with his gun ready to fire. I looked into the darkness, but saw nothing. Akbar crawled to my side, put his hand before my eyes with two fingers wide apart, and signed to me to look through his fingers, with one eye, closing the other. After a time I whispered to him:

"All I see is a light far away."

"Burning like a candle?" he whispered back.

"Yes," I replied.

"That is the tiger."

By and by the light came nearer and I heard a commotion in the stable and the hard, loud breathing of the horses. Presently the light shone almost before our eyes and there were two candles instead of one. It was the most nerveracking sight I ever beheld! I knew perfectly well that no tiger could possibly escape a dozen rifles and spring over Akbar's dagger besides but I felt myself in the presence of a supernatural monster.

In another second he came so near that I believed he stood on the opposite edge of the ditch. The lights in his eyes were burning fiercely. I huddled against Akbar and whispered,

"Why do you not kill him now? Please do."

"Not yet. Your uncle knows when."

Both Uncle and Akbar stretched themselves flat on the floor, one on each side of the fire. The yellow lights began to retreat and I heard both men on the floor breathing as hard and as loud as the horses themselves.

In a second a great flash like lightning, passed in mid-air before my terrified eyes, and the noise of two shots roared in my ears. After this the lights disappeared and a deadly silence fell upon us. Both men remained stretched full length on the floor. Finally they sat up and broke the silence by talking loudly and asking questions of the jungle man who was now standing in the middle of the compound without taking care to hide himself.

"How do you feel now, my soul?" Uncle said to me. "A little bit frightened?"

"Rather," was my honest answer. "But what about the tiger? Where is he now?"

"Oh, somewhere out there, nursing his pains," he answered with a laugh. "To-night there will be no more light in the jungle and it is up to our good host to search for the sockets which were holding the candles."

"But I wanted to see him killed. I wanted to look at him!"

"Of what use would that have been to you?" Uncle asked. "Our idea was to give you a thrill which only a man like Akbar can afford for his master. To see the flashing of the eyes of the tiger as he sprang—the lightning in the air. If the killing of the beast alone had been his intention, the shots would have been fired when the lights were burning close to the ground."

By this time the horses were calm and Akbar told me to

go to sleep as there was no likelihood of seeing more lightning.

I awoke in the morning with the hope of seeing the wood-
chopper boy, but there was no sign of him. I was disappointed and looked at Akbar accusingly, as if it were his
fault.

"We shall wait for him, even if it takes us a day longer.
The others can go on."

"Oh, no," I said to Akbar. "Let us not wait in this
shack!"

"I do not blame you," my doctor brother said to me, "but
if you care to you may stay here until noon, then follow
us to the next resting place which we shall choose after
half a day's riding. Does that proposition please you?"

"Very much," I said, and half an hour later they rode
away, leaving me with Akbar and the servant, "Allah's
Lieutenant," whom Akbar had asked to remain.

Shortly after mid-day we decided to leave. Our party
had an advance of more than four hours and we had to
catch them before evening. Another reason we could not
delay longer was that we were to pass over a road at the
base of a mountain which was supposed to burn with fever
at this time of the year. Now, when a mountain had this
fever, stones and sometimes large rocks would roll over its
slopes, descending like lava onto the road. This was not
always dangerous in the daytime but in the evening it was
quite different.

I was disappointed about my boy but we left a message
for him, saying we were on the road to Amol, travelling
only half a day, and that in case he should arrive later and
be overtaken by the night, he should seek shelter in the
shack.

On the way Akbar prepared me for the strange sight of
the mountain in fever. Akbar had passed this road more
than fifty times in his life and knew every inch of it. He

said that on many occasions he had preferred to walk over the mountains, with the added pleasure of playing "Jumping Goat" with the rolling stones.

"Why can we not walk now instead of riding?" I asked him.

"This is not necessary now. We have the daylight, and besides," he added, purposely speaking very loud to be heard by our servant, "our brave man, 'Allah's Lieutenant,' knows the country and the roads, and were you to go alone with him I should trust him implicitly."

"Yes, Ghorban," said the man behind us, "Vali-Ollah knows his way and is not afraid of the mountain."

I cannot say how long we had been riding, but according to Akbar, it must have been three quarters of an hour, when he halted at a point where the jungle ended and the mountain began. Akbar, by planting the handle of his whip on the ground, and looking at its shadow, could tell the hour almost as accurately as by watch. Our road lay between the sharp slope of the mountain and a precipice which separated it from the forest. The tumultuous roaring of a mighty river which we could not see came to us from its depths.

"I am sure," said Akbar, "that the boy is on his way to us and he might turn out of the mountain path at this point instead of coming out of the jungle opposite the shack where our message waits for him."

"Then shall we wait here?" I asked Akbar.

"It would be too risky," he replied. "You must be across the road before the sun goes down. A mountain is too treacherous when in fever. But if you do not object to my staying here I shall wait another hour while you ride on with our man. He knows the road and is familiar with the mountain fever."

"Yes, Ghorban, I know the country very well," declared "Allah's Lieutenant" again. And after a few minutes discussion I decided to take the road, leaving Akbar behind to join us in an hour or two.

"Take care of your master!" he shouted to the man. "And God be with you."

After ten minutes we rounded the huge cliff and the road became narrower, but still wide enough for two horsemen to ride abreast. Contrary to our usual custom I was riding before my man, trying to go as slowly as possible. I was thinking that Akbar, after his hour's wait would naturally ride very fast to catch us before we arrived at our destination. The scenery before us, if not beautiful, was very fascinating. The grey, thick mist hovering above the river looked like a river itself, and the dark green of the jungle on the other side of the precipice was so even that it looked like a curtain drawn between the river and the sky, which was still blue.

Out of the peace of the evening something crashed down from the top of the mountain, rolled for some seconds and fell at a slight distance in front of us. Then a second one and a third. After that they stopped as unexpectedly as they had started.

"Mountain fever, Ghorban," said the man behind me, trotting up. "It is better to go fast. Those falling stones were a warning."

While he was talking a few more stones fell, this time behind us. I thought I had better ride on without Akbar. Besides there was no use in going slowly and risking being caught under the stones. Just when I thought to put my horse to the gallop, the man cried to me:

"Oh, Ghorban, the cinch seems loose, your saddle may turn with you at any moment. Wait, please, and let me tighten it."

I drew in the reins and jumped off the saddle as fast as I could. The man did the same thing, ran to my horse, fidgeted with the saddle, and pretended to tighten the cinch.

"It is altogether too large. I must make an extra hole in it," he said.

"Do whatever is necessary, but do it quickly," I answered.

He turned his head sharply, staring at me with his abnormally large black eyes from under his thick brows, and all at once, without my knowing why, a chill went through my body as if I had been attacked by a cold fever. The "breath of the jungle" was on me!

He loosened the cinch and asked if I would take hold of it with both hands to hold it taut while he made a hole in the leather. I took it at once, stretching the leather over my fingers to make it easier to punch the hole. He drew out his dagger, placed its point on the belt and pressed it with all his force. I felt my fingers scorched as if hot iron had been stamped on them and drew away, feeling that all my fingers had been cut in two. The sight of my own blood made me sick but I forgot the blood and the pain when I saw the man make a half circle in the air with the dagger, preparatory to a hard stab at my heart. I was sure that my last minute had come. But his hand remained in the air, and the sight of his face, which had turned livid, horrified and sickened me more than the sight of my own blood.

I vaguely wondered what had prevented him stabbing me, and dizzily began to calculate how long it would take a man to kill another man with a dagger. My eyes closed and I had a hazy notion that I was falling. A terrific crash on my head—was it a rock dislodged from its place hurling itself against me? Or was it the man? Why should I bother myself to know what or who it was? I—wanted—to —sleep. . . .

When I opened my eyes it was daytime and I was stretched on a soft warm mat near a fire in the centre of a compound like the one we had left behind. The first thing I saw was the head of the wood-chopper's boy peeping at me from behind a saddle which was laid on the floor not far from where I was lying. He was smiling at me!

"Ohoy, Riga!" I cried to him, "So you did come at last!"

He smiled again but instead of coming to me he ran outside and returned with Akbar—my Akbar.

"Where have you been, Akbar? Where are the others?" I cried to him.

"May God send your Akbar to hell," he cried out, "for exposing his soul of souls to such a horrible——Oh, may God forgive me or give me a chance to sacrifice myself for you!"

I was much astonished by these words and tried to move my hand. This caused a sensation much like the edge of a dagger cutting through my fingers. I remembered now how the man had tried to cut my fingers off.

"Where is that man? What happened to him?" I asked.

The little boy understood and, instead of speaking, he made a sign by rubbing his hands together and then opening his palms wide, making a second gesture as though he threw something away.

"Just that! Nothing more or less!" said Akbar, referring to the boy's gesture.

"Did the stones fall on him?" I asked.

"Yes, two stones," said Akbar. "First that one,"—indicating the boy—"and then this one,"—pointing to himself. "And now, my soul, you had better try to sleep a little more."

"But I am not sleepy," I protested. "Go on, tell me the rest. I feel a little pain when I move my hands, but that is all."

"And you have had a little fever which I happily see has now left you altogether," he answered.

"Where is my brother and the rest of our party?"

"They were all here, but they have gone now on horseback back to the place where that plague attempted your life, to make sure that he is dead."

Bit by bit he gave me the details. I had been in bed for two nights and a day. The boy had been found by Akbar on the day we left the jungle shack early in the morning. But Akbar, for a reason of his own, had, instead of taking him to me, despatched him to the mountain.

When he had sent us on our way, pretending to wait for the boy, he had already caught sight of him hiding behind a rock, and that had decided him to let me go alone with the man. As soon as he saw us disappearing behind the cliff he called to the boy, to follow us, while he climbed over the mountain, cutting the distance in two, through passes known only to him. He arrived twenty minutes before the man and I did at the place where the mountain ejected the stones. The first volley of stones had been rolled down by Akbar but the second had been genuine and caused really by the mountain fever.

Akbar had for a long time had suspicions about the man, not because he was an opium addict, but because he had learned that he was a professional murderer, with the blood of many innocent persons upon his soul. The Shah's mule-drivers would, long since, have put him on the point of their swords, had it not been for the craftiness of the man in attaching himself to my brother. Akbar was aware that the shadow which I had one night detected in our camp, was none other than this man and that had I not been awakened by "the breath of the jungle" he would have killed me then. Akbar was sure he was after me and not my brother. His first intention had been to kill Akbar, but when he saw how impossible that was he had tried to avenge himself upon the one human being whom Akbar loved— his little master Firuz Khan!

Akbar had half planned to kill the man back at camp and throw his body into the river, but his sense of justice made him refuse to accept hearsay against the man. Hence all this effort to give him an opportunity to be alone with me. If he had succeeded in killing me on the mountain he could easily have run away into the jungle, taking care first to push our horses and my body over the cliff as alibi.

Akbar's appearance prevented this. The struggle had been short and the man was now, in all probability, an unsightly mass of human debris in the depth of the chasm. The cuts on the back of my fingers were deep, but not dangerous. The bones had not been broken. First aid had been given me by the little wood-chopper, who was an excellent doctor in his own way. He had chewed up some herbs, known to him as having medicinal properties, into a paste with which he dressed my wounds. Even my brother, declared that the boy's treatment was the only one to which he, himself would have had recourse under the same circumstances.

Two or three days of inactivity on my account and on the fourth we were on the road again going north, where I expected more adventures. Our first destination was Amol, the beautiful and picturesque town where oranges grew in the streets; from there we expected to go to Barfurush, where the climate was mild and balmy; and after that to Sari, the seat of the Governor General and the capital of the entire province.

II

FARTHER ALONG THE ROAD

OUR ARRIVAL in Amol was marked with great attention
from the Lieutenant Governor. A beautiful house was
placed at our disposal where we were to live until the Governor came. I had never seen so many orange trees. Even
the streets were planted with them and the town looked
like a vast orange grove. In Teheran we used to get oranges
only during the season, and they were very expensive. The
orange grove at home was an ornament and not to be touched.
The houses in Amol were quite new to me. Unlike those
in Teheran, they were of wood, beautifully decorated. My
brother said Amol was a miniature Paris, and that it would
be possible to make it as attractive to outsiders as Paris if
only Persia could afford to build a railway.

During the week we were there, I did not see a single woman, either on the streets or inside the house. I asked Akbar
if there were any women in Amol and he answered, probably
more than men, but they all were busy looking after their
children and households and weaving a certain water proof
woollen material, known as tchoukha.

After we had been there three or four days the Governor
came. Several days of festivities followed, and then we bade
Amol good-bye and set out for Barfurush where we were
to remain for some months. Before us lay a dangerous road.
I had already, so it seemed to me, gone through all the dangers
there were, but I was to find out that there were many left.
Travelling in Persia was not easy.

We had not gone far before the road became a narrow

356

slippery path between rice fields. By and by we came to a jungle and it began to rain. Our horses found a foothold in the narrow path, which under the rain was as uncertain as a whale's back. This continued for two days. Then we came to a muddy path somewhat like a corduroy road. The mud came nearly to the knees of my horse. It was the most dreary journey I had ever made. Hour after hour we trudged along, till I noticed the ground was becoming flat and covered with wet grass. I was happy at the sight until it was explained to me that this was not a green plain. The green was only moss. Under it was a deep sea of mud. A step in the wrong direction, and good-bye forever! Once, they told me, a horseman made the fatal mistake of believing the ground safe and, taking the moss for grass, set out to gallop over the treacherous plain. In the twinkling of an eye he and his horse vanished forever. After this I kept quiet as a mouse, focussed my eyes on the tail of the horse before me and prayed God to help the guide.

Then another thousand yards of muddy walls and again another "invisible death." "No wonder oranges were expensive in Teheran," I thought to myself! A second night in the jungle, and on the third, after a half day's crawling in the mud or going over the unseen paths on the sea of mud behind the guide, we finally came out into an open plain, covered, this time, with real grass. Everyone was happy and our horses were uncontrollable. We galloped like madmen, and oh, but we were a sight! We were literally covered with mud. Before facing the crowd that was sure to come out to welcome the Governor, we succeeded in finding a stream to wash our faces and boots. Happily our arrival coincided with the setting sun. The city was asleep and in semi-darkness.

Barfurush itself was very clean. In fact, it seemed to me that Teheran was the ugliest and dirtiest town in Persia. The government palace was a beautiful building in the middle of a vast park in the centre of a lake by name Bahr-Eram (Paradise Lake). Orange trees were everywhere and the lake a dream of beauty. There were small boats in which we could row in the morning. The water was so clear that we could see the bottom of the lake, which was covered with fantastic plants. Two columns of marble could be seen under the water in one spot and these were supposed to have belonged to a palace in the old days of the great kings; the people believed great treasures were still hidden under it.

One of our favourite pastimes during the three months we were here was catching wild ducks at night. This was very amusing and peculiar. I had to row the boat as quietly as possible. We had to choose a dark night. A candle was lighted and stuck in a bottle. On Akbar's knees was a copper bowl which he beat as on a drum with a small stick. Hundreds of wild ducks, swimming on the water, would swarm toward the light at the sound. When they were near, Akbar would simply reach out with a hand and catch them one by one, gripping each by the neck and lifting it up, then putting its head under its wing—and that was all. The duck made no noise, and was left in the bottom of the boat. On a dark evening we were able to catch as many as thirty or forty of them.

When we grew tired of catching ducks we caught foxes. All we had to do was to take a boat and leave it on the opposite side of the lake, with a duck for bait. During the night a horde of foxes came regularly near the lake and gave a most uncanny serenade. One or two of them were sure to smell the duck and jump on the boat, which, being loose, would start to float on the water. Many times in the morning we were surprised to see a fox standing in the boat, very unhappy and miserable, in the middle of the lake. One of us would then shoot him down. It was no use to try to catch him alive.

It was when we reached Sari that my conviction grew that the saying was very true that "Each servant gets the master he deserves and each country the government due to its national merit." It was clearer than ever to me, after our arrival here that the Sardar was Governor in name only; the real governors, were first, the farrash-bashi and second, the executioner. The weapons with which justice was meted out were the bastinado and the dagger. To keep his post the Governor had to let these people work out their schemes according to their own whims. Everybody was robbing someone. Only the peasants were guiltless. Clothed either with spiritual or temporal powers, all the officials were thieves, liars, and rascals. The few exceptions were of no avail to the public. The mollahs, counting on the protection of the government, robbed orphans and widows. The officials robbed the public and were robbed in turn by the governors who in their turn had to surrender a part of their spoils to the central authority in Teheran, who was robbed by the Shah!

There was nothing so sad and at the same time so ridiculous as the way the Persians were fooled by the military officials into believing that Persia had an army. The army existed only in name. I was told that there was a great army in Sari capable of reconquering all the provinces which the Persian Shahs had lost to Russia, but so far as I could see, it was composed of a number of half clothed soldiers, nearly all of whom were under the influence of opium or shireh. The general was a boy called Ali Khan who had never seen a real soldier in his life. He owed his rank to his father, who had been a general before him! I was told that before his birth his father had applied to the Governor for the rank of colonel and a pension for old age for his unborn son! Both these demands had been accorded, but the pension had gone by a mistake of the pen of the military mostowfi into the Governor's pocket!

This famous general was so friendly with us that during the month of Ramazan he let us fire the cannon which was to inform the public to break their fast. The cannon was in itself a perfect representative of the army; both wheels were broken and kept in position by a small wall of brick and mud built after each firing. Every time the cannon was fired, it raced a yard after the shot and the wheels scattered. We had to ask the General to give us a long rope to fire the gun! But it was the best cannon I had seen. In Ashraf, we found that the single cannon, an old and funny-looking thing, large as a barrel, had been taken off the wheels by the peasants, who used it for churning the milk to make butter! Yet these peasants were supposed to be the army quartered at that important frontier to keep away the Russians!

This parody of an army was nothing however, compared with the ignorance of some of the mollahs, who were so stupid as to think prayers and a few days of fast were all that were necessary to defeat the enemy. One day I went with my brother to visit a great modjtahed, the highest religious authority of the Mazenderan. Some of the visitors said they feared much for the safety of the country, but the reverend clergyman replied, "You must understand that so long as men like myself live in the country no nation can make war on Persia. A few peasants from my country place, with their spades as weapons, and our benediction, will be sufficient to defeat all Russia!"

Another aspect of the people which sent me to Akbar for enlightenment was the sight of so many men well known in literary and religious circles who were sightless. Such was the case of a great poet, by name, Adib, and of a mollah who had been one of the few among the string of the turbaned heads whose honour and fairness had been vouched for by my brother. Both these great men had been at one time or another the only ones with courage enough to raise their hands against the injustice of some of the governors. My brother always kissed their hands whenever we went to their houses, and told me to do the same.

I asked Akbar if they were born sightless.

"Oh, no, Ghorban, their eyes have been taken out in payment for their honesty, courage and righteousness against injustice and wild despotism," was Akbar's answer.

Once in the bazaar I met a young man begging for bread. He was weak and suffering. Akbar gave him some money and told me he was the son of a wealthy father who had been murdered by one of the governors, who confiscated his wealth in the name of the Shah and threw his wife and son into the streets.

We met a lot of poor people who seemed unlike the so-called class of beggars and to my inquiries about them Akbar invariably told the name of each and the history of injustice done to him or his family by the Shah's representatives.

"But this is nothing, Ghorban," Akbar would tell me whenever we met a man without an arm or a hand or a leg. "Go with me in the evening to the different quarters of the town and see how miserably people live, suffer and die. Every caravanserai is filled by people who are in a state of suffering which will sicken us."

We went sometimes in the evening, before dinner, to the poor quarters, where I not only was able to get a personal glimpse of the public condition, but also to see with my own eyes that the vice of opium was more prevalent here than in Teheran.

Among the smokers Akbar pointed out a number of men who were working in the palace or were in the service of different officials and members of the Governor's suite. The result of this inspection was an arrangement with Akbar to go every Friday evening, either alone or with Riga, to distribute food or money to the needy. The work had been progressing for some time when one evening, in the month of Ramazan I decided to accompany him to the great mosque where one of the well known mollahs was to conduct a religious service. When I asked my brother if he had any objection he said that, on the contrary, he was very glad, and asked his own servant to give some money to Akbar to buy dates to present to the passers-by. This was an old custom with many of the Persians and each man who accepted a date was supposed to send a benediction to the departed members of the family of the donor of the dates. We started immediately for the bazaars, taking Riga to present the plate of dates to the passers-by. When this was arranged Akbar and I went into the mosque, washed our faces and hands at the basin, and entered the sanctuary. After the prayer was over, I read half a chapter of the Koran and left the Mosque. We were standing beside Riga when I caught sight of a man with his head covered under his aba as a protection against the rain. For a fraction of a second he stopped as if to speak to me but as quickly changed his way.

"Did you notice who he was, Ghorban?" asked Akbar excitedly. "It was the man you saw in the imperial camp with the strange glass bulb," he said.

"Oh, you mean that strange man with gray eyes?"

"Himself, Ghorban," said Akbar.

"I thought he had gone back to Teheran."

Akbar turned to Riga and told him in my name to go back to the palace and wait for us. The boy bowed and hurried away.

"Now," said Akbar, "let us go after that man. I want you to meet him again."

We caught the man just going inside the gate of a caravan-serai, where travellers, mostly mule-drivers, found lodgings and cooked their food. The vast courtyard had a cistern in the centre covered by a raised roof forming a platform. All around were small rooms for the guests and in front of us the huge arched opening, the entrance to the stable where mules rested for the night. The place was black and quiet except for the sound of bells hanging under the mules' necks, jingling at every move. There was nobody in the courtyard and no light in any of the rooms except a faint glow which was visible behind a single door, half closed, next to the stable. "That must be his room," said Akbar. We approached the door Akbar gently pushed open, and, putting his head inside, said, "Harmless friends and well wishers. May we come in?"

"Certainly," said a voice. "I am in such a state that the unexpected visit of a dreaded foe has no effect on me but a friendly call is always welcome." I looked at him over Akbar's shoulder. He was trimming the wick of a candle that he had just lighted. He placed the candle on the floor and said to us: "Befarmaid"—"Please come in,"—while bowing and showing the bare floor. "I apologise for being poor," he said. "Nothing has been left to me, not even a rag to sit on."

"And yet you refused to accept money when I met you for the first time in the imperial camp!" I said.

"I never accept money from officials. I do not mean to offend you, sir, but it is a matter of principle!"

"Perhaps you will be our guest during this last week of Ramazan."

"I am leaving to-morrow for Teheran; for to-night I have had enough food; for to-morrow God is Great and mindful of His creature."

"Are you a dervish?" I asked him.

"No, sir. I am a simple man with no pretension to any knowledge except the desire that burns my heart like a flame —the desire to see my country rid of the Evil."

"The evil of opium?" I asked with interest.

"No. That is indeed an evil, but the one that I pray God to destroy is far more dangerous than opium. God will lead me to him. I shall destroy him and save my country."

III

THE JINNEES PURSUE ME

LIFE in Sari seemed very stale after our exciting sojourn in Neytal. All the care-free atmosphere of the camp was gone. Everything was scheduled to the minute and everybody was supposed to behave in the grand style of the Orient. Even my brother was always accompanied by a servant wherever he went, and he insisted that I should be also. We had had no lessons in Neytal, but here the ghazi was supposed to teach us the Koran and the Arabic grammar. None of us took his duties seriously, nor did he. But we were wise enough to pretend to be deeply interested in our studies. One of our daily prayers was performed under his leadership, and that was about all.

Every day, whether we were in the school room or out hunting, he gave a good report of our behaviour to the Governor, with most florid praise of the wonderful progress we were making in reading the Koran. Every now and then we had to provide funds for his poor relations though he was not married and had no relations!

I was beginning to be very tired of Sari until one evening in the room of the ghazi I heard a tale of jinnees that roamed in the dark corridor between the Governor's palace and part of the ruined palace that had been built by the great Shah Abbas who ruled over Persia when Elizabeth was Queen over Engelestan. Our quarters were beyond this ruin. I had passed through this corridor about ten times a day ever since my arrival in Sari on my way from our quarters to those of the Governor, but it had never occurred to me that it might be haunted. I determined to have a good look at the whole Shah Abbas building in the daytime.

In order to get to it from our quarters I had to go through a small door into a courtyard covered by a glass roof, with an orange grove in the middle and a single room, facing the entrance and opening onto a balcony which could be reached by two staircases, one on either side. This room was occupied by a fat scrivener, the military mostowfi of the Government—a very amusing man who mingled his conversation with such flowery quotations from the poets that no one could understand what he said. He ate like a mollah, slept all day long, and drank clabbered milk all the rest of the time—except when he was drinking tea. I never could understand why he chose this remote and peculiar room, especially since his rank was high enough to entitle him to a beautiful apartment in the palace.

Next to the mostowfi's room was the arched entrance to the jinnee corridor. This corridor was long, narrow and very dark; on one side high arches at regular intervals opened into a desolate ruin which Akbar told me was an ancient summer house.

I was told—not by Akbar, who was very reticent about the place—that every Saturday evening at midnight the jinnees held a meeting there and that there were many rooms, halls, passages and underground corridors. Akbar was sure that it was filled with devils and told me not to go near it. Cries and moans were frequently heard in the passage as if somebody were being strangled, but these, it was believed, could have come from the prison, which was not far away. My brother laughed at these stories but I myself heard a cry not unlike a woman's voice one evening when I was crossing the passage. Goose flesh covered me, but I was not afraid because I always took care before venturing into the dark passage, to invoke the mystic phrase: "Besmellah Rahman Rahim!" "In the name of the Almighty God, the merciful."

At the end of this corridor I had to be careful and watch my step because the floor was steep and slid down to an arched hall almost dark, that led into a place which in the reign of Shah Abbas was the famous Zoor-Khaneh (wrestling arena) for the heroes and athletes attached to his court. What surprised me most the first time I entered this hall was an uncanny feeling as though my feet touched some soft and living material. The reason, explained to me later, was that the floor of this compound was evidently made of a thick layer of special clay mixed with straw, then covered with a second layer of soft red clay that shook whenever it was stepped upon. In fact, this floor was a shock absorber in case of a fall. The hall itself, octagonal in shape, was twenty feet across, with four arched niches and next to each niche a doorway leading outside. Only two of these doorways were open; the others had been walled up for hundreds of years. Each niche was large enough for five persons to sit in it, and there were four balconies without stairways to afford access to them. Apparently they were reached from outside in bygone days. Old pieces of beautiful tiles still remained here and there on the walls and some broken pieces piled in a corner indicated that this place must have been a beautiful hall in the days of the Shah Abbas.

I was warned not to cross this hall after sunset and by no means after midnight, and was further warned that every year two or three men had been victims of the jinnees, who were so devilish that the least they would do would be to strangle you. Many who had ventured into this hall after midnight, challenging them, had been found next morning dead or unconscious, with a most uncanny expression on their faces.

We used to have dinner with the Governor every evening, and afterwards I used to return, as a rule, to our own place with my brother unless he wished to remain longer with the Governor, in which case I returned alone. One evening I stayed longer than before. The Governor had gone to a dinner with some of his officials, among them my brother, and I had my dinner with the ghazi and the Governor's sons in their apartment.

When I was ready to go home I stepped outdoors. It was terribly dark. We had no lights at that time except a few oil lanterns here and there against the walls of the palace which burned for only a few hours, sometimes finishing before dinner was over. As a rule, I would call a page to carry a lantern for me, but to-night I was irritated, for the ghazi had suggested that I call for Akbar to take me home. "Silly ass," I said to myself, "he thinks everybody is like a mollah, afraid of the dark."

I crossed the courtyard, went through a small door into the covered orangegrove and was just going through the corridor leading to the dark hall when I heard a cry which sounded as if the mouth of whoever made it had been closed to keep him from finishing it. I felt a cold shiver running through my back and halted in spite of myself.

"It is nothing!" I said to myself and stepped into the passage, turning my head toward the entrance to see if, perchance, somebody was behind me. The darkness was complete.

I made my way through it and then stepped into the hall! Cold shivers began to run up the back of my neck. The floor, shaking under my feet, seemed wet and cold, and the vibrations were more pronounced. Was it really shaking more,—or was I shaking? When I was in the centre of the hall—I do not know why—I looked up at the arched balconies above my head. They were jammed with thousands and thousands of creatures, all dwarfs, looking like pigmies, with abnormal heads, hideous eyes and mouths, lurching and grinning at me while pointing with their long uncanny fingers, all the time swaying their appalling bodies to and fro. Their hands with long fingers like daggers were growing longer and longer. In another minute they would reach me. I felt I was going to fall, my heart was beating loud and cold perspiration was running down my face. I thought to run away before the hands could reach me, when I noticed—my thought of escape must have been known to them—each one of the hideous creatures putting one hand on the edge of the balcony and lowering its body ready to pounce upon me at my first sign of action. I was breathing hard and trying to raise my voice to cry out the Talismanic words from the Koran, but my voice failed me. It would not come out. Yet I tried and tried to cry. That was the only thing that could save me from those terrible fingers which, now—O my God!—which were about to pierce my flesh like an eagle's claws! One more effort, before I die! Yes, I could, I could, and at one mighty effort a yell issued from my throat that must have been heard all around. "In the name of Allah the Merci——" and the next second my feet were carrying me through the long corridor with a horde of jinnees tumbling over one another, chasing after me. I felt the tail of my coat in their hands but I was yelling the words of the Koran at the top of my voice and beating the wall with my sword, running, running to the orange grove, where the dim light from the single room was now my only goal! I cannot tell how it came about that I found myself on the balcony before this room. All I know is that I crashed against the door, the jinnees still behind me, only to behold one of them, who bore a strange resemblance to the mostowfi sitting on the settee, as if he had been waiting for me, with a pipe of opium in his hand! I slashed at his head with my sword and fell.

When I opened my eyes I saw Akbar sitting near me, saying: "Come, my own soul, drink some tea; it will do you good." Little Riga was standing in a corner watching me and in front of me a man was sitting with bowed head, the head covered with a white towel. When Akbar helped me to my feet, the man with the white towel looked at me in a most sorrowful manner, and I saw that it was the good and peaceful Mostowfi! "Please send your Khan brother to me as soon as possible, will you?" he asked me with a pathetic voice, placing his hand against his head to indicate that it pained him.

Next day, with the morning light filtering through the window into my room and with Akbar and Riga bringing my breakfast, I remembered I had had a fight, but with whom? Had it really been against the jinnees or was it all a dream? It could not have been a dream, for Akbar told me my brother had found the poor fat mostowfi with a nasty cut that I had given him on the crown of his head! Moreover, the Governor had sent word that he wanted to see me as soon as I was up. In a little while my brother came in with uncle Mostafa Khan, and the chief banker, to hear me explain my behaviour toward the mostowfi. I told them as best I could, without omitting anything. While I was talking I saw my uncle and the chief banker laughing behind their hands, but my brother looked serious and tested my pulse. After a minute or two he turned to uncle, saying: "No, he has no fever," then shaking his head at me he said, smiling: "You funny, funny boy, I do not know really what you will be doing next!" Then he left the room saying "Go to the Governor, he wants to know what happened to you last night."

When I was ready to go uncle took my hand and said he was going with me.

I asked him about the mostowfi. "Oh, he is all right, only you should do him a kindness in return for the cut you gave him," said my uncle.

"I shall be delighted, Uncle," I said.

"Very well," he said, "when you tell the Governor about the jinnees, don't mention the one with the opium pipe in his hand; you understand what I mean, do you not?"

"Very well, Uncle," I said, "you may depend on me."

IV

A STRANGE WALK

AFTER the incident of the night battle with the jinnees my brother thought a change of air would do us good and took me for a voyage to a different locality on the border of the Caspian sea. The expedition, so far as I was concerned, was successful. I brought back more than a dozen wooden clocks, the gift of a Russian official, which hung by my order in my bedroom.

These innocent timekeepers were the cause of many changes in my household. First of all, my brother refused to sleep in the same room; he said he had no desire to hear the call of the cuckoos at every hour, particularly during the night.

Consequently, Akbar was ordered to sleep in the vestibule and the door was left half open. He took his new office in a most dramatic manner. He brought his bed from the empire's stable (as the stable belonging to the Shah or his Governor General in each capital was called) to the Palace. Every night he lay on the mattress with a naked sword at his side, swearing by all the Prophets that he liked the cuckoos as much as I did.

The excessive formality of the life in Sari made Akbar and me doubly glad to be left alone. We still had our adventures, but the difference was that now we kept them to ourselves. In our nightly sight-seeings we used to get the sort of information that never came to the ears of the Governor—tales of extortion of money and the seducing of innocent young girls. A hundred or so servants and officials had been added to the Governor's retinue, and half

371

of them were perfectly strange to us. Among them was a young man, Vali Khan, son of a lieutenant governor. He was reputed to be wealthy, and being an official besides, lived a life of pleasure. Akbar said he deserved to be hanged, I shall have more to say of him later.

At six o'clock sharp we had to go to the Governor for the evening and dinner. The dinners—which were served about midnight—were most elaborate. The Governor's chef had two score of kitchen scullions under his orders.

Among the latter were two coloured men whose duties were to roast for every dinner a dozen or more young grain-fed chickens three months and ten days old. One day more or one day less would have made them ineligible for the Governor's table. The chickens were killed the day before, plucked, cleaned, and washed many times in hot water. Then they were stuffed with onions—grown under the special care of the gardener—salt, pepper and curry, and put in a copper stewpan and covered. Another servant took the pan, carried it to the ice-cell and buried it under the ice. Next evening the pan was unearthed, the stuffed ingredients were removed, and the chickens were brushed and prepared for the fire.

The fire was made of charcoal in a copper brasier. By the side of it was a bowl of melted butter mixed with saffron and other spices. At a sign from Mohammad Ali, the head butler, a chicken was put on the fire and in a slow and rhythmical way the broached chicken was carefully turned on all sides. Every now and then the roaster would dip a soft brush made of the finest feathers collected from the tail of a royal pheasant (known for the delicate and refined taste of its flesh) into the bowl of melted butter and sprinkle the birds with it. When ready, the chicken was put on a piece of long, thin bread made of whole wheat covered with poppy seeds. The bread was laid on the plate with one half hanging over, which served as a cover when the broached chicken was placed on the plate. Each person was served one and no more.

Nearly every evening now, after dinner, my brother and I, followed by three servants and Akbar, would go for a long walk before retiring for a night's rest. My brother told me it was a good thing for everybody, especially for young people, to walk after dinner and get fresh air. This habit of his was known to everybody in and out of the palace. The ghazi considered it outlandish and due to his relations with Faranguis. This high cleric believed Faranguestan (Europe) the Land of Zolmat (Darkness) where devils lived and schemed to bring men to Hell. When I asked my brother if this was true he said the ghazi was a mule.

What baffled me was the way my brother would visit all the narrow, dark streets in the vicinity. Every evening dozens of ill-looking men, sometimes women, were met as though by coincidence. To each of these he gave money with his own hand instead of allowing a servant to dispose of it.

He would return abruptly to the palace when his money gave out. He never asked his servants to give him more when his pockets were emptied. Even Akbar could not or would not give me an explanation of this matter. Once I asked my brother and he answered: "My dear boy, if you give money to the poor, it is one pleasure, if you give it with your own hand it is two pleasures."

All went as usual until one evening my brother was kept by the Sardar. He asked me to go home with the assurance that he would follow shortly. I started with Akbar at my heels, and I was determined to show him that I could also take notice of beggars, like my brother.

Once outside, I said rather timidly to him: "Akbar, give me some money!" My voice sounded very strange to my ears and I wondered how it sounded to Akbar's. It was out of order to ask Akbar for money, but to my astonishment he took out a handful of silver coins and gave them to me with both hands, without a word.

Presently I saw a man approach us, but when he realised that I was not my brother he turned away as if disappointed. Akbar made a sign to him, and he came and stood in front of us.

He was an old man and a sad-looking thing, with a shaved head and bearded face. His tears were running. He clutched a piece of dry bread in his hands as though it were a bag of money. His shirt was a thin, soiled and tattered rag. Fragments of a worn out pair of trousers hung loosely down his legs barely covering them. His bare feet were trembling as though he were shaken by fever. He glanced first at the money and then at me. I thought he was going to refuse the money, but at a sign from Akbar he stretched his hands saying: "May God protect you and your brother and give you power to vindicate the humble and uphold the right!" As I passed by I heard Akbar whisper that the doctor would be along shortly.

We passed two other men, more destitute and mournful than the first, both of whom readily took the money I gave them. A fourth was standing against a shuttered wall and made no advance. Akbar whispered to me that he was lame. I approached him, but Akbar intercepted me quickly, saying: "Ghorban, if you will allow me, I shall take the money to him. Now let us go to the street, I am sure there we may find other poor wretches," he suggested, pointing to a dark and lonely lane.

We had hardly entered the street before I saw a black form huddled against the doorstep of a ruined house. I clutched my sword but Akbar said it was a woman. We approached and learned that she was waiting to warn my brother against two desperate men who were waiting in ambush. While we were talking to her we saw two men running under the shadow of the wall ahead of us, and a moment later we saw my brother coming with his lantern bearer in front of him, but instead of going away we hid behind the wall to see what would happen. My brother stopped and apparently gave the old woman some money. Then he continued his way and the woman disappeared almost as if by magic. My brother was just turning a curve in the street; when we reached it we saw him go into a house a little further down. Taking care not to be seen by the lantern bearer, who was waiting outside the door, we stepped into the courtyard and slipped quietly up to a spot from which we could see inside the room. Almost at the same moment the two men disappeared behind another door on the opposite side of the house.

My brother was sitting on a bundle or box listening to the pleas of a young woman who sat sobbing before him. An older man and woman—the father and mother of the girl, I afterwards learned—were standing near. After a while my brother helped the young woman to her feet and said something which was apparently very comforting.

All this was very strange, but stranger still was to follow. My brother left and I was about to turn away when Akbar motioned me to stop, saying that we had to see where the two men were hiding. He had hardly finished speaking before one of them rushed out of the darkness and struck the old man to the floor. With a loud curse Akbar sprang into the room at him just as the second man appeared. A wild scrimmage followed, in the course of which Akbar felled both men. He had no sooner put them out of the way, however, than a third shadow form appeared, creeping along the side of the house. In an instant Akbar leapt upon it and rolled it into the light and we saw that it was the old woman who had been begging on the doorstep!

We learned—I shall make the story short—that she was in the pay of Vali Khan, but in a moment of regret had warned my brother. Vali Khan had tried through her to persuade the girl to come to him although she was already married. He had tricked her husband into jail and was trying to get the marriage annulled. Grief had fallen upon the whole family. The old man, for thirty years the official sweeper at the great mosque in Sari, had been dismissed. They were in despair when my brother's attention was drawn to the case. With his help and Akbar's, the young man was very shortly after this night released from prison. This accomplished, we emptied our treasury to send them to a small farm that the old man owned in Neytal near the home of Riga's father.

This is the sort of incident that made me ashamed of Persia—an incident all too common throughout the kingdom when the Kajars sat on the throne.

V

YAGHOUT, THE EXECUTIONER— PRINCE OF WRATH

BUT the strangest of all my adventures in Sari was yet to come. Near the entrance gate of the ruined Shah Abbas' Palace, not far from where my brother and I were quartered, a low, thick wooden door was conspicuously in sight with a heavy copper knocker designed in the shape of the ace of spades. Behind this door lived a negro whose name was Yaghout, which in Persian means Ruby. He was a colossus —about seven feet tall—when standing erect and calm, but a monster when at work. His muscular body, perfect in proportion, was a marvel to see—sturdy as an Auroch bull. His eyes were fearful, unusually large, bulging, and blotched with red spots. Because of them he was nicknamed the "Bloodthirsty Executioner" or "Prince of Wrath." His fists, when clenched, were perfectly enormous. I once saw him extend his thumb and small finger, which was twice as large as the middle finger of an ordinary man, and boast that he could strangle anyone with them. His fame as a strangler without equal kept him his position as executioner and holder of the "Sword of Justice" under all the different governors. Some of the natives jokingly called him bastard, because his teeth were discoloured and uneven—unlike those of the true-blooded Persians, which generally were white and healthy. I was told he was fond of arag, which discolours the teeth, but he was not an opium fiend, as were many of the Governor's servants.

Notwithstanding his faults, and his position, he was unfailingly fascinating to us young boys. He was an able story-teller and in return for a few tips used to relate amazing tales of his boyhood: how he was sold to a carpet seller in Constantinople, how he finally landed in one of the largest harems of a wealthy Pasha. It seems that he was caught attacking a white Turkish woman, and the Pasha thought it would be safer to get rid of him. As he was a slave, it would have been easy to throw him in the Bosphorus with a stone attached to his feet, but the Pasha thought it a waste of money and consequently, got rid of him in a more practical manner by selling him for a large sum. In the service of his second master, Yaghout committed a murder and was finally assigned to a Greek slave merchant, who was told to sell him outside of Turkey. So it happened he arrived in Persia.

We wanted Yaghout to tell us of his experiences as executioner; how many persons he had killed, and for what crimes, but the Governor objected, and Yaghout was threatened with the loss of his tongue, by the hand of other executioners, if he allowed it to run loose. Consequently, we had to content ourselves with the stories of his earlier adventures.

When telling stories Yaghout's pose was in itself a study. He would stand at a respectful distance, both arms crossed on his strong chest, full of modesty and humiliation, as if he were the most innocent man on earth, never looking one straight in the eye, speaking in a soft and melodious voice. His diction was far better than that of most of the dignitaries of the court. I never learned what his religious beliefs were, if indeed he had any. Many a time I found him in prayer like the rest of the people, and I heard that he never broke fast during the month of Ramazan. Sometimes he had even been seen in the mosque!

His stories had a bad effect on my imagination. They made me nervous; and those he told surreptitiously about

the governors, and their cruelty to the common people
made me angry with him, the Shah, and the governors. I
used to suffer from nightmare, and cry out and disturb my
brother's sleep. He advised me not to listen to Yaghout's
yarns, and, knowing that I would probably not heed him,
went directly to the executioner and told him that he must
stop telling me horrible tales. In my position, any sign
showing lack of courage would have brought an end to my
prestige, and I was rather glad to see that Yaghout avoided
me as much as possible, after my brother's order. Very few
had seen the inside of Yaghout's room, and those who had
never desired to repeat their visit. My childish interest was
aroused when I heard that it was a chamber of horror, and
I was strongly seized with a desire to investigate it. To ask
Akbar to accompany me was out of the question. He was
not afraid of Yaghout, but he disapproved of him in every
way. He often told me that if ever Yaghout crossed him,
he would pass his sword through his body without the
slightest hesitation. The executioner was fully aware of
Akbar's aversion and took great pleasure in taunting me
about it.

"Well, Ghorban," he would say, "your famous Akbar
seems to have a dislike for me, and has the *good* intention of
helping me out of this rotten life. I have no grudge against
him, nor have I any objection to his *kindly* designs. I did
not laugh when I was born, and I do not care how I am
to die!"

My brother heard of my desire, but instead of discour-
aging me he warned Yaghout to be on guard. He told
him that on the day Firuz Khan set eyes on his chamber
of horrors he would be given a thorough bastinado, that his
tips would be stopped, and no excuse would be accepted.

Yaghout used to declare to anyone who would listen that
the little master, Firuz Khan, had a way of coaxing even
the devil to do things against his will, and since he, poor

Yaghout, was only a human being how could he hope to stand against me? He felt that he was destined to give way sooner or later. Khoda willed it; it was inevitable. He therefore resigned himself to submit dutifully to the bastinado, but not to the cessation of tips!

His "museum," as he called it, had only one door, and a single window facing the street behind the palace. I finally succeeded in entering it, and the sight which I beheld made such an impression upon me that even to this day I abhor the name of the Shah, the Governor, the court, and the whole institution of Persian Shahdom.

It was on a day when we were outside the town riding some horses which had recently been presented to the Governor. We were breaking them into our ways by crossing rivers with them and galloping up hills. We had been out since sunrise, and were back late in the afternoon. I came in a little earlier than anyone else. At the palace door I dismounted and Akbar took my horse to the stable. There was no one in sight—not even a soldier. I knew that the guards took advantage of our absence to sleep inside their room, or loaf in the bazaars. I rested one foot on the small platform in front of Yaghout's room and began to brush the mud off my boots with the handle of my whip. The door was closed, but not locked. I peered through the opening. The interior was dark and the faint light that came from the window seemed far away. I experienced the keenest desire to enter the room. Yaghout was nowhere to be seen, and I thought he might have gone to the bazaars like the rest of the servants.

Very gently, I pushed open the door with my whip, and stepped inside. As would be the case with any room on a level with the ground, it was very damp and gloomy. It contained no furniture, and no apertures for light other than a window with iron bars. After a while I began to see more clearly. A soiled black carpet was thrown on the floor in one corner, with a large bundle of cloth which, I surmised, must contain the necessary blanket, mattress and pillow of Yaghout's bed.   Upon closer inspection, however, I saw a figure of a man stretched full-length and fast asleep. Evidently, Yaghout himself.   A few empty bottles were scattered here and there, but nothing more.

Now I began to reproach myself.   I felt I was in a position where I could not afford to be seen, not because the room held any terror for me, but simply because I was unattended, and visiting a servant's room while he himself was asleep, and unaware of my presence.   Not only my own dignity, but the prestige of the Sardar would suffer by such informality.   The conventionality of Oriental life was not a matter to be trifled with; the ceremonies prescribed for the behaviour of a full-fledged Khan were not to be violated. I walked to the door, and was about to go out when the prostrate man jumped to his feet and pounced upon me like a tiger.   It *was* Yaghout!

When he saw my face, he fell on the ground, actually rolling, as if he were in pain.   "O Ghorban," he cried out, "what has brought you in my poor room when your slave was deep in sleep?   How terrible for me, this neglect of duty, when I ought to have been on my feet and at your command!"

"Do not talk so loudly!" I commanded, and then, after a second thought, added in an angry tone: "Is this the way you guard the gate of the palace and the door of your room?"

Due either to his fear, or his weariness, he seemed incapable of keeping himself erect.   The sight of the empty bottles made me wonder if he was drunk or sober.   I thought that Akbar might have been right when he said Yaghout was nearly always half drunk.   He finally succeeded in keeping a sort of balance—enough to save the decorum of our positions and crossed his arms on his chest.

"Where is your museum?" I asked him.

"I have none, Ghorban," he answered, "nothing worth your highness' looking upon! Besides, if I may be allowed to venture a remark, I should beg to say, with all due respect, that some people amuse themselves at my expense by attributing all sorts of stories to your poor slave, and others go so far as to pretend that I am always drunk with arag, when, as a matter of fact, I do not even get enough money to clothe myself properly. How could I get arag when it is scarce, and a bottle of this dirty water is sold for as much as a kran by the wine smugglers!"

When I did not make any comment, he continued in his subdued tone:

"A number of men call me 'Prince of Wrath.' And yet for many weeks I have had not a single head to cut off. Yes, Ghorban, not one head, nor even a nose to make a hole through! I can only say that if the Sardar is going to run this government with his soft-heartedness, your poor slave soon will be forced to beg in the streets for a piece of bread. Believe me, Ghorban, your compassionate eyes will one day see me, your slave, stretched out dead at your feet through starvation. And who will wield the 'Sword of Justice' then?"

He looked so dejected I did not know what to say. His manner baffled me, but the thought that he probably got drunk with arag in order to execute the command of justice did not cause me to think the worse of him. Besides, had he not just told me that he had not done a job for many, many weeks? I was even moved to pity.

"No, Yaghout," I said, "you will not starve, even if your service is not demanded for years. I shall order Akbar to see that you are provided with necessary money."

"Khoda will preserve you for us, the poor, who are always at your service and command!" he cried out.

"Now show me your museum," I urged him.

The prospect of money put new life into him. He stepped back and said: "This way, Ghorban," and waved his hand toward the gallery. I took a few steps, but saw nothing.

"Look up, Ghorban." Yaghout waved his hands toward the wall.

Then, for the first time, I looked up, and noticed many objects of different forms and size arranged on it, some hanging from short bits of string attached to a peg. The darkness still prevented me from ascertaining the nature of these objects, and Yaghout urged me to go nearer to get a better view; this I did. Closer inspection showed me that these were actually human limbs! Not effigies, not wax forms, but parts of real flesh and bone!! Heads, arms, hands— even ears, and smaller parts which I could not distinguish, formed a ghastly exhibition. Some thirty cured and stuffed heads, arranged in a line, were nearest. These were unspeakably grotesque, but not so gruesome as the repulsive sights that first caught my eye. The whole display filled me more with anger than anything else. I remember clearly that at the moment I could not centralize the object of my anger. Was it with the black man, the Governor, the Shah, or myself?

"Whose heads are these?" I asked, without looking at him.

"Turcomans' heads, Ghorban, all of them; chieftains and rebels."

"Were they killed in war?"

"No, Ghorban. Those killed in war were left for the wolves and the jackals. These were captured alive, and justice has been meted out to them by the hand of your slave."

"Did you torture them before beheading them?" I asked again.

"No, Ghorban. Yaghout is not a torturer; he is only an executioner," he answered haughtily. "Torturers are cowards who never dare handle a man unless he is shackled from head to foot.

"Ghorban," whispered Yaghout to me, "will you sit on my back and have a close look at those hanging higher up on the wall?"

"No," I answered, but I looked without his aid.

The sight this time was horrible indeed. I felt nauseated. My head whirled, and I became dizzy.

Three heads hung in a line close to each other. They were not dried, and they looked as though they had been torn from their bodies. Above them hung another head with such a vivid look on its face that it seemed alive. The eyes bulging, the mouth in twisted derision, and a loathsome and fearful stare held me till I felt my legs shaking, and I tried hard to keep myself from falling to my knees.

My back was turned to Yaghout, so that he could not notice my revulsion, and I tried to keep him talking to divert his attention. I could only utter the words: "Those three heads!"

"Ah, Ghorban. They are the three chieftains of the Turcoman tribe, where I was in captivity. The one nearest is the very son-of-a-dog that sold me after branding my back with burning tongs with his own hands, and cutting off one of my ears with his own knife while I was tied to a tree, and my neck was flattened to its trunk by a belt. Ah Ghorban, think of it! When the pain made me crazy, and I hurled insults at him, he roared with laughter and purposely took several hours to torture me. Ten years afterwards I was given the sublime pleasure of looking at him alive and chained like a dog. Even then I did not desire to avenge his cowardice without giving him a fair chance, so I loosened the chain and set him free to give him an opportunity to fight. He grappled like a tiger! Three times he forced me under him! He bit the remains of my ear, already cut by his knife! At last I threw him on the floor, stunned, then stripping off my clothes, showed him my back where he had scorched me with the flaming tongs. The sight crazed him and he hurled himself against me like a mad dog, and bit a big piece of flesh from my back. While he was chewing it, I seized the back of his neck with one hand, forced him to his knees, and cut off his head with one stroke!

"The other head is that of his younger brother, who strangled two of my fellow prisoners, each with one hand, and threw a child up in the air and caught him on the point of his sword. But I must confess that before I cut off his head I did an extra bit of work. I pushed the point of his own sword into his heart, as I told him who I was and reminded him of the child he had murdered."

"When did all this happen?" I inquired.

"Oh, before the arrival of the Sardar, and, between ourselves, our dear Sardar is very soft-hearted, and Turcomans and other rebels are becoming bold again. We need a strong hand to hold the reins of government."

By this time my faintness was increasing! I was dizzier than ever, yet I knew I dared not reel, for I had to uphold my dignity. A single word about my sickness, a grimace of disgust, or loathing, would be interpreted as lack of courage and I should have no more significance for the black slave than a tramp.

As the mist cleared before my eyes, I said to Yaghout in a cutting tone, "Is that all you have done during your life?" and jerked my head toward the walls.

"Yes, that is all, and yet people give me the devil's reputation and pretend that no man's head is safe with Yaghout."

I turned to go, but for dignity's sake looked once more around the room and said: "We have seen all there is to be seen. Let us go away."

But just at that moment, my eyes rested on a most appalling sight: On the side of the wall, near the door and almost hidden from view, a pair of eyes were leering at me from a grinning head, which seemed alive.

My knees began to shake, my throat felt dry. Something burned in my mouth.

"Yaghout," I cried out, "you told me you had been doing nothing for a long time, and yet this head seems to be freshly cut off, and not the head of a Turcoman. Do I understand that you are daring to tell me a falsehood?"

"O Ghorban, I swear by all the prophets that this head was cut away more than six weeks ago."

I left the room and with fresh air on my face gradually became myself again.

Yaghout shuffled behind me, saying, "Whoever can pretend that Yaghout has been passing his time in leisure? Not one week passes without doing some part of my duty. I have never failed to do service. No one can accuse me of lack of unselfish work for the establishment of this governorship. If the Farrash-Bashi has blackened me before the eyes of the public and the Sardar, he is a liar. If I were allowed to open my mouth, I should say that nothing would give me greater pleasure than to cut off the unworthy head of the Farrash-Bashi. Khoda will strike me dead if I say an untruth when I swear that Yaghout cuts the heads and the Farrash-Bashi gets the money."

I motioned him to keep quiet. A vision of all these heads, arms, hands, ears, of so many human beings—some guilty, others no doubt thoroughly innocent—upon whom the evil of corruption had passed its sentence, began to turn before my eyes. I felt cold. The poor devil at my heels had no idea of what was happening within me. He was only an instrument in the hands of scheming monsters who were conspiring to get money. He was ignorant, and knew no better, a slave from his birth, and a blind tool in the hands of devils.

After this visit I knew more deeply than I had ever known before, that Akbar was right: the roots of the tree of Shahdom had to be dug out and burned. I, too, was ready to pray for deliverance through the "Unseen Hand."

VI

THE "UNSEEN HAND" STRIKES

WE WENT back to Teheran a little before the winter was over. We had intended to stay until spring, but messengers came to summon the Governor. In May the whole country was to celebrate the fiftieth anniversary of the Shah's reign, and all the governors were requested to come to the capital and take part in the festivities. The messengers said that it was rumoured that during the jubilee his majesty was to declare himself a kind father to his people. His reign had been a bloody one, but he had decided now to win back the hearts of his subjects. Elaborate preparations were to be made to celebrate this jubilee as the beginning of a new era. All the regiments of warriors were ordered to parade on that day and universal amnesty had been promised to all prisoners. I was very happy at the idea of going back. I was tired of Sari, and homesick.

The messengers told us that the mountains were practically impassable because of snow and hurricanes. Already there had been a series of ahmans and bahmans, two fearful and disastrous agencies of death in the mountains. When a whole section of a snow-covered path was dislodged under the feet of a caravan and a hundred men and animals swept over a precipice this was called an ahman. When a section of snow covering the surface of a sharp cliff for a distance of a mile or more raised itself like a monster shaft, fell from a height of thousands of feet, and engulfed a whole caravan this was called a bahman. Neither man nor beast had ever escaped either of these two calamities alive. They said that the mountain passes we had traversed during the spring were covered with ice, but this made no difference. We had been summoned by the Shah; dead or alive we had to reach Teheran as quickly as possible. There were more than two hundred of us, besides the guides, when we finally set out. We prepared for the worst, and as we came out of the jungles and started up the mountains we redoubled our precautions. We put on high boots, rain-proof coats of tchoukha, woollen jerseys, and gloves, and covered our heads and faces with woollen scarfs and black glasses. Our rifles were in woollen coverings. They were useless. The barrels were ice cold; when I touched mine, I felt a shock as if I had touched a piece of burning charcoal! Our horses were also protected against the cold. Their bellies and necks were covered with woollen mats which left only their ears and eyes exposed. I was surprised to see Akbar, who was a teetotaller, with a bottle of arag in his hand, but he said it was for our horses.

Thus equipped we were about to fight a battle against Almighty Nature, in which we had only one single weapon to defend ourselves—the experience of those who had made the trip before. All else was useless—our rifles and swords, even our strength. The path that the messengers had cut through the snow had since been covered with some twenty inches of new snow. Under the snow was a layer of solid ice. The snow was a great help in climbing, but none at all in going down. The poor horses could do nothing. They simply slid down like sleighs, the heavy snow massed under their bellies preventing them from going too fast. It was impossible to see the difference between heaven and earth, both had been turned into a vast world of white snow whirling in the air, slashing our faces, winding around men and horses like a shroud. Sometimes I glided down the icy path for five minutes without a stop, with my horse's legs stretched straight in front of him. Akbar was sliding in front of

me, guiding my horse as best he could in view of his own
difficulties, and shouting instructions which I was not able
to hear. Esmail Khan was somewhere behind me.

When we reached the summit of the plateau my first
impression was that we were in a room filled with thick
vapour floating in the biting cold air. I tried hard but was
unable to see five yards beyond me. We moved forward
in silence, like ghosts. The snow was falling thick and our
advance was very slow. When presently we came to the
part of the plateau called Adam-Kush (Man-Killer), a wind
suddenly began to blow, at first mild but in ten minutes
so strong that I thought it would blow us away. The falling snow began to whirl and spin in circles, and in a short
time the whole plateau was alive with the swirling flakes.
Huge cones of snow were whirling like dervishes, starting
in tiny circles and growing until they formed columns as
high as a minaret. A muffled cry from one of our guards
brought the party to a sudden halt. One of the horsemen
hurried ahead in front of the rest, and Akbar pushed my
horse toward him. Others followed, and the rest of the
horsemen formed a large circle around us with the heads of
their horses turned outside. When the circle was complete
one rider forced his horse backward twenty feet and soon
another and another until a second circle was formed. Again
a rider separated himself from the rest and in this way a
third circle was made, each time smaller and nearer to us,
till at last we were inside a series of circles, the backs of
the horses turned to us. My hands, in spite of the heavy
woollen gloves which covered half my arms, were so cold I
had no control over them. I felt as if I had no hands at
all. A snow whirlwind which had started around us shot
up almost instantly into a pillar, which circled frantically
higher and higher until we were hidden inside a thick wall
of snow that was turning like a screw. The sight of it made
me sick at heart. There was a hissing in my ears, but I

could not tell whether it came from the wind or the snow. I was glad we were so jammed against one another that we could not be blown away and scattered. But I did not rest long in this serenity. The hissing gave way to ear-splitting shrieks. My heart came to my mouth. My horse shivered and shied backward and forward as if possessed. Had it not been for the horses around me I am sure he would have taken the bit between his teeth and rushed us both to destruction. My hair was standing on end and my cries to the men to tell me what these howls were that sounded so like human screeches brought no answer.

My terror made it seem that this had lasted an age, but in reality it was not a great while before the whirlwind of snow began to subside. The howling died away and the riders began to push their horses aside. In a few minutes I saw that they were going through the same manoeuvre in reverse. The howling stopped completely and the small circles widened into a single big one, which broke at the point nearest the path. Two by two the horsemen turned, and in a short time we were in a long line leading toward a yellowish light which proved to be the sun, but hardly looked like it. Here and there a few small snow eddies were trying to whirl, but since the wind had stopped, they died. Again we looked like ghosts shrouded by falling snow. We moved in silence like a funeral procession. Eventually we reached the edge of the plateau and descended an icy path by letting our horses slide down on all fours. After many hours of this acrobatic riding I saw the black form of a jungle ahead and I knew that we were safe. Our passage was really remarkable. We had crossed the Man-Killer plateau without a single casualty to man or horse.

Akbar, happy and excited, told me that by forming the defensive circles we had also escaped a most terrific encounter with a horde of hungry wolves. The circles had brought the beasts and horses face to face, opposing the glaring eyes of the charger to the snarling wolves. Had we been scattered, with the backs of our horses to them, very likely none of us would have escaped.

After another day of riding we came to my mother's girlhood home, Firuz-Kuh, where we halted for rest and sleep for the first time since we started from Sari. The fourth day brought us in sight of Teheran.

My home-coming was that of a prodigal son. I was as much of a stranger as a man from the jungle. The cold had done its worst. The skin of my face was peeling off as if it had been scorched by fire. For a day or two I had to remain in my room, my face smeared with a coat of cream. My Dadeh said I was a sight, but notwithstanding that, a sight which gladdened her heart to the brink of bursting for joy.

All day long friends and comrades swarmed to my room and all night long I had to tell of my adventures to the crowd of servants sitting in a circle around me, listening with wide eyes. Akbar was going through the same performance with the menservants. Laleh had asked permission to remain with me, and slept in the next room to make up for the time that I had spent away from him. But my heart was missing one great delight, the soul of my soul, the blood of my heart—my mother.

My impression of Teheran after my return was of a population stirred to a frenzy, although it was yet some weeks before the jubilee was actually to begin. It was whispered that the day of the Shah's celebration was to be the greatest in the history of Persia. Throughout the land, feasts and merrymakings were to be arranged to render the day really a national jubilee. Shops were to be decorated and business suspended for a week. Children were to have a holiday and new clothes, as on the New Year. Warriors and nomadic cavalry, rushing from the different provinces, were to line up in the streets and at the side of the highroad to the shrine; afterward, to enact a pageant such as never had been witnessed before in Teheran.

Prisoners were to be released without condition and a general amnesty was to be proclaimed; peasants were promised exemption from taxes for at least two years; young men who were enrolled for the army were to be sent home to their parents. The town was to be illuminated for weeks with triumphal arches and the poor were to be fed for months. Ministers and officials were already intriguing for honours and pensions from the Shah.

Shrines and sacred places were to open their gates to all wayfarers and pilgrims, and the seyyeds and mollahs were taking cough medicine to clear their throats to sing and chant the praises of the Shah in all the pulpits. The mosques were swept and repaired for general meetings and public prayers in behalf of the sovereign. Thousands of holy men and priests were swarming in from all corners of the country to solicit pilgrimages to the holy places. Sacred fountains were enlarged to hold more holy water and the rightful authorities had foreseen that many miracles might take place on the day of the jubilee, with the aid of these fountains. It was whispered that his majesty intended to vacate the harem of its present inhabitants and replace them with an entirely new set of women! The talk of the jubilee was on every tongue.

Having, by the help of my Dadeh, succeeded in growing a new skin on my face, I was to call on my friends and to arrange with Abol-Fath, long before the day, for our entry into the Shrine of Hazrate-Abdol-Azim, outside Teheran, where we were to witness the Shah's prayer. Moving about the city, I came to understand that the jubilee day was to be a most startling occasion for Persia. To think that an Oriental monarch, like Nasser-ed-Din Shah, coming to the throne when a boy, now, after a fifty years' reign notorious for absolutism, was to reform himself in a day, was most unbelievable!

The Shah had declared—it was no longer a rumour but a fact—that he would, after a prayer in the Holy Shrine of Hazrate-Abdol-Azim, renounce his perogatives as despot and proclaim himself "The Majestic Father of all the Persians." The city authority was to relax its vigilant watch. No record was to be kept of the strangers who flocked to the Caravanserais and the population was to be left free to wander the streets during the whole night.

In our own home, there was nothing else to think or speak about, except the coming event. Carpets were to be spread on the space before our house, rugs and brocades to be hung over the walls; we were to receive uninvited guests for tea and sherbet for as many days as the feast lasted.

Even her majesty, the Queen Ghamar-ed-Dowleh, whom I had the pleasure of meeting again after my arrival in Teheran, was now so enthusiastic about her imperial spouse that she said she was sure that, from the day of the jubilee, Persia was to face a new destiny and a great future. Many who had never believed in the Shah before now felt that a great change was about to take place.

Her lovely lady-in-waiting, Tuberose, who never paid any attention to politics or anything else outside her immediate surroundings, seemed converted to an enthusiastic admiration of his majesty. She was now back at the palace of the Shah's sister, and, by reason of our having passed the summer with the Shah, she was allowed to call on my family and remain the whole day with me. On one occasion, she told me that her departure from the imperial harem had been rather difficult. His majesty had seen her and had made it known that she should be kept there. Only the Princess's most urgent call for her to go back had won her release; but she was not altogether sure that she would be allowed to remain long. Fortunately, the jubilee had turned the Shah's attention to other matters.

The only man who seemed quite indifferent to all these preparations was Akbar! He took no notice of what was said or done, and when I asked him what he thought of the declaration of the Shah, he smiled and shook his head. "My dear little master, it is impossible to whiten a black face with soap or transmute a black heart to white. Nothing will change the Shah, and prayers and feasts will not keep the country."

"Then you do not believe in the goodness of the Shah?"

"No good ever has come from a bad subject; a folus tree will never bring forth oranges; the Shah is not the man to bring happiness or prosperity to the country by simply calling himself 'The Kindly Father.' The destiny of the country lies in 'The Unseen Hand'!"

"I understand. You have been to the Shrine to see our grand old man, have you not?" I queried.

"No, Ghorban, I have not been to the Shrine, because the grand old man is not receiving any one."

"Are you not living with him?"

"No, Ghorban. Since our arrival, I have taken quarters with the chief of the stable of the Princess Ezzat-ed-Dowleh, the man called Gagou."

"Why did you change?"

"The grand old man is leaving the city in a few days; he is busy preparing for a long journey," he answered.

I asked Akbar if he were going to the Shrine to see the Shah.

"I do not believe so. I dislike comedies played to fool the public," was his answer.

"I hear that the great modjtaheds have decided, for the time being, to discontinue persecuting the babis and other infidels," I said.

"Another comedy! Let the Mohammedan clergy save

their own skins from the fire of Hell and leave the souls of the Persian people at rest—that is what I say!" added Akbar vehemently.

I concluded that it was no use to talk to Akbar any more, and spent the rest of my time preparing for the great day.

I thought no more about the grand old man in the Shrine, until the following Friday, when I came out of the Garden of Pesta Beyk, where I had been with Laleh visiting the tomb of my forefather. I turned toward the shrine and caught sight of a man, who seemed familiar to me, stepping inside the gate. I halted, my face toward the shrine, and began to pray in silence. The man who had entered the shrine was now walking toward the sanctuary. I was sure I knew him. After a moment I saw that it was the man with the glass bulb to measure the pressure of the blood. He took off his shoes, and disappeared inside the sanctuary. I finished my prayers and walked away.

On my way home, I thought, "Can it be possible this man knows the grand old man and is one of his friends? He knows Akbar, surely he must know Akbar's friend and companion."

When I arrived home, I found Akbar waiting to ask me if, on the jubilee day, I was going to the Shrine of Hazrate-Abdol-Azim with the officials of the court, or alone. I informed him I was going there with my comrade, Abol-Fath, who told me he too was to be in attendance upon his majesty inside the sanctuary.

"That will be fine," Akbar replied, " for I know that none of the officials will be allowed to go inside the shrine when his majesty enters. His majesty has said he wishes to be alone in the shrine and mingle with his people, like one of them, without attendants. He also said that any one of his subjects will be allowed to go to him direct, without interference."

"So much the better," I said.   "Abol and I will be the only privileged ones!"

"Yes, Ghorban, Abol-Fath Khan and your good self will be the only ones to have the privilege of seeing the grand day—a very grand day, indeed!"   I was somewhat surprised at Akbar's change of attitude, but too busy with my own affairs to pay much attention to it.

The Shah was expected at the shrine at one hour and a half after noon.   Abol-Fath Khan went early in the morning and I met him shortly after.   The whole road, from the city to the shrine, was jammed with thousands of men and women, on foot, on mules and on donkeys.   All along the road, hundreds of vendors had set up small tents, to sell ice cream, sherbets, and other refreshment to the passers-by.

The town of Hazrate-Abdol-Azim, near Teheran, was crowded to such an extent that Laleh and I were obliged to go to the garden belonging to the family of the Shah's sister, and ask the gardener to shelter our horses.   The whole park was crowded.   We had decided to obtain food from the bazaar and have luncheon in the garden, as it was impossible to walk through the crowd.   I believe all Teheran was at the shrine.

I intended to wait and see the cavalcade of the Shah arrive from Teheran, but Laleh told me it would be impossible to get into the shrine if we delayed.

"I am afraid we shall never arrive there any way!" he said.   "I am sure hundreds will be suffocated in the crowd."

We left the garden, and went to the shrine, (where I waited for Laleh), to find Abol, who was entertaining his mother and sister at luncheon, in one of the many gardens around the shrine.   After a short time, Laleh ran to me, saying, "Come, my soul, Abol is waiting for you."

"But the Shah will not arrive for an hour," I protested.

"You must go inside now; the shrine is to be cleared of all this crowd," he answered.

I ran to Abol, who immediately took my hand and started away. Laleh said he would wait for me at a particular spot, pointing to the place where the man who took care of the shoes of the public was already preparing himself for the extra work.

The shrine was filled with people. We forced our way to the sanctuary, only to find ourselves pressed against the wall by hundreds of women who were pushing against one another to touch the sanctuary with their hands.

"We are in the place where we must stand when the Shah arrives, and it is just as well to keep it, if only some of these honourable khanoms will be gracious enough not to push us into the wall!" said Abol.

"You must consider yourself very happy to have reached this corner alive," remarked one of the khanoms under her veil. "Many have fainted in the crush!"

It seemed a very long time before we heard voices, commanding the crowd to vacate the shrine. His majesty had arrived! In ten minutes the place cleared.

Abol breathed deeply and addressed himself to the shrine: "Please, O Highness Emam, see that my comrade and I depart from here alive!"

Presently, a hush of such ominous character fell over the whole building that I shivered. The silent shrine and the gorgeous sanctuary seemed to be waiting for some great event, far more important than the Shah's jubilee. All at once, I felt "the breath of the jungle," which always foretold an unexpected danger.

"Are you afraid?" asked Abol.

"Afraid of what?" I replied somewhat haughtily.

"I do not know," he said, "but you seem nervous."

Then he pulled at my sleeve to hush my answer.

His Majesty, the Shah of Shahs, the Standard Bearer of Islam, the Shadow of Allah, the Shah of Persia, was inside the sanctuary!

We flattened ourselves against the wall when he came in sight. He threw a glance at us; we both bowed deeply to him, with hands crossed on our breasts, and stood at attention. He passed us, making the rounds of the Shrine and touching the silver rail around the mausoleum with his forehead, murmuring prayers. After a while, he came back and stood against the wall opposite us, looking now at the shrine, now at the ceiling, then again at the shrine. He was dressed very simply—no jewels, no sword.

Presently he looked toward the entrance, where a man was standing with a letter in his hand. Abol hurried toward the man, intending to take the letter and bring it to the Shah, and I followed. We were both near the man, when I saw his majesty make a sign for us to let the man deliver his letter himself. We stepped back, bowing to the Shah and walking backward, with such respect that we did not halt in our retreat until we felt the wall. We were about to straighten our bodies when a shot rang out, echoing in the arched dome of the shrine like a cannon. Only a hundredth of a second the Shah remained standing; then he fell headlong to the ground! The shot was so unexpected, and the sight of the Shah so appalling that my head began to swim. The dizziness lasted only a second. I opened my eyes and was about to rush to the Shah, but the whole place had so filled with courtiers and officers, that Abol and I could not move. I wanted to cry, but Abol clutched me by the hand and after a while dragged me outside.

We rushed out into the courtyard, and thence to the street. I was about to be forced into a closed carriage by an official, when a hand seized me by the shoulder and a voice said, "Into the other carriage, here; here, I shall take you to it."

It was my Laleh. He rushed me toward a carriage, and though I was a big boy, he picked me up and put me on his shoulders, shoving the crowd away, and elbowing with all his might until we reached the bazaar. He put me down, but took my hand, and hurried me toward the garden where our horses were. He helped me to the saddle, and soon we were galloping away by a side road, to the city. The main road was crowded with carriage after carriage racing for Teheran.

When we arrived in the city, he helped me down, and instead of taking me home, brought me to the house of the brother who had been with me in Mazenderan. "My soul, remember, you know nothing! We have been in the shrine and that is all!"

But all through the city the cry rang:

"The Shadow of Allah has been assassinated by a babi!"

"Killed by a babi!" I thought to myself. Then dawned in my mind all I had been told about the mysterious hand, and I knew that it had struck.

*   *   *

A week or so after the fall of the most picturesque figure among Oriental monarchs: Nasser-ed-Din, Shah of Persia and Shadow of Allah, I was standing on the roof, just before sunrise, thinking about the events of the last few days. The scene of the Shah's assassination was in all clarity before my mind's eye; in fact the expression I noticed in his eyes when very quietly and with dignified calm, he turned his glance towards the Holy Sepulchre, then another glance at Abol and myself who, rooted to the spot, saw him turn a final look upon the assassin who had dropped the pistol and was leaning towards the dying Shah, as if anxious to prevent his fall.

The expression in the Shah's eyes as they were closing was that of weariness, a cessation of care and love of the world and its glamour. He appeared tired of it all, tired of the corporeal pleasures and mundane pomp and circumstance.

It seemed almost incredible to me that He, the Shah of Shahs, Shadow of Allah, favoured creature of Khoda, could die by a mere bullet! Did I ever consider a rifle or pistol as anything other than an ordinary toy with which to amuse myself? Deadly, perhaps, but only to ordinary mortals or beasts. Delightful instruments of game and chase, just utensils for punishing criminals of greater or less degree, but for extinguishing a potentate—banish the thought! No catastrophe was impossible now! I was beyond astonishment, nothing could shock me.

He had been shot! *He* had fallen dead! He had gone the way of all flesh. Yet, the fascinating blue sky was in its usual place, the verdant foliage and solid earth, the soil of my beloved land, my adored Iran, the sacred ground which held in its close embrace for all eternity the bodies of my ancestors and all my kin that had departed this life, was as undisturbed and flourishing as beautifully in its lovely spring garment, as ever!

I had already been to the palace with my father to see the man who murdered the Shah. He was then a prisoner. One look, and I caught my breath as if I had been choking. The man in the heavy chain was none other than the man with the glass bulb, the tester of the blood! I looked at him in horror. Then I recalled the grand old man of the shrine and his prophetic words that I was to witness the "evil" destroyed and I wondered for what reason I, of all the members of my family, had been selected by Destiny to witness that tragic event, the most momentous in the modern history of Persia.

Pandemonium reigned. Always at the Shah's death, whether natural or not, confusion sweeps over the country. To keep down the disturbance as much as possible Nasser-ed-Din Shah's death was kept a secret for three days, in fact until the Crown Prince was actually en route from the north to the capital. When he was picked up in the shrine he was taken out to his carriage, propped up in the seat, his attendants beside him, dressed as was his custom when riding, the populace saluting him as was the duty of his subjects—all this in order to defer the news that his imperial majesty had moved on to make room for a successor. But there was little danger, at that time, of the removal of the Kajars from the throne of Persia. That did not occur until a very few years ago, when Nasser-ed-Din Shah's grandson was deposed by the Persian parliament.

The promises of the Shah and my appointment to a post of honour such as any mortal might envy were swept away. With loneliness, disappointment, and grief in my heart, my woes were augmented by the disappearance of Akbar. Was he afraid suspicion might attach to him? And the old man of the shrine—he too was absent. Did his prophecy come true? He had said he would die when the Unseen Hand had fulfilled the Destiny. Had it come to pass? Had they gone together, he and Akbar? Who knows? I was desolate. Even my Laleh, on whom I depended for all solutions, only shook his head as one who would say: "None knows." Had my mother been present, she might have told me, but alas, she too, had gone.

What was left for me to love? The sun was slowly rising behind the majestic peak of the Demavend Mountain, transforming its snowy dome into a sea of purple light. I stood as one in a trance. The blood of my ancestors—worshippers of the Sun—was urging me to fall on my knees and worship the glorious symbol of Ahura, the God! Suddenly the seven shafts of light, flaming towers, shot into the firmament, and a thrilling warmth permeated my body. Was it the warmth of the sun or was it the touch of a hand, soft as velvet, gentle as the breath of spring, perfumed as a rose? The hands which framed my face were prompting me to keep my countenance towards the sun, while a sweet voice seemed to whisper in my ears. There was no other touch so gentle, so fond, so soothing; it was the touch of my *mother's* hand!

Just as truly as if she had not passed on before, I heard her sweet voice saying:

"Oh, son of my heart, there is no sky like our own sky, no Sun like our Persian Sun! Only our eyes can read the divine inscription written in letters of fire—origin of all creation—on its disc of molten gold. Only our Persian minds can imagine how long and by how many billions of devotees has the Sun been watched, honoured and worshipped in its rising and setting. Nowhere does the Sun rise in such glory and majesty as in Persia. It inspires awe and fear; at the same time it fills our hearts with hope, courage and an abiding trust in the Almighty Khoda! Did the Sun ever rise and set as it does in our beloved country, the whole wide world would be Sun-worshippers."

I listened, enraptured. Yes, there was something greater, more lasting and worthy my affection, my loyalty, my service,—something to love, to live for, to die for if need be,— something more than all the glitter of the Shah's court. There was Iran! glorious land of the Persians!

THE END.